ROYAL HOSPITAL SCHOOL
HOLBROOK

PRIZE

AWARDED TO

J. Moffett

FORM **VIB**

FOR **History**

at the Annual Distribution

on **8th July 1978**

[signature]

Head Master

Ancient Japan

The Making of the Past

Ancient Japan

by Edward Kidder

Advisory Board for The Making of the Past

Frontispiece: popularly known as Yumedono Kannon, this gilt wooden figure is often said to be an effigy of Prince Shōtoku, the Buddhist saint, made not long after his death in the early 7th century. It is preserved in the Yumedono in the eastern part of the Hōryū-ji and rarely shown to the public. Height 2·15 m.

ISBN 0 7290 0047 8

Elsevier-Phaidon, an imprint of Phaidon Press Ltd,
Littlegate House, St Ebbe's Street, Oxford

Planned and produced by Elsevier International Projects Ltd, Oxford, © 1977 Elsevier Publishing
Projects SA, Lausanne. All rights reserved. No part of this publication may be reproduced, stored in a
retrieval system, or transmitted, in any form or by any means, electronic, mechanical, photocopying,
recording or otherwise, without the prior permission of the Publishers.

Origination by Art Color Offset, Rome, Italy

Filmset by Keyspools Ltd, Golborne, Lancashire, England

Printed and bound by Brepols, Turnhout, Belgium

Contents

Preface to the series

This book is a volume in the Making of the Past, a series describing the early history of the world as revealed by archaeology and related disciplines. The series is written by experts under the guidance of a distinguished panel of advisers and is designed for the layman, for young people, the student, the armchair traveler and the tourist. Its subject is a new history – the making of a new past, uncovered and reconstructed in recent years by skilled specialists. Since many of the authors of these volumes are themselves practicing archaeologists, leaders in a rapidly changing field, the series is completely authoritative and up-to-date. Each volume covers a specific period and region of the world and combines a detailed survey of the modern archaeology and sites of the area with an account of the early explorers, travelers, and archaeologists concerned with it. Later chapters of each book are devoted to a reconstruction in text and pictures of the newly revealed cultures and civilizations that make up the new history of the area.

Titles already published

The Egyptian Kingdoms	**Biblical Lands**
The Aegean Civilizations	**The New World**
The Spread of Islam	**Man before History**
The Emergence of Greece	**The Greek World**
The Rise of Civilization	**Barbarian Europe**
The First Empires	**The Roman World**
Rome and Byzantium	

Future titles

The Iranian Revival	**Indian Asia**
Ancient China	**Prehistoric Europe**
The Kingdoms of Africa	**Archaeology Today**

Introduction

Only a few years ago the frequently asked question, "Who were the Japanese?", was regarded as completely valid, but after the intensive studies in history, linguistics, mythology, sociology, geology and archaeology the chief question of this kind with any validity today is "When did they become Japanese?" Until a distinctive piece of geography was shaped by nature that could be called Japan, the people living in the area would not be "Japanese."

This book tells the story of the discovery of the origins of the land and people of Japan. Although, as elsewhere in the world, the chance discovery of antiquities and the rifling of tombs have proceeded for a thousand years and more, purposeful and scientifically directed archaeology is quite recent. From speculative investigations by a few foreigners from the west in the years between 1875 and 1914, we pass to Japanese pioneers of the first half of this century and so to the enormous increase in archaeological work since the end of World War II. Nearly all the discoveries discussed in this volume date only from the last 30 years; but they are set against the background of Japanese mythology and the early written records, both Chinese and Japanese, of the first millennium A D. Japanese prehistory has been extended deep into the Palaeolithic and there are now more scheduled sites than in any other country, so rich is the potential for archaeological investigation.

What begins to take shape is an account of the cultures of generations of dwellers in the islands, their diet, living space and beliefs. The contribution made by the introduction of rice and iron from China and of Buddhism from Korea is shown to have combined with earlier traditions of community nature cults and shamanistic divination in a hierarchical society. A developing concept of the divine origin and right of Yamato rulers was formalized by the 8th century as the backbone of a political system borrowed from China, composed of a supreme emperor supported by a subordinate bureaucracy. As it unfolded, the practice of one-family control of the government furnished the major buttress for the imperial principle.

Not all archaeology has involved excavation: the repair of temples has revealed ancient guide marks to their builders; stone bases reveal the plan, position, size and structure of lost palaces, temples and cities. But such sites have also been lately explored by excavation in the widespread growth of "historic archaeology," all the more necessary because of the population explosion and its concentration in the areas of the great conurbations. Japan had never been successfully invaded in historical times from overseas until the close of World War II and consequently has never been looted; but the violence of internal strife and of natural phenomena – typhoon, earthquake, thunder and flood – has taken a heavy toll. Nevertheless great tenacity to old traditions has led to systematic restoration through the centuries of ruined buildings and sculptures, while traditions of craftsmanship have persisted through history even down to the present day, and sculptors can still be found working in the old techniques with the old tools and materials and in the old spirit.

The regular periodic renewal of the Shinto shrine has meant the perpetuation of structural forms for well over a thousand years and can still today present features of domestic architecture current in the Yayoi period in the first centuries A D.

Chronological Table

30,000		Small bands of people hunted big game, made pebble and flake tools
20,000		Land-bridges broken; big game dying out
15,000		Unifacial scrapers and points, and bifacial blades
		Microliths
10,000	Jōmon	Simple pottery made
		Hunting and gathering subsistence; inland fishing
7000		Coastal fishing, seafood collecting
5000		Scattered pit-dwellings
3000		Nut gathering
		Clustered pit-dwellings, elaborate pottery
2000		Large shell-middens formed; stone circles in north
1000		Population diminishing
300	Yayoi	Domesticated rice grown in north Kyushu; some barley
200		Bronze introduced
		Iron introduced
100		Chinese grave-goods with jar burials
BC		Bronze weapons locally cast
AD		Iron tools locally wrought
		Bronze bells cast in Inland Sea region
100		Rice-growing communities already north of Kansai
107		Wa sent 160 slaves to Chinese court
c. 220		Himiko, female shaman of Yamatai kingdom
240		Chinese court sent 100 bronze mirrors, two swords and other articles in return for gifts from female ruler of Wa
300	Old Tombs	Building of mounded tombs
258 or 318		"Emperor" Sujin, probably first chief of federated tribes under the Yamato
c. 380		Mimana colony in Korea secured
c. 420		Emperor Nintoku, head of Yamato state
c. 475		Consolidation of Yamato state under horse-riding nobles
c. 507–31		Emperor Keitai reigned
538 or 552		Buddhism introduced from Paikche and accepted by the Soga
539–71		Emperor Kimmei reigned
588		Asuka-dera started
592–628		Empress Suiko reigned
593–622		Prince Shōtoku acted as regent
607		First Hōryū-ji built
		Embassy sent to China and many monks went to study; language of greetings offended the Chinese
643		Family of Prince Shōtoku killed
645–46		Taika Reform, following the assassination of the leading Soga
		All land came under imperial control
660		Dōshō returned from China and introduced Hossō sect
662		Ōmi civil and penal codes promulgated by Emperor Tenchi
663		Japanese fleet destroyed off Korea by Silla; north Kyushu fortified
670		First Hōryū-ji destroyed by fire
672–86		Emperor Temmu reigned
684		System of eight ranks (kabane) introduced
694		Empress Jitō established a formal capital at Fujiwara
702		Taihō codes promulgated
708		Copper and silver coins officially minted
710		Empress Gemmyō established a new capital at Heijō

712	*Kojiki* completed
718	Yōrō codes written by Fujiwara Fuhito; enforced in 757
720	*Nihon Shoki* completed
724–49	Emperor Shōmu reigned; first emperor to abdicate
724	Taga-jō built in the north as chief fort against the Emishi-Ezo
729	Kōmyō, wife of Emperor Shōmu, a Fujiwara lady, broke precedent by becoming empress
741	Provinces ordered to build provincial monasteries and nunneries
752	Dedication of the Great Buddha at the Tōdai-ji in Heijō
754	Ganjin arrived from China, founded Tōshōdai-ji and Ritsu sect
765	Priest Dōkyō became prime minister (disgraced in 770)
781–806	Emperor Kammu reigned
783	Structure of government reorganized, the number of officials reduced and building of private temples in the Home Provinces forbidden
784	Capital moved to Nagaoka
789	Japanese troops suffered serious defeats by Emishi-Ezo
794	Capital moved to Heian (Kyoto)
801	Sakanoue Tamuramaro appointed field commander against the Emishi-Ezo and defeated them by 804
805	Saichō returned from China and founded the Tendai sect on Mt Hiei
806	Kūkai returned from China and founded the Shingon sect on Mt Kōya in 816
810	Ex-Emperor Heijō tried to move the capital back to Nara; Emperor Saga formed the Kurōdo-dokoro, an imperial office to handle administration and the content of decrees
816	*Kebiishi*, Imperial Police established in Heian capital
838	Twelfth and last embassy dispatched to China
858	Fujiwara Yorifusa became regent for nine-year-old Emperor Seiwa, marking the beginning of the Fujiwara domination of the government
894	Official suspension of travel to China
985	Priest Genshin wrote *Ōjō-yōshū*, the doctrine of Jōdō (Pure Land)
995–1027	Fujiwara Michinaga controlled the government
1010	About this time Lady Murasaki wrote *Genji Monogatari*
1052	Date given for Mappō, the End of the Law
1053	Byōdō-in in Uji converted to temple for Fujiwara Yorimichi
1069	*Kirokujo*, a Documents Office, established in reign of Emperor Go-Sanjō to certify the legal acquisition of manor lands
1086–87	*Insei*, rule by retired emperors started by ex-Emperor Shirakawa
1156	Hōgen civil war over succession; the Taira defeated the Minamoto and put Emperor Go-Shirakawa on the throne
1159	Heiji revolt, an unsuccessful revolt against the Taira, and Taira Kiyomori became prime minister
1175	Hōnen Shōnin founded the Jōdō (Pure Land) sect
1180–85	Gempei War between the Minamoto and the Taira families, saw the burning of the Tōdai-ji and defeat of the Taira by Minamoto Yoritomo

Opposite: Mt Fuji, the eternal symbol of Japan, rises 12,365 feet from almost sea level. Now climbed by thousands of hikers during the summer, it was given a wide berth by ancient people since it was violently active and only fully subsided about 300 years ago, justly meriting the ancient term Fire Mountain.

1. Japan and her Archaeology

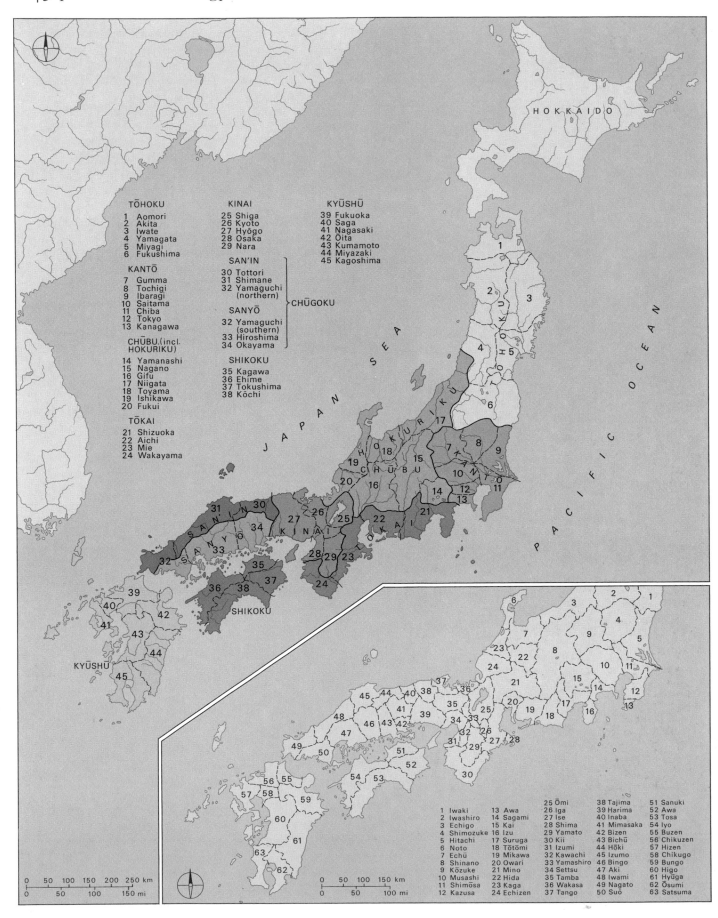

TŌHOKU
1 Aomori
2 Akita
3 Iwate
4 Yamagata
5 Miyagi
6 Fukushima

KANTŌ
7 Gumma
8 Tochigi
9 Ibaragi
10 Saitama
11 Chiba
12 Tokyo
13 Kanagawa

CHŪBU.(incl.
HOKURIKU)
14 Yamanashi
15 Nagano
16 Gifu
17 Niigata
18 Toyama
19 Ishikawa
20 Fukui

TŌKAI
21 Shizuoka
22 Aichi
23 Mie
24 Wakayama

KINAI
25 Shiga
26 Kyoto
27 Hyōgo
28 Osaka
29 Nara

SAN'IN
30 Tottori
31 Shimane
32 Yamaguchi
   (northern)

SANYŌ
32 Yamaguchi
   (southern)
33 Hiroshima
34 Okayama

CHŪGOKU

SHIKOKU
35 Kagawa
36 Ehime
37 Tokushima
38 Kōchi

KYŪSHŪ
39 Fukuoka
40 Saga
41 Nagasaki
42 Ōita
43 Kumamoto
44 Miyazaki
45 Kagoshima

1 Iwaki
2 Iwashiro
3 Echigo
4 Shimozuke
5 Hitachi
6 Noto
7 Echū
8 Shinano
9 Kōzuke
10 Musashi
11 Shimōsa
12 Kazusa
13 Awa
14 Sagami
15 Kai
16 Izu
17 Suruga
18 Tōtōmi
19 Mikawa
20 Owari
21 Mino
22 Hida
23 Kaga
24 Echizen
25 Ōmi
26 Iga
27 Ise
28 Shima
29 Yamato
30 Kii
31 Izumi
32 Kawachi
33 Yamashiro
34 Settsu
35 Tamba
36 Wakasa
37 Tango
38 Tajima
39 Harima
40 Inaba
41 Mimasaka
42 Bizen
43 Bichū
44 Hōki
45 Izumo
46 Bingo
47 Aki
48 Iwami
49 Nagato
50 Suō
51 Sanuki
52 Awa
53 Tosa
54 Iyo
55 Buzen
56 Chikuzen
57 Hizen
58 Chikugo
59 Bungo
60 Higo
61 Hyūga
62 Ōsumi
63 Satsuma

HOKKAIDO

JAPAN SEA

PACIFIC OCEAN

KYŪSHŪ

SHIKOKU

0 50 100 150 200 250 km
0   50   100   150 mi

0 50 100 150 km
0   50   100 mi

Japan's geography. Japan, a corruption of Marco Polo's *Jipangu,* is a part of an extended line of islands that at first glance on the map resembles the back-row seats in the theater of Asia. The three main islands have always been "Japanese": Honshu (Main Island), Kyushu (Nine Provinces) and Shikoku (Four Provinces); and Japan has always looked on itself as having a residual sovereignty over Hokkaido (North Sea Route), but the northernmost island was of little interest as long as it was thought not to be able to grow rice and while it was inhabited by relatively hostile people known as Ainu. When the Russians started to move into their maritime provinces c. 1820, Hokkaido was viewed as a potential buffer and it was then brought into the Japanese orbit, but equal status has been long in coming. For good measure the Japanese nibbled off two rather large Kurile islands, and later, after the 1905 war with Russia, the southern half of Sakhalin.

The Ryukyus had been wrested from China early in the 17th century, so they were deemed to qualify as "Japanese" when Korea, Taiwan and other more recent acquisitions had to be surrendered following Japan's defeat in World War II.

Both the Ryukyu island chain and Hokkaido have been rather marginal to developments in Japanese history. But both played important roles in Japanese prehistory, as natural links between other regions and Japan. Nevertheless, this book will deal chiefly with the core areas of the country from before the formation of the islands to the 12th century AD, the period the Japanese call *Kodai,* or ancient, at the end of which starts the period designated "medieval."

The orientation Japan has had toward Korea and the China mainland is an unavoidable result of geography. All the notable cultural incursions entered through south Japan; commerce and trade came the same way. The north

Above: the surface appearance of rural areas looks as though life has changed little over the centuries. Traditional methods are still in use: here persimmons are dried for storage through the winter.

Opposite: ancient and modern Japan. The early provinces (inset) had taken their rough shape as administrative divisions by the end of the 8th century, but these were all changed to larger prefectures by the Meiji government in the 19th century.

had some gold, and was eventually found to be richly blessed with coal. Good railroads became essential in the last century for industrialization, but the "bullet" trains are far behind the construction schedule north of Tokyo.

In the 7th century AD Japan was divided into provinces (*kuni* or *koku*) for administrative purposes. These were streamlined to a smaller number of prefectures (*ken*) in the Meiji period around 1868, but the names of provinces remained in scholarly use long after the public had forgotten them. It still seems pertinent, however, when dealing with the cluster of administrative units in the cradle of Japanese culture, to speak of the Go-Kinai, the Five Home Provinces, which had a special physical and political relationship with the court. Recent post-office administrative divisions place large areas under the jurisdiction of cities. It is useful to know this, as sites listed under a city are often well out in open country.

The islands form natural physical regions. Tōhoku (Northeast), the northern part of Honshu; Hokuriku (North Coastal Region), the northwestern area; Kantō (East of the Mountains), the large eastern plain and surrounding foothills; Chūbu (Middle Section), the central mountains and lower land running to the east coast but more or less north-south in orientation; Kansai (West of the Mountains), the Yamato Plain and surrounding country; the Chūgoku (Middle Provinces), the Seto Inland Sea side and the opposite side of the long leg of Honshu. The east side is the San-in (Sunny Side of the Mountains), the west side the San-yō (Shady Side of the Mountains). Shikoku and Kyushu keep their familiar, historically descriptive names.

Archaeologists find Japan's history laid out to order. It is stratigraphically layered, since the Japanese tended to accumulate cultural habits and social practices and discard few in the process. It is regarded as a normal perpetuation of tradition to have a new car blessed at a Shinto shrine that may be prehistoric in style and to drive it to a festival of community dances for better harvests which have changed negligibly in 2,000 years.

Pride in this continuous sweep of history was justifiably acquired. Geography in the last 20,000 years has provided natural isolation from east Asia. An insular invulnerability gave a sense of security and allowed time to develop a general homogeneity based on physical appearance and language. Salvation from two attempted Mongol invasions served to increase the sense of divine protection. Conservatism developed early. The Japanese discovered how to live with each other through Confucian principles of harmony, and conformity through language, agricultural methods, uniform education and communal celebrations has produced a group spirit known for its formidable collective action.

There are within the country, however, numerous islands, narrow valleys, sequestered pockets – isolation within isolation. This accounts in part for the great number of prehistoric pottery types, for instance, so that despite the national racial characteristics, many regional differences exist in dialects, ceremonies, food preferences and assorted customs. This makes Japan internally rich in culture, and enhances greatly the interest of traveling in different parts of the country.

Japanese society. The Japanese also learned how to live in relative harmony with their Pacific neighbors – until the last 50 years before World War II, when the scramble for resources to fuel an industrial state became too keen. Except for rare occasions it is safe to say that Japan's influence in Asia has been slight. She could withdraw into her shell for long centuries, following the proper practice of sending emissaries when desired, and trading and dispatching a few perceptive monks. Japan was not prey because her resources were known to be limited. But geography is not the sole answer. Japan had a political system that did not normally give rise to undue ambition, being more likely to produce struggle on a secondary level, one step below the single perpetual source of authority.

Above: the Deer Park in Nara, to most people the cradle of Buddhism in Japan.

Left: Japan is said to be symbolized on the physical side by Mt Fuji and on the spiritual side by Shinto. In some cases the Shinto *kami* protect Buddhist temples, as here at Ishiyama-dera near Lake Biwa.

The Japanese replaced rulers without disrupting the whole political and social system and without involving their neighbors. It is often said that Chinese emperors came and went, but Japanese emperors came and stayed. A change of regime in China resulted in great national turmoil and political upheaval, often involving direct invasion, with reactions occurring throughout Asia. A change of regime in Japan was usually between families for control of the power of office and the collection of taxes. Not that it was necessarily bloodless, but assassinations on the imperial level were almost unheard of – the emperor's position was hallowed, and an assassination would not make that much difference – and the ordinary person and the country as a whole continued in their accustomed way. By the 8th century AD it was not unusual for the emperor to abdicate and so use the power of the imperial office to select his successor and smooth over the transition.

In another comparison, constant external threats to China from the north made the Chinese more sensitive to internal threats, which they handled with an equal degree of violence. They could eradicate wantonly, perhaps drawing confidence in their ability to rebuild from their history of periodic invigoration from outside sources. Buddhism as a foreign religion was almost wiped out in the 9th century when monasteries were destroyed and monks evicted. The Japanese preserved things almost neurotically, as though uncertain where the next source of inspiration might come from. When Emperor Kammu

faced excessive clerical power late in the 8th century, instead of using physical force he simply moved the capital away from the temples, leaving the establishments and their patronage dangling, looking for a new place in the social system.

Many natural and social factors helped mold the Japanese way of life: the native, animistic religion of Shinto which involves an appreciation for land and country; the tolerance embodied in Buddhist thought and escape from the harsh realities of this world; the Confucian idea of harmony; the tribal spirit that regards what is good for the group as good for the individual; and the system of hierarchy which fitted everyone in his place in the social scale.

Japan's place in history lies somewhere between two commonly held extreme views: the one of mainland Asians and many westerners who regard Japan as little more than a derivative culture, lacking in genius, made up of bits and pieces of Korea, fragments of south Asia and massive parts of China; and the other, usually more locally held view, that ignores most external factors and concentrates on seeing things by their very Japaneseness as being original.

Since the history of Japan is distinguished by its remarkable continuity, few points can be found to demarcate major changes. One lacks the invasions, the forcible imposition of new religions, and radically new political systems. By most standards, the changes were so

Above: the Aoi festival, usually translated as hollyhock, is held every year in Kyoto on 15 May; leaves of *Asarum caulescens*, like a wild ginger, are offered to the *kami*.

Below: Kyoto's Jidai festival or festival of time periods, held annually on 22 October, is a parade of traditional Heian costumes and great historical events.

smooth as to make pigeon-holing difficult. The arrival of Buddhism in the 6th century AD, the Taika Reform of the 7th century and the moving of the capital in the late 8th century did not occur without considerable internal dissension but caused no breaks in development. Nevertheless, it is possible to define major phases of early Japanese history.

Early history. Early man arrived by land, and went through a hunting and gathering Palaeolithic stage until he invented pottery. The cord-marking on the pottery gives the name of Jōmon (cord pattern) to the succeeding, more or less Neolithic, period of about 10,000 years' duration.

As political changes occurred on the continent and their repercussions reached Japan, rice began to be grown and metals introduced. This is the Yayoi period, dating to the last centuries BC and the first centuries AD; the name comes from a site in Tokyo. This farming revolution brought about territorial claims among developing tribal groups which Chinese records refer to as "countries." The power center shifted to the Yamato Plain, where it was to remain until the late 19th century.

Competition between tribal groups, territorial expansion and controls of resources resulted in the rise of a dominant tribe, the Yamato, who built large tombs for their nobles. The term *Kofun* (Old Tumuli) is applied to about a 300-year span, which witnessed the materialization of the Yamato state in the cradle of Japanese civilization.

The claims made by this tribe for supremacy are spelled out in great detail in two books, *Kojiki* and *Nihon Shoki* or *Nihongi*, both compiled in the early 8th century AD as

Heijō, the old city of Nara, occupied from 710 to 784, retains landmarks of pre-Buddhist history in the mounded tombs and the early temples set into the grids.

propaganda to validate the Yamato position. The imperial line was accorded great antiquity with special rights attributed to its divine origins. The pattern of hierarchy of both deities and aristocracy took shape. The "emperor" was a priest-king, the head of religious ceremonies for the state and the director of its political affairs.

Cultural connections with the southwestern Korean kingdom of Paikche grew increasingly close, as political differences with the southeastern kingdom of Silla intensified. Buddhist cult articles arrived from Paikche as one result of this relationship, and the three major families at the court – Soga, Mononobe and Nakatomi, the Soga with some historic foreign connections – were more sharply pitted against each other. Buddhism finally became acceptable at the court through the power politics of the Soga, and the residences of the rulers were constructed in a small region in Nara prefecture known as Asuka.

The historical period. Asuka (552–645 AD) thus constitutes the first fully historical period in Japanese history, with a rising priesthood, a nucleus of literate personalities at the court, and sophisticated art and architectural forms. Encouraged by Empress Suiko and Prince Shōtoku, families undertook the building of modest-size temples. There was a rapid increase in temple construction after the fall of the Soga and the edicts which produced the Taika Reform in 645–46. The pattern of government was modeled on the Chinese bureaucratic system, the emperor being the focal point. Formal palaces and a city were needed to make the system work.

The first of the grid-plan cities that were built in Japan was Fujiwara, which was located north of Asuka and occupied by Empress Jitō in 694 AD. This period would best be called Late Asuka-Fujiwara (645–710), but it has only the woefully inadequate art-historical designation of Hakuhō.

The capital of Fujiwara, though certainly planned on the ground, could never have been fully inhabited in the span of 16 years for which it was used. In 710 Empress Gemmyō built a new city called Heijō further north. This is now known as Nara. Japan had lost her last friend in Korea through the hostile action of Silla, and now found sources for new ideas in China itself.

Male and female *tennō* – now formally titled emperors – made cultural contributions through their interest in Buddhist affairs and the arts, by far the greatest being made by Emperor Shōmu. But the sharp increase in the number of temples and in the corresponding power of the clergy was an uncalculated factor that had ultimately to be reckoned with.

After only one century of history, and with a brilliant record of opening up larger areas of the country, the court had to move. Emperor Kammu first tried Nagaoka for ten years, then settled in Heian in 794, leaving the temples behind. This is now the city of Kyoto.

Heian remained the capital until the late 19th century. After the overwhelming Sinicization of the previous 100 years, the pendulum swung almost as far back. Absorption went on. Imperial power began to slip as landownership passed into private hands, and official foreign contacts were neglected. China under the late T'ang dynasty was in a period of decline. Court life gradually dominated the city, while parts of the country were being introduced to Buddhism through the medium of the native gods. Esoteric sects brought back from China by Saichō and Kūkai were made more palatable by being amalgamated with traditional Shinto.

The Early Heian period (794–893) saw a consolidation of the Nara achievements and imperial retrenchment. It was also the beginning of the subtly changing relationships that witnessed the resurfacing of the tradition of family dominance. This was on a far grander scale than can be claimed for the Soga. The Fujiwara family was installed in every corner of the government, at the height of their long climb to power since a Nakatomi, renamed Fujiwara, drafted the Taika Reform edicts. The Late Heian period (893–1185) brought a remarkable expression of Japanese taste. Yamato (Japanese) literature and art were fashionable and consciously different from Chinese style. The Fujiwara worshiped Amida intensely, building many temples which were gorgeously ornamented. After the psychological depression caused by Mappō (the End of the Law, the belief that the power of the Buddha would drastically subside) there followed a brilliant period in the cultural field, though politically and economically far from spectacular. It was broken when the Fujiwara were destroyed by the Taira, who in turn lost out to the Minamoto. This marks the end of what is called the Kodai (ancient period), and opens the way for the Middle Ages, when the government was manipulated from Kamakura, contacts were again frequent with other parts of Asia, and vigorous leadership and religious crusading wrought a change in national spirit.

Taboos and tomb robbers. Many taboos, stories of the supernatural and rumors of disasters attributed to relics hampered the advancement of archaeological investigation. The oldest records make it clear that the finding of relics was little different from that of other unusual phenomena, such as albino animals, two-headed calves, etc., many of which were looked on as bad omens and for safety's sake were usually reported to the court. As early as 839 AD an entry in the *Shoku Nihonkoku* mentions white, black, blue and red stone arrowheads appearing along the northeast coast following heavy storms. Since these materialized after the spirits of nature had run riot, they were obviously of supernatural origin. The local official sent them to the Heian court where a special ceremony was held to neutralize the chance of any execration.

A few years later another book tells of the finding of arrowheads inside Akita castle when it was being built for the battles in the north against the people the old texts called Ezo. The official in this case sent a report to the central government. Archaeologists now know that a small Neolithic shell-mound existed within the grounds of this old castle that was destroyed by the Ezo in 878 in their last major battle of the war.

In most instances the actual objects were probably dispatched to the court, accompanied by an explanation of their discovery. Several bronze bells dating to about the 2nd century AD are mentioned in early records, the first in a document of 668, and others in old texts dated 713, 821 and 842. The finders of these bells were quite ignorant of their use and reacted with considerable awe to their discoveries. They sometimes called them Ashoka's bells, referring to the great Indian Buddhist ruler, as though the bells had been associated in some way with early Buddhist ritual in Japan.

The *haniwa*, the clay objects made in the shape of animals and human figures and placed on the slopes of burial mounds of the 6th century, are credited with apparitional powers in one of only two references in the ancient literature. During the reign of Emperor Yūryaku (5th century AD), according to the *Nihon Shoki* (Chronicles of Japan), a man by the name of Hyakūson was returning from visiting his daughter who had given birth to a child. As he was riding home at night, while passing the huge tumulus of Emperor Ōjin he noticed a "red courser" running alongside his horse "which dashed along like the flight of a dragon, with splendid high springing action, darting off like a wild goose. His strange form was of lofty mold; his remarkable aspect was of extreme distinction." The rider of this marvelous steed sensed Hyakūson's desire to own such a horse and offered him his in exchange. No time was lost and Hyakūson rode off on the magnificent red courser. When he arrived home, he put the horse in the stall, fed it and retired. Early the next morning he went out to look at his steed and there, standing in the stall, was a *haniwa* horse of clay. Hyakūson retraced his steps and found his own horse wandering around on the slope of the emperor's tomb among the clay horses keeping silent guard.

The only other reference to these tomb sculptures in the early literature is a description of their beginnings and the rationale for their use. The *Nihon Shoki* says they were first made during the reign of Emperor Sujin, as substitutes for the practice of human immolation, and were so satisfactory that an imperial edict was issued proscribing live burials and ordering the making of *haniwa* instead.

The Taika Reform of 646 put such severe restrictions on the building of mounded tombs for even the highest social strata that they eventually ceased to be made. It is a well-known fact that they were already being widely pillaged

Haniwa figure of a woman seated on a high stool. Period of the Great Tombs, 5th–6th centuries A D. National Museum, Tokyo.

by the 8th century, despite Shinto's general prohibition against associating with the dead and primitive man's irrational fear of the spirits of the dead, as Shinto practices so clearly demonstrate. Since so many tombs were in some way related to the imperial family, it behoved the government to keep a protective eye on most.

Despite official efforts, the rewards were always high for the tomb looter: tombs traditionally claimed to be imperial, and imperial family tombs, made special targets. Priests whose names would otherwise have been lost to history are now in the records for their escapades.

The person who rifled the tomb of Empress Kōken (718–48) died at an early age of a bloated body, shocking his friend (and probable accomplice) into replacing the grave-goods out of fear for his own life. A group of priests living near the tomb of Emperor Daigo (885–930) all died young for no known reason, but the record leaves little doubt that the public connected their demise with the proximity of their residence to the tomb.

This fear of the spirits of the dead may still be present today, as local people often conform to taboos that archaeologists blithely ignore. Excavations of a tomb may start with a Shinto ceremony, which makes for an understanding between the spirits and the diggers on the intended procedure. Such rituals counteract any ill effects.

The first Japanese archaelogists. Japan's first recorded archaeologist was Tokugawa Mitsukuni (1628–1700), a man of unquenchable curiosity about his country who in years of painstaking research wrote an extensive history called *Dai-nihon-shi*. He excavated a pair of tombs at Ishioka city in Ibaragi prefecture, but having studied the contents, he had them reburied. The mounds were then restored and landscaped and a purification ritual ensured the safety of all concerned.

Not long after Tokugawa Mitsukuni judiciously explored the tumuli in a way that offended neither man nor the gods, there began to evolve a very respectable practice of collecting ancient and exotic things. Stones were of particular interest. No special distinction was made by the collectors between worked and natural stones, largely because they were unable to do so. At best the stones were said to come from the Age of the Gods, Japan's mythological period. Slowly, more rational men came to see arrowheads at least as not supernatural. Their presence on the ground was now accounted for by the fact that the Ezo (Ainu) used them for shooting down birds. Every hit brought a bird (and an arrowhead) to the ground!

The most archaeologically minded of the early collectors was Fujii Teikan (d. 1797), who acquired a unique collection of old roof tiles and ink squeezes of their decoration. His collection of antiquities might well remind us of a junk shop today, but Teikan takes the credit as the first to publish full descriptions of artifacts, including their measurements. His *Kōko-nichi-roku* (Report on the

One of the earliest collectors of archaeological beads, arrowheads etc. was the Kyoto man, Kiuchi Sekitei (1724–1808), who was described as "crazy about odd shaped stones." Here he tells a visitor that the stones change weight each day.

Old Days) catalogs in 119 pages a wide variety of items, marking him as one of the first Japanologists, or students of "things Japanese."

What distinguished these stone collectors from earlier dilettantes of the arts, such as Emperor Shōmu and Ashikaga Yoshimitsu, was that they occasionally dug tombs. They knew where the good sites were located, and that they should be visited after rains, after spading for new crops and when the vegetation was low, and they traveled considerable distances to make ink rubbings of epitaphs. Slowly they added metal items to their acquisitions, then pottery and eventually miscellanea.

The Meiji emperor moved his national headquarters from Kyoto to Tokyo in 1868–69. Archaeological materials were concrete evidence of ancient history and the traditions of the state, and so were important to the Meiji view of Japanese history. The National Museum was established in 1871 and the building dedicated in the following year. By 1876 the first law was passed to protect cultural properties and national treasures; all unearthed objects were to be sent to the museum. An appreciation of the antiquity of the objects was greatly sharpened through official sanction, but even the most enlightened could do little more than guess at the age of the relics, speculate on what order they came in, or conjure up a very general idea of their use.

In the Meiji period (1868–1912), as the Japanese sped toward modernization, the imperial ancestors were the object of great reverence as part of the policy of enhancing the position of the emperor, and the imperial tombs received special attention. There was also, despite what one might expect, an occasional private individual who investigated the authenticity of the imperial tombs, made his own suggestions as to their identification and occasionally had some influence on their redesignation. One of these was Gamo Kumpei (1813–59), the author of *Sanryōshi* (Mountain-mausoleum-will), written as a protest against the seeming lack of concern shown by the Tokugawa rulers toward these tombs.

The Tokugawa did magnanimously pay their respects to the memory of imperial rulers. Fences were set up around the tombs in the Five Home Provinces in 1697. Identification sign boards were erected in the 18th century. Major repairs were carried out between 1861 and 1864 on the eve of the collapse of the regime, when they were put in substantially the form in which they may be seen today.

The *Koji Ruien*, a book published in 1896, contains drawings of the imperial tombs. These may be free drawings, but in some cases the details of the tombs look so different from how they do today that one must assume that other changes have since taken place, some perhaps not formally disclosed to the public. The Imperial Household Agency does not publish its investigations.

Western archaeologists in Japan. This was the incubation period. Japanese archaeology was just waiting for someone to usher it into its modern age. A Harvard-educated, American natural scientist came to Japan in search of certain types of marine shells. Edward S. Morse (1838–1925) arrived in July of 1877. Tokyo University recognized his wide knowledge and experience and appointed him professor of zoology. On his way from Yokohama to Tokyo, when passing through Ōmori where land was being leveled for more train tracks, he noticed workmen cutting through shell-mounds.

Morse knew shell-middens to be a sign of Neolithic cultures and within two months had set about excavating them. He measured an "89 m. length of deposit along the embankment" and was amazed by the "pottery in such great abundance" and its "infinite variety of form and ornamentation." He found "50 vessels more or less complete ... The pottery is rude, and ... bears the impression of the well known cord mark." The shell-mounds were "nearly half a mile from the shores of the Bay of Yedo."

The methodically written and illustrated book *Shell Mounds of Omori* was published in 1879, a remarkable piece of work for all the difficulties of English typesetting at that time and of instructing a Japanese in the finer points of western-style drawing. Interestingly enough, the book is also dated 2539, the year of the official chronology that started with 660 BC when the governing of the country is said to have been begun by Emperor Jimmu.

Delivering lectures on zoology, botany and anthropology at Tokyo University, Morse encouraged the inclusion of these subjects in the regular curriculum. With Darwin's concepts of evolution percolating through the learned societies in England, Morse introduced them to Japan, where they brought him into conflict with the

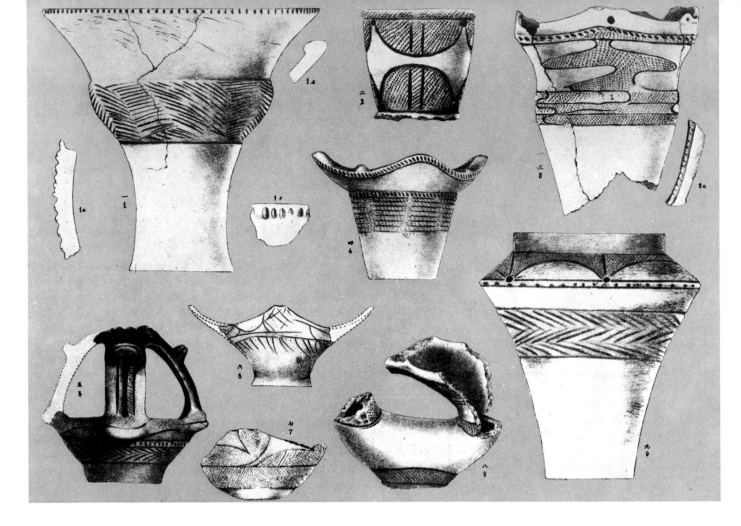

Edward S. Morse (*below left*), newly arrived in Japan from the United States and appointed professor of zoology at Tokyo University, dug the Ōmori shell-mound in 1877 (*below right*) after recognizing it as the remains of a prehistoric culture. The frontispiece of his site report (*above*) shows Japanese workmen in a cut removing debris along the train line; other plates show remarkable drawings of pottery, tools and shells.

Opposite: shell-mounds in the Kantō Plain.

missionaries who were teaching in the Japanese universities and who far outnumbered him. Morse found only the word *hensen* – transitional change – to express the idea of evolution, but it caught on and was gradually accepted.

Morse stayed about two years, and made two other trips to Japan. He was an avid collector of pottery, but was very shaky on its historical attribution. From 1880 to 1914 Morse was director of the Peabody Museum of Salem which today houses many quaint items of everyday use from the 19th century, rarely seen outside Japan. It also contains several *haniwa* and other antiquities.

The great popularity of archaeology today has brought about a revival of Morsiana, and the *Shell Mounds of Omori* has been reissued. Morse's omnivorous interests in the daily scene led him to record everything of a material nature. His *Japan Day by Day* is a descriptive piece well outside the range of a simple diary, and his *Japanese Homes and their Surroundings*, complete with 307 of his own drawings, has never been surpassed.

No one knows today exactly where Morse dug at Ōmori. His innumerable successors there have entirely gutted the shell-mounds over the years, leaving only the legend and two monuments, one erected in 1929 and the other a year later. Signboards also decorate the spot now, but all the markers are hemmed in by buildings and are best seen from a little park across the train tracks.

Japanese use the word *kaizuka*, literally mound of shells,

to describe these remains. The abundance of such middens (refuse heaps) in the coastal areas of Tokyo Bay provided a field day for excavators in schools and institutes of the Tokyo area and their chief field experience in archaeology. Many of the 1,000 or more shell-middens in the Kantō have since been wiped out by the boundless expansion of the cities of Tokyo, Kawasaki, Yokohama and Yokosuka in recent years.

Other foreigners drifted in and out, several looking at Japanese prehistory in different ways and making their own special contributions. Henry von Siebold (1852–1908), an Austrian diplomat stationed in Japan, wrote *Notes on Japanese Archaeology with Especial Reference to the Stone Age*. He claimed the shell-mounds were the remains of the Ainu, or perhaps a pre-Ainu people. A freelance English volcanologist named John Milne (1850–1913) had worked his way across Asia and into Japan, where he spent 18 years after his arrival in 1876. He believed the shell-mounds were Ainu sites.

Milne excavated a few tombs in Hokkaido and investigated other sites, but he is best remembered for his efforts to calculate the age of the shell-mounds by their distance from the existing shorelines. Since the water has now receded by as much as ten miles, Milne based his estimates on annual land rise from old maps and calculated the Ōmori shell-mounds to be about 2,600 years old. It is interesting to note that his calculation was hardly more than 1,000 years out, though the material he used was in fact totally unreliable from a scientific view.

Gowland and Munro. Two other foreigners well known for their early studies of Japanese prehistory are William Gowland (1843–1922), adviser to the national mint, and Neil Gordon Munro (1863–1942), a medical doctor with his own practice. Gowland's interests were centered on the mounded tombs, which he referred to as dolmens. He did extensive fieldwork, making meticulous measurements and recording specific dimensions of 130 tumuli. While most of these "dolmens" are in the Home Provinces, Gowland studied them in all parts of the country except in the north.

Gowland arrived from England in 1872 and remained in Japan until 1888. Most of his collection, in particular the Sue pottery from the tombs, was given to the British Museum.

Munro opened a medical office in Yokohama and set about investigating prehistoric sites with a scientific inquisitiveness. He dug the Mitsuzawa shell-mounds in Yokohama for seven months, distinguishing nine separate middens. His observations are still echoed by archaeologists in Japan: "There are few countries where the vestiges of ancient culture are so apparent and abundant as in the case with Japan." His monumental opus, the 705-page *Prehistoric Japan* (1911), was the summation of all his early studies, and stood the test of western readership on ancient Japan for almost half a century and received much

grudging praise from Japanese scholars.

There were two points in which he was years ahead of developments in Japan: he dug stratigraphically, and he discovered the remains of pit-dwellings. He put it this way: "... as the layers gave evidence of having been deposited at different times, an account was kept of pottery and implements from the different strata." He knew he had the remains of houses; he even spoke of a "neolithic village" because he could see the "distinct vestiges of habitations" below the shell layers: "three primitive hearths were seen under a small shellheap... near these, holes, apparently for house posts..." But the more difficult job of finding the outlines of the pit-dwellings was still many years off.

Munro married a Japanese and settled in Japan for the last 50 years of his life. He moved to Nibutani, an Ainu village in Hokkaido, practiced medicine, and studied the local people. His house there has been preserved as a museum. Munro may have known too much about Japan. He was interned during World War II and died in 1942.

The growth of Japanese archaeology. The Archaeological Association of Japan first met in 1895 and the following year saw the publication of its journal by the National Museum, which still takes responsibility for issuing the *Kōkogaku Zasshi* (Journal of Archaeology). At this stage in Japan's archaeological history there were three chief centers: Tokyo Imperial University, the Imperial Museum in Tokyo and Kyoto Imperial University. Tokyo University and the Museum were receiving unearthed material from all over the country, but it would not have taken a very observant eye to notice that neither space nor personnel would be enough to manage such rapidly accumulating masses of artifacts. Today Japan may well put more money into excavations and the elaborate preservation of her sites in proportion to her size and wealth than any country in the world – and may ultimately allow more to be destroyed because of their sheer number.

The earliest listing of sites known to me was done by Tokyo University in 1900. About 3,500 were then noted. The 1925 law required the compilation of site lists, and some of these are still valuable for their identification of sites with place names that have disappeared from the scene through urban expansion in the second half of this century. The last official list in this series came out in 1929. Every prefecture has recently recorded its sites in a

A *haniwa* horse found by Munro, now in the Royal Scottish Museum, Edinburgh. Munro's observations are still echoed by archaeologists in Japan.

standardized form in lists and on maps, which are all now published in a consistent format.

Archaelogy received formal recognition as an academic discipline when Tsuboi Shōgoro (1863–1913) was appointed to the chair of anthropology at Tokyo Imperial University at the time the Anthropological Institute was established in 1893. What was meant by anthropology until World War II was in fact archaeology and was directed toward the investigation of prehistory and prehistoric physical remains. Tsuboi, called the "father of Japanese anthropology," died prematurely of an intestinal infection while attending a conference in St Petersburg and was succeeded at the university by Torii Ryūzō (1870–1953) who combined archaeology with the study of northern coastal peoples.

Progress made in Jōmon period studies was quite steady. Japanese archaeologists credit Matsumoto Hikoshirō (d. 1975) with digging the first site stratigraphically in 1919, the Satohama shell-mound at Takaragamine in Miyagi prefecture, and Yawata Ichiro (1902–) and Miyasaka Mitsuji (d. 1975) with proving the existence of pit-dwellings when they exposed a number under the shell layers of the Ubayama shell-mound at Ichikawa city in Chiba prefecture in 1927.

Kantō Plain archaeology moved forward rapidly after Kashiwa Ōyama (1889–1969) founded the Institute for Prehistory in 1929. Within a short time he had solved the major chronological problems of the shell-mounds near the shoreline of Tokyo Bay.

To put it briefly, Ōyama discovered that the proportion of marine and fresh-water shells may vary by layer in the shell-mounds. Changes from one to the other and from lower to upper layers indicated that the people tended to stay on or to return to the same spot despite the recession of the ocean, gathering shells from closer riverine sources. Within a cluster of mounds, in other words, the ones

Above: Professor Kōsaku Hamada, who started the department of archaeology of Kyoto Imperial University in 1916, here digging at Kō in Osaka in 1917.

Below right: part of a pelvic bone, found in 1931, once claimed to be earlier than Peking Man.

Below: human skeletons dug from shell-mounds in 1917, most with the heads turned toward the east.

Above: the first serious investigation of tombs, from 1912 to 1917, revealed some fine objects, especially horse trappings; but the publication was inadequate.

Below: archaeology today in Japan involves meticulous, time-consuming field techniques, laboratory analysis and mandatory publication. Here "loam pipes" are being investigated.

wholly of marine shells and furthest from the present coastline are the oldest, while the ones wholly of riverine shells and closest to the ocean are the youngest; the others, in which the proportion of shells changes from one to the other, fall in order in between.

Yamanouchi Sugao (1902–70), to whom goes the credit for the Jōmon chronological scheme, was a superb typologist with whom few could argue. But where he worked on individual sites his typology was sometimes so complicated even his close followers could be mystified. The backbone of the system was the typology of the Kantō Plain. The broad stages were called Sō-ki, Zen-ki, Chū-ki, Kō-ki, and Ban-ki, adequately translated into English as Earliest, Early, Middle, Late and Latest.

Yamanouchi's views were formed long before modern scientific dating systems stretched the chronology, and his belief in a precise ordering of pottery types of roughly equal duration allowed little room for the great antiquity of Jōmon pottery that the radiocarbon dates later implied.

He died still trying to make a case for the Jōmon period starting in the neighborhood of 3000 BC.

Kyoto Imperial University had concentrated more on the excavation of mounded tombs and it was there that Hamada, Umehara and others were honing their theories on the dating of the tombs and the origin of the particular keyhole shape. On the basis of the bronze mirrors in the Kuzugawa Tomb, dug in 1934, Umehara initiated a chronology for the keyhole-shaped tumuli.

Japan in her thought-control period had an official line requiring unquestioning respect for the emperor, do-or-die patriotism and total acceptance of the orthodox national history. The actual act of digging was not so much affected, but speculation on antiquity was discouraged and historians were obliged to accept uncritically the early mythology as fact and the succession of "emperors" as traceable without break to Jimmu. School children memorized the names of the emperors, and history books included nothing which put the imperial family in a bad light. Anyone questioning the integrity of the ancient history books or the political stance of the government found himself behind bars, as did happen to a number of university professors and others.

Post-war archaeology. The historians especially benefited from the intellectual freedom won by defeat in World War II, but all the disciplines were relaxed, open to foreign influences, just waiting to explode in a characteristic frenzy of Japanese academic literacy. Post-war archaeology is the essential substance of this book. Its history is a splendid achievement of the training of two generations of archaeologists, innumerable excavations, governmental awareness and support for the work, and floods of site reports and monographs, at every level from the most abstruse to the most popular, from Palaeolithic to subway construction, Tokugawa period archaeology. The discoveries have frequently been spectacular, the excavations often extending over many years, the results published in the most minute detail. The identification of palace sites, the discovery of Japan's Palaeolithic, the understanding of the Yayoi culture, the plan of the first Buddhist temple, and others could be listed as the major post-war developments, but the single discovery that ranks top in the list was the opening of the Takamatsuzuka painted tomb in Asuka on 21 March 1972 by Suenaga Masao (1897–), climaxing a lifetime of archaeological work in the Kansai.

Two of the essentials for good archaeology are manpower and money. Japan has both. There is no dearth of good sites, and people to dig them. The archaeology departments in the bigger universities are large. For all its controversy, salvage archaeology has shown spectacular results since the archaeologist tends to have the upper hand in controlling the time, and the budgets are diversified for excavation, analysis and scientific studies, and publication.

2. Geology, Prehistory and Anthropology

Geological movements. The remains of fossil creatures, the survival of plants of continental origin and the results of geological studies leave no doubt that at several stages Japan was part of the Asian land mass. It is probably only the last of these land-bridge stages, the Late Pleistocene, that is pertinent for the arrival of man. Remains of elephants are frequently fished up in the Inland Sea and in other coastal areas. With periodic lowering of the water level of Lake Nojiri in Nagano prefecture thousands of people descend on it in winter to dig in groups for fossil bones.

The first break in the land-bridges which started Japan on her long road to geographical isolation was the formation of the Tokara Strait between Yaku Island of the Ōsumi group and smaller islands of the Ryukyu chain to the south. The seabed of this and the Tsushima Strait between Japan and Korea lack irregular conformations and must be the original continental shelf which once acted as a natural land connection.

Layers of volcanic ash were laid down over large areas of the country in the later Pleistocene. In central-eastern Japan they form collectively the Kantō Loam. Most of the cultural remains with which archaeologists are concerned are in the top main layer, called the Tachikawa Loam. Very few sites are as ideally stratified as they are in the Kantō Plain and it therefore stands to reason that chronologies should be built around such safely stratified conditions.

The first tool makers. Hundreds of sites are now known, more inland for central Honshu and more coastal for the Inland Sea and Kyushu. Throughout the country certain broad traditions can be recognized for which the generally accepted starting dates are around 30,000 years ago. Large flake and pebble tools were widely used with few recurrent forms; pebbles were worked along one edge to produce a chopper. Occasionally, edge-ground ax-like tools are found. Backed knives were the first to be retouched, made from a long flake and bifacially worked along one lateral margin. The prolonged use of pebble and

Previous page: "goggle eye" figurine of the Latest Jōmon period, the last millennium BC, from Aomori prefecture. Height 34·8 cm.

Left: land-bridges and animal types. The Oriental elephant was largely replaced by the Naumann elephant between 300,000 and 200,000 years ago, and joined by the Giant Deer. The large animals died out after the land-bridges were broken.

Opposite: the Kokubunji Bluffline runs for many miles along an old bed of the Tama river. The Nogawa site, on the south bank, then on land of the International Christian University, west Tokyo, was dug in 1970 (*above*). It was the first to demonstrate vertical stratigraphy in one spot (*below*), yielding eight Preceramic culture layers in a depth of 3·25 m, that is, to Layer VIII, dating to about 24,000 years ago.

Below: a worked Naumann elephant tusk, 11·5 cm long, perhaps used as a tool, from the bed of Lake Nojiri.

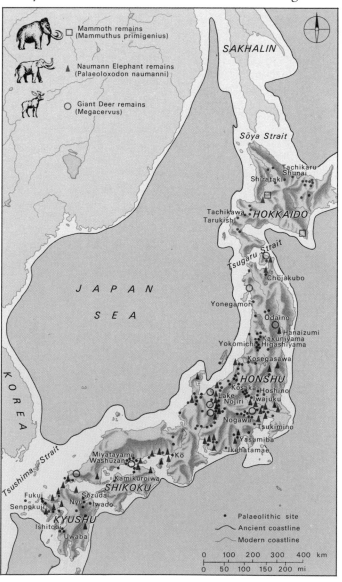

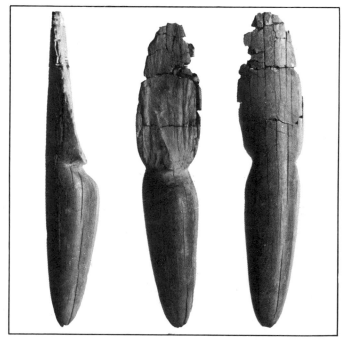

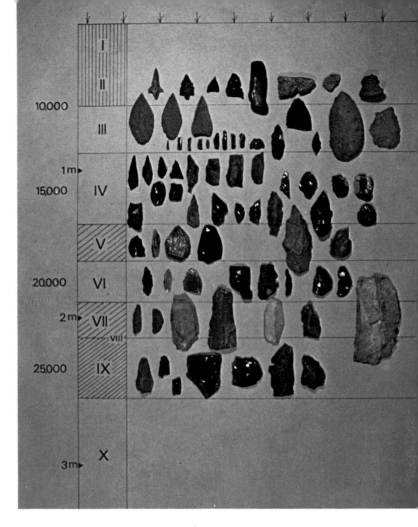

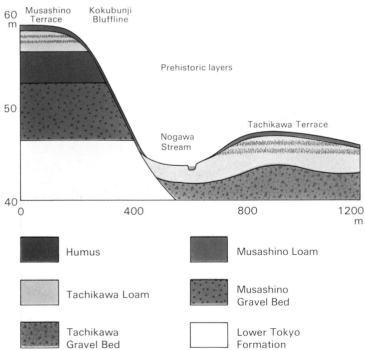

Above: the stone tool sequence at Nishinodai in Koganei city, dug in 1973, the most complete in a Kantō Loam site. The tools are chiefly of chert and obsidian. Part of a clay figurine (*top right*) of Earliest Jōmon was included.

Below: tools from the Shirataki site in Hokkaido, Layer III. They are probably about 15,000 years old.

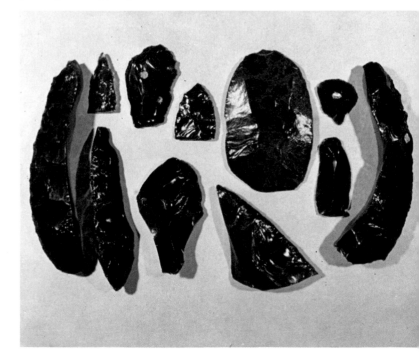

Humus

Tachikawa Loam

Tachikawa Gravel Bed

Musashino Loam

Musashino Gravel Bed

Lower Tokyo Formation

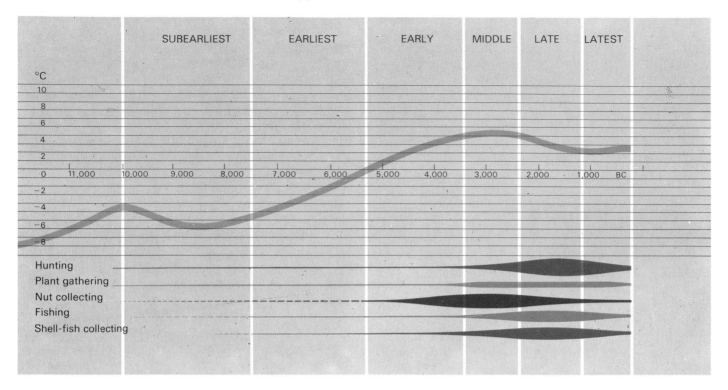

	SUBEARLIEST	EARLIEST	EARLY	MIDDLE	LATE	LATEST

Over a span of about 10,000 years, temperature change had a major bearing on the primary food sources of the Jōmon period.

flake tools makes it perilous to ascribe them to a specific cultural level or time period unless they are stratigraphically recovered. The hand-axes of Iwajuku belong to this early stage. Geologically, all of the artifact-yielding layers in the Kantō sequence from the earliest to Layer V belong to this flake-pebble tool stage.

In the chronology that Japanese archaeologists have adopted – now with much more validity since the stratified sites in the Kantō Loam have yielded such plentiful data – a notable trend toward recurrent forms started around 18,000 years ago. These were tools of smaller size and greater variety, perhaps inspired by efforts to improve the tool kit through the acquisition of better-quality stone. The wide distribution of sites of this stage marks the first country-wide participation in cultural development. The population was exploiting more of the natural resources, staying longer in one place, refining its tools and defining the shapes for greater hunting efficiency, food preparation, the making of clothing and what other needs it may have had.

Throughout all the stages of the Preceramic traditions there are heavy-duty tools which tend to go less noticed. But blade-making techniques were highly developed only in the north, due to borrowing from northern Asia, and were applied primarily to burins (cutting tools). In the last phase of the Preceramic – where the word becomes truly paradoxical – the Palaeolithic tool tradition overlaps with the appearance of pottery around 10,000 BC. Microliths were accompanied by linear relief pottery.

The first potters. A worldwide warming trend about 12,000 years ago was aided in Japan by a slackening of volcanic activity. There was considerable increase in broad-leafed trees, especially birch, and also in spruce and the omnipresent pine, and annual plants, making the acquisition of food easier and encouraging the multiplication of small animal life.

This stage became known as the Jōmon period, after the cord-marked pottery that is so common. A spread of radiocarbon (C-14) dates is available for the decorative developments starting with linear relief in Fukui cave in Nagasaki prefecture, Layer III: 10,750($\pm$500) BC; Layer II, nail-marking: 10,450($\pm$350) BC; Kamikuroiwa rock-shelter in Ehime prefecture, a finer linear relief: 10,750($\pm$500) BC; Iwashita cave in Nagasaki prefecture, plain and nail-marked: 9250($\pm$130) BC; and Kamikuroiwa rock-shelter, Layer VI, undecorated: 8135 ($\pm$320) BC.

This stage, which I have called Subearliest in order to relate it unmistakably to Earliest, is of extraordinary interest because it appears to have the oldest well-dated pottery in the world. The pattern of dates for samples tested in different laboratories is in harmony with the stratigraphy and style changes, and makes it unlikely that any extreme error has occurred, despite the well-known need to adjust C-14 determinations.

The invention of pottery need not be a one-time-one-place event. It required intelligence, but not genius. Observation of hardened clay in firepits which collected a little water might be the start. The practical application from unfired to fired clay was the important step. It required no special drive for the improvement of living, but it did enhance the quality of existence. Cooking made foods more palatable, and pots offered safer storage facilities and the relief of not being so closely shackled to the water sources.

During this 3,000-year period, the temperature gradually warmed enough to attract many varieties of shellfish to breeding grounds along the east coast and in the lower rivers. These rich resources were discovered by Earliest Jōmon people, who left piles of shells where they lived, along with other waste.

The Earliest and Early Jōmon periods represent only nominal cultural progress. A bullet-shaped pot was standardized for boiling the seafoods after the bivalves had been allowed to stand for several hours to extrude their sand. There were also oysters and scallops in smaller numbers.

The modest-sized boiling vessel was decorated in south Japan by rolling a carved stick over the surface in a rouletting fashion, in central-eastern areas with early forms of cord-marking, and in north Japan usually by some kind of shell-marking. Hokkaido is quite marginal to the main island changes.

Shale, sandstone or clay-slate ax-like tools were used for extracting roots and bulbs from the soil. Among the sparse animal bones in the middens are those of the Siberian mountain lion, probably a rather important food source at the time. But these bones rarely show up in later sites, as though the creature had been unable to survive the changing climate or had been over-hunted by man.

Houses may have been used primarily for poor-weather shelters. The few remains that are found are of rather small, shallow pits of more or less square shape, about four meters to a side. Slanting roofs of thatch or bark were supported by an irregular number of posts over the pit. Fires were generally made outside and some sites have 20 or 30 cone-shaped firepits, dug on the opposite side of a rise from the houses. The so-called Kayama type of pottery of this stage is fiber-tempered and shell-scraped and still with sharply tapered bottom.

For about 2,000 years no effort was made to put a flat bottom on the pots, perhaps because most were being used outdoors and set down into rather soft ground. But as more living took place indoors on hardened floors, flat bottoms became more convenient. This minor achievement is recognized by archaeologists as one of the traits that signify the start of Early Jōmon. Fiber-tempering was going out, and heavy dense cord-marking and marking with the crescent-shaped split end of a bamboo stick were coming in. Surface coverage of cord-marking increased greatly in more northerly areas, with a variety of unusual twists and knotting of the cords. These vessels were still imperfectly fired in the open at a rather low temperature. Any minor variations in shape were aimed at improving the usefulness of the cooking pot.

Three or four houses grouped in an arc composed an Early Jōmon hamlet, situated near a spring or small river.

Left: all finds are plotted after being bagged; flecks of charcoal are shown ready for horizontal plotting in west Tokyo.

Below left: pieces of basketry, the oldest so far found (5000–4000 BC), from the Torihama shell-mound in Fukui prefecture.

Below: the same mound has yielded valuable cultural information: shells, tools, pottery, bones, pieces of wood and nuts.

The house design was quite traditional, although a rare one had an indoor fireplace and so necessitated larger posts and higher roofs, since a center pole was still the main supporting unit.

The appearance of storage pits both inside and outside the houses reflects a new need. Nuts were becoming more plentiful and adding greater nourishment to the diet. There are unexpectedly few animal bones in the shell-mounds.

Recent excavations at the Torihama shell-mound in Fukui have substantially elevated the Early Jōmon people in the estimation of the archaeologist. A more diverse daily fare accompanied a richer cultural life than was previously thought. Gourds amplified the diet of shell-foods, nuts, deer, boar and bear. Miniature stone tools are perfect replicas of regular implements. Advanced woodworking techniques account for wooden tools, parts of boats, oars, boards and lacquered combs used as ornaments. Bone needles, a thimble and fine twine are little different from today. Weaving, rope nets and basketry are all represented by remarkable surviving pieces.

The end of Early Jōmon and the beginning of Middle witnessed the maximum Yūrakuchō transgression – after which the water level began to fall – and the warmest temperature of prehistoric times. Beginning about 3500 BC, the culture rose spectacularly in the upland areas of the Chūbu. Sea foods were still enjoyed, but the proliferation of deciduous, primarily nut-bearing trees and animal life in the central mountains was an irresistible enticement, heightened by proximity to the obsidian sources in the present prefecture of Nagano.

Essentially, the main nut crop in the cool-temperate north was walnuts, in the warm-temperate central area chestnuts and in the subtropical south acorns. Horse chestnuts supplemented the Chūbu-Kantō diet. The central mountains had the special advantage of the availability of all three of these nuts. Storage pits abound both inside and outside the houses and large pots were made for the preservation of raw foods. Nuts, in contrast to rice much later, need large-capacity vessels. Most of the acorns of eastern Japan are bitter and need to be soaked in peat before they are really edible. The acorns of west Japan can be eaten directly. Chestnuts can be collected and preserved in large quantities almost indefinitely – in fact, for as long as 100 years.

Other foods consisted of lily bulbs, yams (*imo*), dogtooth violet, mushrooms, roots and wild grapes. Starch was leached out of bulbs and tubers in springs, grinding was done on stone mortars of scoria and the starch could then be made up into cakes like lumps of bread. *Tochi-mochi* is today a thick paste made of horse chestnuts.

Archaeologists disagree on whether there was actual cultivation, or only manipulation of plants, or whether it was a matter of collecting what grew naturally. Bumper crops of seafoods had allowed for a degree of sedentary life and perhaps even less time spent in food gathering, but had failed to produce the logical population expansion. Some other invigorating factors were involved.

Middle Jōmon society. The new degree of social stability and the rich mountain plant and animal life worked to produce a number of cultural changes. The middle geographical belt of Honshu has numerous large sites featuring house pits by the score and occasionally by the hundred. But pottery typology suggests that only a few were in use at a given time and these accommodated bands of probably not more than 25 or 30 people. A common view is that an average of five people occupied a house.

The pits of these houses have rounded outlines, with a central fireplace and five or six postholes. A more spacious plan, resulting from the elimination of the center pole, made the hearth the core of family life and added enormously to the intimacy of the house and its comfort. The fireplace sometimes had a large bowl or pot without bottom and was often outlined with stones. Like postholes, fireplaces that were moved around the interior leave a record of enlargements and reductions of house size.

Houses were frequently rebuilt and the pits are often found to overlap each other. Many are full of the debris of broken pots, implements and heat-cracked stones, in some cases in sufficient quantity to show that abandoned pits of houses were used for the disposal of the village's garbage and waste. It may be that postholes were enlarged to be receptacles for human bodies, as some are remarkably large.

There is an enormous increase in grinding, digging and tree-cutting tools. Over 200 ax-like implements have been found in a single house pit in the earlier part of Middle Jōmon when pottery of the Katsusaka type was in style. Many of the stone implements in the houses are only the butt ends, leaving one to assume that the users often did not change a broken head until after their return home. Ranging from a soft shale to a hard andesite, in triangular, rectangular or bowtie shapes, they were chipped only as little as was needed to be useful.

The sheer quantity of pottery in the sites is staggering. For the first time it was made in shapes and sizes intended to serve a variety of purposes, some of which were ritual. Vessels were made as steamers. In fact, food was boiled, stewed and steamed. A cup-shaped rim could hold a wicker tray lodged in the neck. Luxuriant ornamentation includes symbolic and magical features. The fact that the decoration was often so excessive as to interfere with the function of the pots must mean that it had more than simply esthetic value. Snakes and heads of animals or sub-humans range from explicit to stylized. Other clay ritual objects are lamps or "incense burners," stands and female figurines. Houses on mountain sites occasionally had platforms on one side, on which stood upright stones. Phallic symbols were widely made.

Hunting utilized traps and bows and arrows. Arrowheads are somewhat less numerous than one might expect, and most are rather small. Preference for good-quality stone doubtless affected their size. They are triangular or roughly V-shaped in most cases and made of varieties of chert or obsidian.

Obsidian was brought from the mountain sources in Nagano, chiefly Wadatoge and Kirigamine, and from the Hakone area into the Kantō Plain. There may have been a steady, perhaps seasonal, trek at that time, since even then the mountain winters could be blustery, snowy and unpleasant. If there was any exchanging going on it was with the processors of salt. Japan has no natural salt mines and all salt has to come from evaporation sites along the coast. From at least Late Jōmon it was processed in special vessels, and eventually a way was developed for molding portable cakes.

Deteriorating climate, heavy rainfall, cooler temperatures and a considerable lowering of the coniferous tree-line made life in the mountains scarcely tolerable and the people drifted down toward the coasts, abandoning many of their forest-related customs in the process. Most of their symbols and particular artifact forms disappeared from the archaeological record. Supplementing the population along the east littoral, they joined forces to form the many large shell-middens that are characteristic of the Late Jōmon period. This took place around 2400 BC.

The Late Jōmon periods. Some of these shell-mounds are among the better-known names of Japanese prehistory. Ōmori, Kasori, Horinouchi, Ubayama and others are landmarks in Japanese archaeology, pottery type names, or otherwise noted for the information they have yielded. Recent efforts by the government to buy the sites and preserve some of them as parks, with small well-planned museums of an educational nature on the site, make for very rewarding visits.

These large mounds are in fact usually clusters of middens, extending for several hundred yards along a knoll above an old inlet. Over 200 kinds of shellfish have been counted in them, mainly mollusks, oysters, abalone and snail-shells, and 30 species of fish, in particular perch, sea bass, mullet, gilthead, snapper, dragonet and seabream caught offshore. Hooks and sinkers are well enough known from earlier midden sites, along with lines, nets and spears, but these increased in size and in efficiency as detachable harpoon heads were now employed. Remains of dugout canoes indicate boats up to six meters in length and many bones are those of deepsea fish.

Among the roughly 30 species of land animals, the Ezo deer is found in northern sites, the Japanese deer elsewhere. Deer bones are largely those of adult males. The females and young were astutely avoided. No such concern existed for the rapidly breeding wild boar, which provided meat, skin and fat, and narrow and long bones for tools. Rooting around houses and storage pits, it must have been a constant pest in the winter, as it still is in some parts of the country today.

Monkeys were eaten. Cat bones give no clues as to their degree of domestication. Dogs, ancestors of the small modern Shiba, were kept as house pets and properly buried.

Left: the Kainohana shell-mound in Matsudo city, Chiba prefecture, was fully excavated to reveal the settlement pattern.

Below: narrow oval pits with tapered walls almost 2 m in length and dug well into the loam, were probably wild boar traps. These are at Nishinodai, Koganei city, greater Tokyo.

Shell area		Clay figurine
Kasori E-1	Middle Jōmon	Clay plaque
Kasori E-2		Stone "club"
Horinouchi 1	Late Jōmon	Stone "sword"
Horinouchi 2		
Soya		
Angyō 3c.	Latest Jōmon	

0 20 40 m
0 60 120 ft

The pits of the houses of Late Jōmon are hard to find, as they penetrated the red loam only slightly, if at all, and so may fail to show the color and textural differences by which the Middle Jōmon pit-houses are recognized. The known houses were more or less rectangular in shape. The settlements were located on a sharply protruding terrace above a large inlet or on the edge of a swampy area, convenient to the water's edge yet out of reach of stormy tides, or in protected spots along rivers. In most cases the level land behind gives the impression that the site was selected for its potential as "backyard" vegetable gardens.

In some sites in the Kantō about one out of every ten house pits has a floor paved with large riverbed stones. There is often only one to a site. If it was not the residence of the village head, it may have been a special meeting house or place. Some contain pieces of unusual pottery and stone phalli; others seem to have no postholes; most have little indication of hearths. Mat marks appear frequently on the bases of pottery to suggest that mats were not a rare feature of a dwelling floor at this time.

Late Jōmon pottery consists of smaller, more wieldy vessels, made of fairly pure clay, baked at a slightly higher temperature than Middle Jōmon and so having a dirt-brown rather than the reddish Middle Jōmon color. Firing was sometimes done in a hollowed-out spot on a gentle slope.

Above: cord-marked spouted vessel from an eastern Kantō site of the latter half of Late Jōmon. Height 20 cm.

Below left: larger sites often have one stone floor among many ordinary pit-dwellings. This one measured 2·37 by 1·50 m.

Opposite: many stone circles have been recorded in north Japan, but few remain. The sites were probably Late Jōmon cemeteries.

Below: an unusual, hollow figurine with tilted head and rows of holes in the body, from Mitaka city, greater Tokyo. Length 11·1 cm.

The large storage pots virtually disappeared, to be replaced by thin-walled, gracefully functional vase shapes. The chief distinguishing feature is cord-marking in outlined zones. This spread rapidly to all parts of the country, a fact that is explained by its first use on practical cooking vessels which had to be made everywhere and were eyed by every neighbor for any adoptable improvements. The decoration again conforms to the shape of the vessels – as though Middle Jōmon had never existed – and many bowls, shallow pots, a few spouted vessels and some bizarre shapes accompany the vases. Some have polished surfaces, especially in the north, done for waterproofing and esthetic effect.

The ritual paraphernalia consist of large stone phalli, stone "swords," a small number of carved stone objects, clay plaques and often many clay figurines on a site. These last have now taken on a definite style, are more anthropomorphic and frequently resemble pregnant females, with grotesque, mask-like faces. They may have been thought to facilitate childbirth, alleviate disease – some are believed to have been intentionally broken – and perhaps to simulate burial in the case of the crouched ones, a position which might also show the throes of childbirth.

North Japan has over 30 remains of stone circles, some quite large in size and presumed to be cemetery sites. The most impressive are at Ōyu in Akita prefecture, where two sets of concentric circles made up of thousands of stones lie 80 meters apart. Rectangular groupings of stones are the size of a human body and must have been markers for graves. In the case of each pair of large circles, at almost the same relative position, a sundial-like arrangement is set apart from and between the concentric circles. The rituals for the salmon-fishing season were probably performed at Ōyu, the ceremony that started a long-standing tradition of depositing stones at sacred spots to ensure good catches.

Ōyu and such circles are the clearest evidence for substantial community rituals, and remind one of a possible setting for dances that inspired the myth of Izanagi and Izanami before their creativity produced the Eight Island Country. The Tohoku and Hokkaido depended greatly on salmon, trout and porpoise at that time. Several sites have large stones bearing engraved fish. Ōyu's pottery is almost all of unusual, non-utilitarian shape, and there seems to be no recognizable residential area in the immediate vicinity.

Ritual became increasingly significant in the life of the Latest Jōmon people of the last millennium BC in the north. Sites thinned out quite considerably elsewhere as the temperature slowly cooled and the resources supported a smaller population. Kamegaoka (or Ōbora) is the family name of the chief pottery types, which are profuse in number, small and often delicate in size, painted or burnished and skillfully made. Cups, bowls, vases, lamps, spouted vessels and odd shapes were decorated with or

without cord-marking, and with elegant, often complicated patterns carved like woodwork. Vessels for daily use tended to be simpler and have coarser features. Each member of the family may have enjoyed his own "set of dishes."

The figurines are a striking phenomenon of this stage. There are several types, some of which are hollow with paper-thin walls. The "eye idols" – the bloated, heavily costumed statuettes with eyes totally dominating the face – were said by Tsuboi to be wearing "snow goggles." Others see in them the window to the soul, or the evil eye. The hollowness was not merely an exhibition of skill; it was intended to provide space for the "soul" of the *kami* (higher spirit).

Latest Jōmon looks much like an extension of Late Jōmon but increasingly ritualized. There are proportionally more carved wooden objects, ornamental bone and horn pieces, earrings and other accessories, phallic symbols, polished stone axes, all stereotyped in their own particular way. In other parts of the country Latest Jōmon is an enigma. Surface dwellings could have been in wide use. Identified house pits are more or less rectangular and arranged in crescent shapes. But the sites are scarcer and culturally inferior. All evidence points to major population changes in much of the country except the north.

One of four "Venus" stones, between 5 and 6 cm in length, found in Layer IX of the rock shelter of Kamikuroiwa in Ehime prefecture, dating to the opening of the Jōmon period.

Who are the Japanese? Who are the Japanese and where did they come from? These questions are still asked by Japanese and foreigners alike, but the day is long past when simple answers could be given. Foreigners often say: they all look alike. This is quite untrue, although the differences are more of degree than kind. There is a great variety of head and body shapes, and some old and gray-haired people in western clothes could easily pass for typical Europeans. About the only consistent features are the black hair and epicanthic fold of the eyes, but these are enough to put them under one heading.

It is fashionable today to emphasize the indigenous physical development of the early Japanese, but this means only that, although alternative views exist, the nationalistic swing is upward. The two views fluctuate between changes attributed to immigrants mixing with the local population and changes resulting from climate and diet.

Japanese history contains well-known instances of migrations of foreigners to Japan, along with locally devised ways of producing certain physical types. At least in the very early stages, physical characteristics were set by the immigrants, but later, internal conditions are more likely to have caused the changes. Breeding was consciously planned to produce white-skinned girls for the court, and the selection of wives for the Tokugawa can be credited with producing the peculiar "Tokugawa skull."

The first people entered Japan from all parts of the "mainland." But throughout the Jōmon period they failed to reduce their physical differences through intermixing. The shell-mounds of Ōta, Tsugumo, Yoshigo and elsewhere have yielded skeletons numbering hundreds, but each group has its own characteristics. The commonly used terms have been Tsugumo Man, Ōta Man or just about any other shell-mound name where skeletons have been found and their physical features fully studied.

By physical standards these people are to be regarded as "non-Japanese." The men stood around 5 foot 1 inch (157 cm), the women several inches shorter. Those that reached adulthood rarely passed the age of 30, judging by deterioration of joints. Over 80 per cent still retain their wisdom teeth. The face was rather low and wide with high projected nose of non-Mongoloid appearance. Earliest to Early Jōmon man was rather prognathic, and became more mesognathic in Middle and later stages as the height and length of the skull increased. These changes corresponded with a slightly greater brachycranic trend, from an earlier, largely mesocranic stage.

The major changes in Jōmon skeletons arose as a consequence of an improved diet and the physical labor required to procure the food. Teeth were badly worn in earliest times, and eating and tearing poorly prepared food took their physical toll. The Hirasaka male skeleton, from Yokosuka of Earliest Jōmon, was a king among gnomes, standing 5 foot 4 inches (163 cm) tall. His right-side, lower-jaw teeth were badly ground down, as though he had spent much of his adult life chewing and pulling leather thongs through them.

The bone structure caused by inadequate nutrition in the diet was remedied in both men and women in the Middle Jōmon period and later. The long bones of both arms and legs became thicker, as they strengthened themselves to support better-developed muscles acquired through heavy physical work. Women dug, carried, ground up foods, and their clavicles, and only theirs, lengthened as the physical labor broadened their shoulders. No other bones lengthened noticeably, other than a very slight overall increase in stature for both sexes.

Changes therefore are attributable to a more nutritious diet, and the strengthening of the body in the process of getting it. The skeletons studied are almost entirely of shell-mound, coastal people, found in conditions in which organic material is preserved. Life was harder in the mountains, but there is little evidence to show how the nut-collectors fared. For none, however, did better diets noticeably increase their longevity.

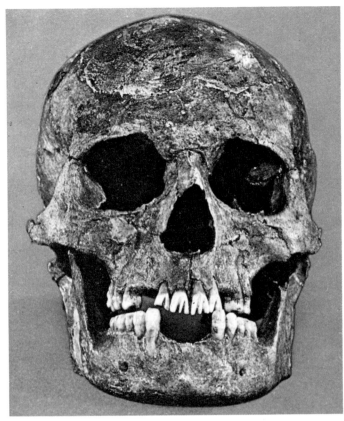

Right: a male skull found in the Ikawatsu shell-mound, Atsumi-chō, Aichi prefecture, of a 30-year-old man (perhaps the village chief) who lived in Latest Jōmon.

Below: Ebijima shell-mound in Hanaizumi-chō, Iwate prefecture, an example of the "cemetery concept" of burial by the Late Jōmon period. It had about 21 human inhumations.

The Ainu in Hokkaido today are probably of ancient Caucasoid origins and are now in the process of rapid assimilation.

Burials in shell-mounds are in flexed or extended positions in about equal number. An occasional one is marked by stones around or on top, or a pot at the head, and some later skeletons bear red paint, especially in the north, where a secondary burial fashion seems to have involved the cleaning off of the flesh and a final interment among the shells.

Pyorrhea was widespread, and many teeth are missing, but where deterioration is otherwise not serious, missing teeth are evidence of an extraction practice indulged in at about the age of puberty, affecting an estimated 70 per cent of males but only about 30 per cent of females. Some minor differences can be seen between sexes regarding the selection of teeth for mutilation. A few of the remaining teeth were filed in a V-shaped way. In no sites did everyone undergo the ritual, and its absence is not necessarily attributable to differences in time. The best explanation is some mixing of tribal groups, especially the taking of wives from neighboring peoples which did not indulge in the practice.

The Caucasoid "hairy Ainu" who reside in parts of Hokkaido today are thought to be very early arrivals from the north Asian region. There is some borrowing from their language into Japanese, such as *kamui* to *kami*, for higher spirits, and quite possibly the associated animistic ideas, but the sweeping claim for Ainu names surviving over two-thirds of the country has now shriveled to the Tohoku and Hokkaido districts, including a skeptical view that Fuji-no-yama (Mountain of Fire) is not necessarily Ainu.

The old name for the Ainu was Ezo, and hence for Hokkaido, the island they occupied. From the 7th century A D in particular, the Emishi were a thorn in the flesh of the Japanese who earmarked them for destruction because their culture and appearance were unassimilable. Population pressures and official policy drove them north, but the fact that they put up such a good fight for more than 100 years, and were still in the Tōhoku in the 18th century according to Tokugawa records, tells something about their hardiness and ability to survive as a tribal group.

It is an article of faith among many archaeologists that the Latest Jōmon in north Japan was an Ainu culture period. Yet it is also thought that there is no cultural break between Late and Latest, implying therefore greater antiquity for the Ainu. For a people who zealously retained their physical and cultural homogeneity through exclusiveness, it would normally be assumed that if skeletal remains existed as evidence, their presence could be traced to considerable antiquity. The Ainu did not cremate, but nor did they bury in cemeteries, and physical remains are scarce. Bones recovered from the Bosuyama shell-mound in north Hokkaido show they can be traced as far back as the Satsumon stage, which is a survival into the Christian era of the Jōmon culture, the so-called Epi-Jōmon, of hunting and fishing people. But before that they might be termed Ainu-related people. Their whole life style has until the last generations been so diametrically opposed to the Japanese way of living that if they reflect a way of life based on the Latest Jōmon archaeological data, then the culture has changed a great deal since that time to become "Japanese." It also shows how difficult it is to understand the real life style of a people simply through the archaeological record.

The Middle Jōmon Subculture

Around 3500 BC, in comfortable, warm conditions, bands of people moved into the central mountains. Their encounter with the flora and fauna and their mountain style of living produced a distinct culture that lasted for about a thousand years, until climate changes and intense rains made life too difficult.

The many large sites, some with numerous pits of houses, quantities of pottery and other remains suggestive of more time devoted to manufacture, are signs of considerable economic stability. New vessel shapes were devised for specific needs, and mountain conditions gave rise to various symbols, especially the snake, female figurines and phalli, along with heads of animals worked into the rim decoration of pots.

For all of its dramatic millennium, the Middle Jōmon culture left few marks in succeeding Jōmon times. The peculiar mountain conditions produced it, and once the mountains were abandoned the particular way of life was forgotten. *Below:* Togariishi in Nagano prefecture where several pit-dwellings have been reconstructed.

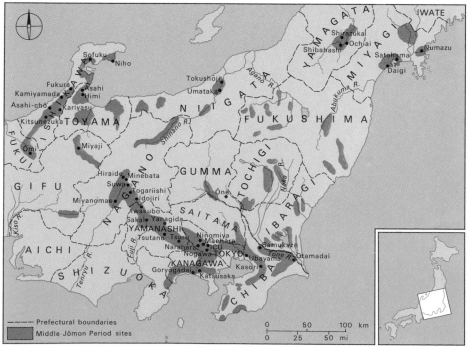

The Middle Jōmon culture rose in southern Nagano prefecture and spread to the west and east coasts. The hundreds of sites that represent it have in common pottery types allied with the Otamadai and Katsusaka types of the earlier half of the Middle Jōmon and the Kasori E or Ubayama type of the later half of Middle Jōmon. Numerous local type names are given to the pottery.

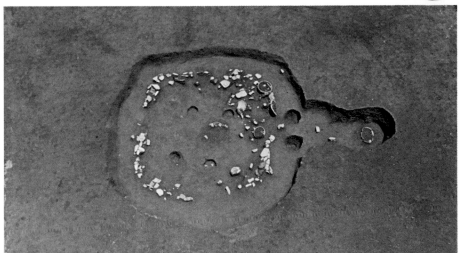

Opposite: reconstructed pit-dwellings at the Yosukeone site at Togariishi are on the south side of Mt Yatsugatake. They have been reconstructed with an off-center entrance on the south and a raised ridge pole to form a ventilation system for smoke from the interior fireplace. Other pit-dwellings, reconstructed elsewhere by archaeologists who believe otherwise, have simply a cone-shape, with no opening at the top.

Right: one of the house pits in the Maehara site, Koganei city in greater Tokyo, appears to have been made into a little cemetery after it was abandoned while people were still living nearby. As it was exposed, there were four clusters of pots and sherds, one stone tool and all or part of a phallic stone for each cluster. A handle-like extension of the pit toward the south had pots buried in it and perhaps marked the grave of an infant or was made for some magical reason. Removal of these artifacts showed a house pit below with an unusual number and uniformity of holes.

Above: for the first time pots were not all exclusively made for cooking. New shapes appear to meet special uses. In some cases, "sets" of large pots and bowls go together, such as these recovered as pairs on the International Christian University campus.

Center left: rough stone tools doubled as axes and adzes, ranging from a soft shale to an andesite in triangular, rectangular or bowtie shapes. They were chipped only as little as needed to be useful. These are from the Maehara site, Koganei city, and they average about 12 cm in length.

Below left: two houses had been built on the same spot of Loc. 24A on the ICU campus, Mitaka city of greater Tokyo, each ditched around the outside and each with a set of five postholes. The outer one is about 7 m in diameter. The fireplace (shown here) had an outline of stones and contained a small pot.

Above : snakes appear on clay vessels in the lower mountains. Some are quite realistic, like this one from a site in Kanagawa prefecture.

Right : 48 cm pot from a pit-dwelling in Loc. 19, ICU sites, marked with a split bamboo stick above and cord-marked below.

Below : this vessel came from a small pit in the Yanagida site in Yamanashi prefecture and has the only snake on the recovered pots.

Left: an unusual ritual type of vessel is this barrel-shaped pot 51·2 cm high from Idojiri in Nagano prefecture. Such vessels have perforations around the rim and a surrounding ridge just below, while this one has a relief figure which looks as if it is dancing. These are probably drum bodies to which skin was fastened with little pegs in the rim holes. The figure may have been inspired by the activities of the ritual in which the drum was used.

Below: male symbols make their first regular appearance in various shapes of stone and, very rarely, clay. The mushroom stone on the right, its cap 22 cm in diameter, stood on a now-broken shaft over 30 cm high. It has blackened holes produced in the making of fire. The volcanic stone was brought into the area from a considerable distance. These objects were all found in the ICU sites in Mitaka city of metropolitan Tokyo.

Right: several shapes of vessels called lamps have been found in sites in the mountains, all with some kind of handle over a small bowl by which they could be suspended. One has little boars on it. These here have been called snakes, frogs and slugs. This lamp comes from Fudasawa of the Idojiri sites in Nagano prefecture and is 16·6 cm high.

Below right: earrings and ear plugs in clay and stone got greater use in Middle Jōmon. The spool-shaped ones were probably inserted into perforated lobes of the ear and are almost always painted red. The stone ones were horseshoe-shaped and slid over the lobe, but few of these are recovered complete. These are from ICU sites in Mitaka city, western Tokyo.

Below: this painted stone 15 cm long was found along the bluffline of the ICU sites, directly above a spring. In what is extraordinarily rare graphic art for Middle Jōmon, there seems to be an animal with head on the right, a humped back and legs, and arched tail to the left. Its imprecision makes the animal next to impossible to identify.

Clay female figurines were made before this time, but they increased sharply in number in Middle Jōmon. This unique one of a mother holding a child, the oldest example of three-dimensional clay sculpture, was found in pit-dwelling 4 of the Miyata site in Hachiōji city of west Tokyo, along with neatly stacked stone tools, fragments of what might have been a standing stone, and a mica-tempered pot in a large pit in the center of the house floor. It had obviously been used ritually. The figurine measures 7·1 cm in height.

3. Mythology, Rice and the Yamato State

Reconstructed house on the Middle to Late Yayoi site of Toro, south of Shizuoka city, in what is now a park.

Where was Yamatai? The greatest mystery in ancient Japanese history has been around since Chinese travelers wrote about their Japanese neighbors in the late 3rd century AD. One book had already described the Land of Wa as consisting of over 100 "countries," 30 of which were in diplomatic contact with China or its colonies. The *Wei Chih* (Records of Wei), compiled in 297 AD, gives a stage-by-stage account of how to reach the "queen country" by both land and sea, starting at Tai-fang on the west side of Korea and going through "country" after "country," usually 1,000 *li* at a time (a *li* is one sixth of a sea mile). It is over 12,000 *li* to Wa. More than 4,000 *li* to the south is an island of dwarfs. Another year of travel in the same direction takes one to a place inhabited by naked men and another by black-teethed people.

Nevertheless, for all this detail, Yamatai, the center of the Land of Wa, cannot be located. If one follows the distances and directions together literally, Yamatai is in the middle of the ocean. Measured by direction only, Yamatai is in Kyushu; by distance only, Yamatai is in Yamato. One problem is that the Chinese could measure distances at sea only in days of travel time.

Where was the power center of Japan as the Chinese understood it? Yamatai is near enough to Yamato to make us suspect a corrupted phonetic equivalent, but differences in writing the characters have blunted the argument.

The "queen" was living in the Late Yayoi period, and Japan is known to have had many female shamans (priests). Wei dynasty writers described the Wa surprisingly thoroughly. Some of this account is verified by other evidence, including that of archaeology. In their daily lives the Wa are law-abiding people, subject to harsh punishment for any infringements. They eat with their hands from wooden trays and platters, and go without footwear. Men live with men, women with women, but there is a community spirit of sex equality. The people are heavy drinkers. Boys and men tattoo themselves and decorate their bodies. Exchange of goods is carried out in fixed marketplaces in each area. Taxes are collected by officials. Nobles are served by people of lesser status, and respect is shown when passing persons of rank by getting

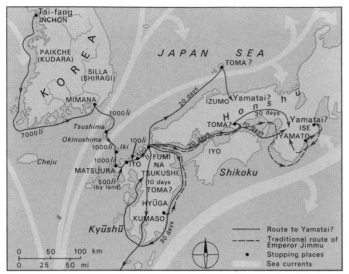

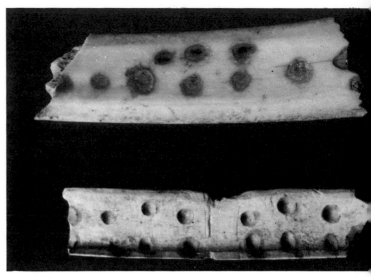

Above: among the practices of the people of Wa was divination through the use of oracle bones. Holes were burned, questions were asked, and the diviners provided the answers.

Above left: the route to Yamatai, the chief kingdom of Japan, called the Land of Wa. Chinese historians went to great lengths to describe their neighbors and how to reach them.

off the road. Squatting or kneeling is required when speaking to nobles. High-ranking nobles have four or five wives; others have two or three, an arrangement the women willingly accept.

The religious practices include divination for future action by burning bones; and there is a class of "abstainers" who remain unkempt and unwashed, and avoid meat and women. As ritual scapegoats, they are killed by their group if things go wrong because it is assumed they have broken their vows.

It is not unusual for Wa people to live to be over 100. They bury their dead in a simple coffin (i.e. not the double ones the Chinese might use), mourn for ten days while musical entertainment is provided by singers and dancers, and then the whole family goes off and cleanses itself by washing in running water.

The Wa were ruled over by a priestess called Himiko or Pimiko, literally "sun-daughter," a title for a queen, who came to power around 183 AD. She was elderly and remained unmarried; she kept her position by her exercise of magical powers. She was served by 1,000 women, but only one man. She lived in a heavily guarded fortified residence and only her brother was in direct communication with her. Himiko died around 248 and was interred in a huge mound about 300 meters in diameter together with more than 1,000 of her attendants, both male and female. Following her death the tribes suffered an inept male leader for a short time, but deteriorating conditions forced them to name a 13-year-old girl called Iyo as successor.

The Chinese were reporting on customs different from their own which they regarded as curious. They were revolted by the flea-ridden, uncombed "abstainers" who accompanied the boats to China, and perplexed at their enormous social responsibility and callous fate. But they noted that the Japanese treated these men well. Perhaps in compensation for their precarious existence they were given slaves. Later Japanese found this reference to slaves embarrassing, as was the account of some of the habits

of their ancestors. Nor was the term for Japan itself complimentary. Wa is "little people" or "dwarfs." The later, more unified Japanese eventually spoke of themselves as people of Yamato when seeking to inspire a native, national spirit; but about the 7th century AD they were happy to settle for a name the Chinese gave them: Jih-pen, sun-rise, the land where the sun rises (for China). Japanese call their country Ni-hon, and westerners corrupted it, perhaps through the Chinese form, to Japon – Japan.

Japanese investigations. Japanese scholars started in the Kamakura period (1185–1392 AD) to try to locate Yamatai. Most early studies took it for granted that the Kinki was its home. Since then it has been located everywhere, from Yamato, the Inland Sea, Izumo region, north Kyushu, west Kyushu to, more recently, nowhere, just a complete and masterful hoax by Chinese writers.

From the first there was some feeling that the female shaman Himiko could be identified with Empress Jingū whose exploits are described in the *Nihon Shoki* as performed in Kyushu. There was always some reluctance to see Yamato as under a female shaman – yet the Sun Goddess must be an embodiment of the same idea – or to accept the authenticity of some of the uncivilized practices.

Arai Hakuseki (1657–1725) systematically identified names given in the *Wei Chih* with old place-names in Kyushu and decided the nominal distances given in the description were meaningless. Soon after the imperial restoration (1868) Empress Jingū was dated about 100 years after Himiko (2nd century AD), and Yamatai – with its many households, as the description goes – was associated with north Kyushu. Himiko was removed from the imperial line and so could be discussed more freely.

Korean records seem to verify the existence of Yamatai. Several notices are given of missions from Yamatai. The trip started at Inchon in Korea, the Chinese Tai-fang, and went by way of Tsushima and Iki, two well-known islands, then Matsuura, Ito, Na, Fumi and Toma. All but Toma have been identified in north Kyushu. But once in Kyushu it still took ten more days by *sea* and 30 by *land* to reach Yamatai. This ought to be through the Inland Sea to Yamato.

Chinese travelers should have been able to locate Yamatai if it was in north Kyushu, only a hop, skip and a jump from Korea where the Chinese had colonies in the north. In fact, it would have been so close it might have been pointless to describe how to reach it.

One idea was tried in 1975. In a cooperative venture between Japanese and Koreans, a boat was built to make the trip. The *Yaseigo* was modeled after a *haniwa* boat (clay sculptures placed on the outside of tumuli) found on a Saitobaru tomb in Kyushu many years ago. The boat was 16·5 meters long and able to accommodate 30 people, with seven oars to a side. It left Inchon, went down the coast, stopped at the islands and reached Japan after a rough spell when it had to be towed. For a while there were Korean rowers, later Japanese. There was no expectation of shedding more light on the location of Yamatai, but a recreation of the trip was thought to make the problems more real. And, to the extent that it took far longer than had been expected, it was useful. Where was Yamatai? This is still the question everyone hopes will one day be finally answered.

Mythology and the Japanese pantheon. To the Japanese the cosmos was a compound of lighter and heavier substances, separated like an egg, one becoming Heaven, the other Earth. The first living thing was a reed. It was a higher spirit (*kami*) which engendered the seven generations of *kami*, the last of which were the male Izanagi and female Izanami, creators of the Eight Island Country. They looked down through the clouds and stirred the brine below with a spear. Drops from its point formed the islands. Among the numerous *kami* they begat was Ōhirume, otherwise known as Amaterasu, eventually the Heaven-Shining Great Deity, the Sun Goddess, chief *kami* of the Yamato myths. She was "produced" from a mirror held by Izanagi in his left hand.

Three levels of existence were dimly divided between immortality and mortality: Takama-no-hara, the High Plains of Heaven, was the scene for many of the events of the so-called Age of the Gods, in an amalgam of two or more myth cycles which decided the supremacy of the Yamato ancestry; Ashihara-no-nakatsu-kuni, Central Land of the Reed Plains, was populated by earthly *kami*, and was created for the divinely originated imperial system to live out its preordained history; Yomi-no-kuni, literally Land of the Yellow Springs, was the subterranean world of spirits, where even the inhabitants of the High Plains of Heaven were forced to retire to and "live" on after death.

During the Age of the Gods the *kami* take on endearing or disgusting qualities; they are heroes and villains, wide enough in variety and number to establish the ancestry for the earth-bound *kami* that follow.

Once the activities move from the High Plains of Heaven to the Eight Island Country, longevity is counted

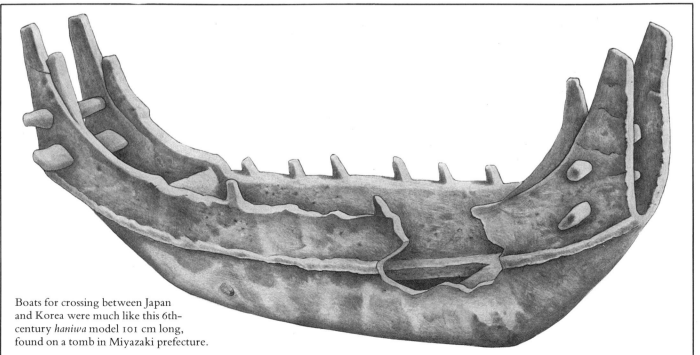

Boats for crossing between Japan and Korea were much like this 6th-century *haniwa* model 101 cm long, found on a tomb in Miyazaki prefecture.

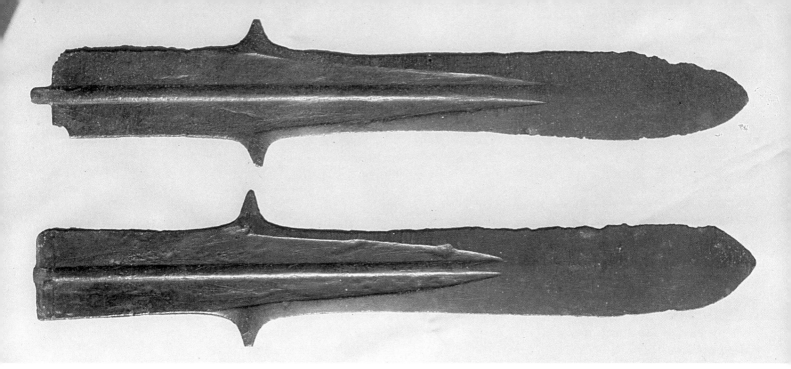

in human years and mortality is increasingly a daily occurrence. The Sun Goddess sent her grandson Ninigi down to take the land for the Yamato, giving him a sacred mirror, sword and string of beads – later known as the imperial regalia – symbols of investiture. He was accompanied by several attendants, destined to be leaders in religion and crafts, and landed on the top of Mt Takachiho, probably the mountain of this name in southeast Kyushu.

Prior to this the region of Izumo had been secured, but its tradition was strong enough to leave a competing mythology. Okuninushi accepted a grand palace and a compromise for his cooperation – the Izumo people were to handle the religious affairs of the state, the Yamato people the secular affairs. This arrangement seems to have had no lasting effect, and proved to be only an opportunistic accommodation made for that region and none other. The Great Shrine of Izumo is the successor of the palace of the *kami* of fishing and sericulture, to which all the *kami* go in the month of October. Even the Grand Shrine of Ise, home of the Sun Goddess, is not favored with such illustrious connections.

After the Ninigi descent the genealogy is unclear, but the man in line to be the first "emperor" marshaled his forces and started out on the long trip to the Yamato Plain. He went up the east coast of Kyushu, through the Inland Sea, around the Kii peninsula and into Nara prefecture, arriving at Kashiwara on the edge of modern Asuka, but only after overcoming numerous obstacles through heavenly signs, divine guidance and miraculous escapes. He built a palace at Kashiwara in 660 BC by the calculations of later Japanese historians.

The Sun Goddess was elevated over the chief *kami* of other tribes by Yamato writers as Amaterasu-Ōmikami, the supreme, but in the view of others she was only one of many, even when the 8th-century *Fudoki* were written. The *Hitachi Fudoki* (Ibaragi prefecture) speaks of Kashima

Bronze weapons were first brought from Korea, then cast in north Kyushu as replicas of imported ones, then modified to wide-bladed ceremonial objects, like these Yayoi period spearheads.

as the highest *kami*, and the *Izumo Fudoki* of Okuninushi (Shimane prefecture) as the creator of the world. In the early sequence leading to the dispatch of the descendant of the Sun Goddess to earth, the male deity Takamimusubi directs the course of events.

At the start of the narrative, largely staged in the High Plains of Heaven, the solar symbol is the sun-spear, *hiboko*. For earthly activities the change was to a mirror, which was formalized when the Sun Goddess gave one to her progeny saying, "When thou lookest upon this mirror, let it be as if thou wert looking on me." Eventually, Emperor Sujin felt that its presence in his palace was causing too much discomfort and enshrined it at Kasanui in Nara perfecture. Later, Emperor Suinin moved it to Ise, where a shrine was built to house it. The first stage of sun symbolism is probably therefore to be tied to the Yayoi use of ceremonial bronze spears, concentrated in north Kyushu, and a later stage to be associated with the Tomb period use of mirrors, centered in the Kinki.

The Inner Shrine at the Ise Grand Shrines in Mie prefecture keeps the mirror of the Sun Goddess; the Outer Shrine is dedicated to Toyouke, the Food Goddess. The Yamato writers placed the building of the latter in the time of Yūryaku, but the Toyouke myth may be the older of the two and have begun in Yayoi times when the idea of a deity of grain began to take shape. As the solar and earth spirits were combined, the mystical union finally materialized at this high shrine of Shinto.

Throughout Japanese history Shinto practices have been a vital social force, communities participating in seasonal ceremonies designed to ensure good crops, fertility, health and the good life in general. The higher beings are coaxed from their customary habitats near unusual land, rock or water formations for such occasions.

The rice-growers. Elements of the Yayoi culture began to take shape in Japan around 300 BC. Extreme views have been taken of this culture, from the older ideas of an "invasion" from Korea or China to the more recent view of a largely indigenous development. Yayoi was a composite product; foreign elements were introduced and adapted, and Japan was "internationalized" and brought into a wider sphere of cultural development.

Bronze and iron were brought in, probably from south Korea. Dolmen-like clusters of large stones over jar burials, and stone cists also, are of Korean origin. It has been suggested that rice was derived from wild species, and that the use and domestication of *awa* and *hie* date to much earlier times. Both are hardy local plants of genera close to rice, the former often translated as millet. But since the reaping knife is clearly a foreign type, it seems a little unlikely that it would have been brought in just to harvest domestic plants. Rice most likely came from the Wu and Yüeh areas of east China, from which some of the

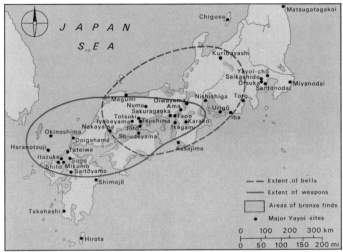

phonetic elements of the language came. This "woman's knife" was part of the package.

Iron tools have been recovered from Early Yayoi middens in Kyushu. In all probability rice was first planted directly in small patches in low, swampy places until water controls made it possible to flood rice fields. And for a century or so rice remained little more than a supplement to the traditional diet, as Yayoi shell-mounds would suggest.

The theory of forceful invasion is now seen as quite unnecessary in view of the fact that the thinly scattered Jōmon population in southern Japan was in no position to resist anyone or any potential change. Foreign to the Jōmon culture are the double-ended celts, the tanged and polished arrowheads and the beveled adzes. Stone daggers, modeled on bronze weapons, were either Korean-made or copied from Korean types during the early stage of scarce metals. Remnants of cloth have come from later Yayoi sites and clay spindle whorls for weaving show it to have been an advanced art.

Itazuke in Fukuoka city is now regarded as the earliest Yayoi site and has been extensively excavated with special attention to the differences from Jōmon. Wooden stakes appear to outline rice-growing plots and farming was done chiefly with wooden rakes and hoes. Itazuke residents lived before the better, polished-stone tools of Yayoi times came into fashion.

No clear shapes of houses were exposed. Pits of all sizes are numerous, presumably for storage. The site yielded

Left: distribution of bronze objects and Middle Yayoi sites.

Below: damp or muddy carbonaceous soil has preserved many Yayoi tools and carved utilitarian and ceremonial objects, mostly of oak and cypress. These are *in situ* in the Ikegami site, Izumi city, Osaka prefecture.

stone reapers, spindle whorls, and stemmed and lidded pots of distinctive Yayoi shapes, but some of the pottery is borderline and difficult to distinguish from the Latest Jōmon Yūsu type in its coarse surface scraping and notched ridge encircling the necks of vessels.

Jar burials number more than 50 at Itazuke, and all were laid horizontally in the fashion of Early Yayoi. Many are double jars. Rectangular shaft graves are rather fewer in number, and in at least some cases must have accommodated wooden coffins. In keeping with a more systematized way of life, Yayoi people isolated their dead in cemeteries, burying the bones in jars, stone cists, mats and wooden coffins, in holes and under large stones, and frequently mixing burial forms within one cemetery.

The remarkable Kanenokuma cemetery in Fukuoka was in use as a burial ground from Early to Late Yayoi. A total of 145 burials were uncovered, mostly single or double jars. Another form of burial, also of the Middle and early stages of Late Yayoi, has been of special interest to archaeologists in recent years. This is a square-shaped grouping of rectangular shaft graves, in which, initially, burials were effected only in the center of the square. In the course of time the four sides also came to be used for interments. These were all on slightly higher ground and were deeply ditched around. Sites where these have been found are rather widespread, perhaps the best known being Ama and Uryūdō in Osaka and Sakachido in Kanagawa.

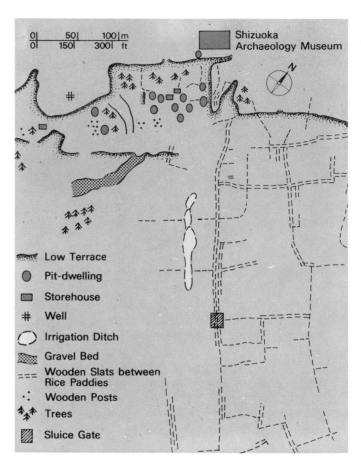

Above: the site of Toro. It was the first excavation to reveal all the major aspects of Yayoi life.

Left: the Ōtsuka site in Yokohama city. At the top, about 25 burials are lined up in square formations, the outlines ditched.

Grave-goods accompanying Yayoi burials were at first Chinese objects of glass and bronze which had probably come in from the Han colonies in north Korea. Many bronze mirrors have been recovered from sites like Sugu and Tateiwa in Fukuoka, and many more are recorded as having been found before the advent of modern archaeology. These finds are largely restricted to north Kyushu, as though their carriers never went beyond its borders to die.

The well-known site of Toro in Shizuoka is the "village that iron built." The thousands of wooden slats used to reinforce the paths between the paddies, not to mention the elaborate woodwork of the storehouses, could only have been made with good-quality iron tools. Toro may not be totally typical, but it represents the elaborate drainage and irrigation systems that brought on the great increase in the size of sites by Middle Yayoi in the first centuries before and after the time of Christ.

Ricefields at Toro lay to the south, a little lower than the dwellings, storehouses and the forest which furnished the large quantities of wood. The Abe river flowed close by and in one disastrous flood inundated the village. Posts of destroyed houses were pointed in the direction of the flow.

Yayoi houses and society. The Toro houses were built alike, facing the ricefields. In fact, Yayoi houses have the kind of dull uniformity that begins to take over after craftsmen start to standardize their work. Oval in shape, a house floor measured about 8 × 6 meters and the superstructure consisted of an *irimoya* thatch roof with ventilator-sunshade supported by four heavy posts crossed by beams and sloping poles. The posts were firmly planted in the soft soil with boards sunk beneath their bases. Banked earth around the outer edge of the interior of the house was secured in place by vertical wooden slats. The original houses had shallow central hearths, though these seem not always to have been built into the reconstructions at Toro Park

Most Yayoi communities kept their rice and other foods in family-owned storage pots. Sets of vessels were now essential for comfortable living: wide-mouthed pots for cooking, narrow-mouthed ones for storage, and cups and bowls with pedestals or with stands for ritual use. But Toro's pottery is negligible. Instead, its inhabitants built storehouses in the approximate ratio of one to a row of five residences. This was a new type of building, seen in scratched pictures on pottery and in thread-line reliefs on bronze bells, but its traces are rarely found by archaeologists. It was a windowless structure, built of boards with raised floor, topped by a simple, thatched roof. A single door on the short, south end was reached by a notched log. The grain was protected from rodents (i.e. field mice) by "rat guards," wooden plates set just below the floor level of the pillars.

A granary like this is a major landmark in architectural development. Planks were used for walls and floors, all of which were squared off in regular shapes. The Yayoi farmer did indeed spend more on his barn than on his wife. And recognition of its social value was not long in coming. In later Yayoi centuries the raised structure was adopted as an upper-class dwelling – its chief disadvantage was its unsuitability for fireplaces – and so became the type of palace and early shrine. Palaces and shrines were interchangeable in both idea and form: the character *miya* or *gū* can have either meaning.

By Middle Yayoi rice planting had moved into upper valleys with residential areas somewhat higher on the hillsides. These are usually settlements of a small number of dwellings, which were otherwise engaged in raising peas, soy beans, red beans, broad beans and millet, along with dry-land rice crops.

As inland progress continued and as bronze casting, iron forging and other crafts increased in proficiency, trade and bartering centers grew up. Stone tools were made and exchanged. Large numbers of tools in differing stages of manufacture have turned up on several sites. Salt was difficult to obtain as branch communities moved away from the coasts, but salt production throve in the Inland Sea, where special sites for this purpose have been identified.

Even in pottery making there was a tendency toward specialization. The large double jars for burials in Middle Yayoi were the work of no ordinary potters. The largest pair together measures about two meters in length. These were the ones laid at about a 45-degree angle; Late Yayoi

Below left: the raised storehouse is the prototype of the palace and the Shinto shrine. This reconstruction is in Koganie Park, west Tokyo.

Below: Yayoi burial jars from the Kanenokuma site in Fukuoka city, a large cemetery with pits, single and double jars.

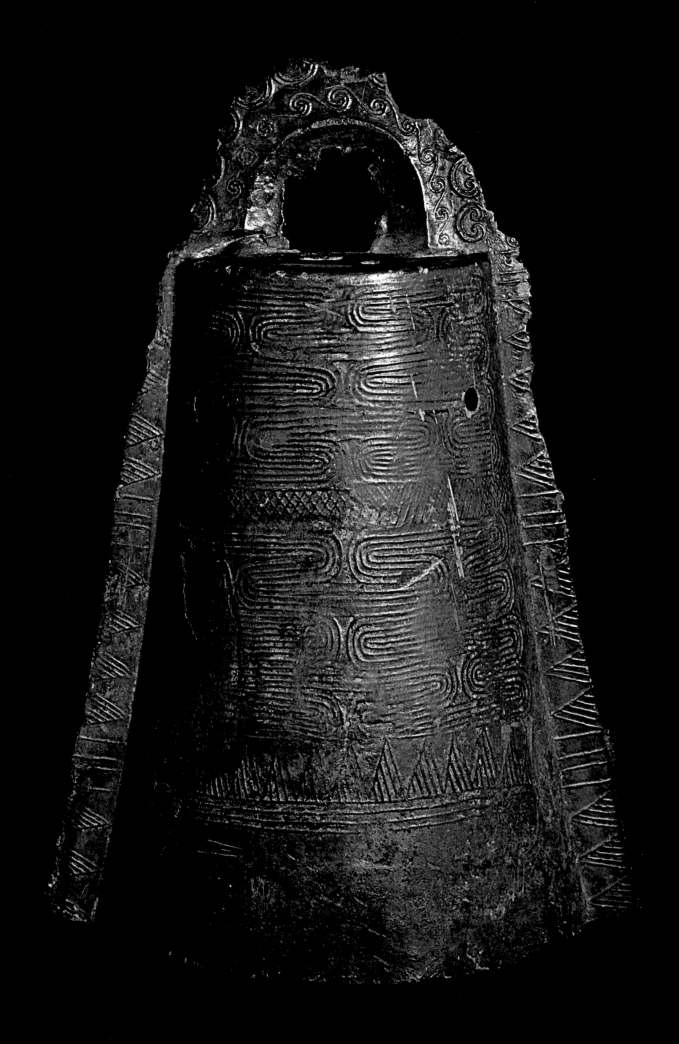

jars were smaller and often placed upright. By Middle Yayoi these were made semi-commercially by craftsmen of considerable skill, probably still without the benefit of a wheel.

Weapons and bells. As in China, iron was the working man's material, bronze the aristocrat's symbol of power. Iron objects were first brought over with bronze, sometimes reworked, and later the ore itself supplied from Korea. Iron was probably wrought locally by the 1st century AD, to judge by the sites containing slag in north Kyushu and on the Japan Sea side.

Four types of bronze weapon came with travelers, three of which were imitated and produced in local versions: a halberd like a Chinese *ko*, hafted to a handle at right angles and used for slashing; a tanged double-edged weapon that came in as a dagger-sword, used for thrusting; and a socketed spear, used as a projectile. The last two were fully accepted by the Japanese and copied in enlarged and non-functional shapes. They were easily adaptable as symbols for current religious beliefs – the "sun spear"

Opposite: a Middle Yayoi bronze bell standing 42 cm high, found beside the Yoshino river in Tokushima prefecture.

Below: discovered in 1964 at Sakuragaoka, outskirts of Kobe city, this bell with 8 panels shows the gathering, collecting and preserving of food. Height 39·4 cm.

(*hiboko*) of a tribally dominant female leader who was later recorded in Japanese history as the Sun Goddess.

The casting of bells lacked the same tutelage or skilled craftsmanship displayed by the weapons. The small, earliest bells show a surprising ignorance of the finer points of the technique. Surface flaws are patched and smoothed; decoration is crude and disorganized. The first bells were a "Japanese" effort. The makers in the middle Chūgoku must have been trying to reproduce little Korean bells brought directly into this region from Korea, and faced casting problems with no recourse to professional advice.

Despite the miserable start, by the 2nd century AD the bells show genuine technical competence, though at no time was there ever an effort to hide the two holes on top, or on either side and at the foot where the two sections of the mold were joined together. Increased confidence in casting stimulated an increase in size. Only small fragments of molds had been found until recently, but a full half-mold of sandstone has now been discovered at Higashi-Nara in Osaka prefecture of the "flowing water" style of decoration. It most likely belongs to the 2nd century AD.

The bells were buried on plateaus overlooking fertile plains, often in caches of as many as 16. They may not necessarily have been deposited at the same time; nor does this preclude periodic retrieval. The most spectacular discovery occurred in 1964 when 14 of different sizes, with

seven Japanese-style bronze halberds, came to light at Sakuragaoka on the outskirts of Kobe city. One with eight panels of stick-figure, thread-relief decoration has already been designated a National Treasure.

The latest of the bells are large, thin-walled and elegantly shaped, and bear body decoration in zones squared off by fine, high-relief lines. Despite recovery in sites great distances apart, it has been found that as many as eight were cast from one mold. From each of five different molds at least one casting has been found in sites in the Kinki, making it almost certain that the workshops were in the Kinki and most probable that control over bell casting had been assumed by tribal leaders of the area. Distribution to neighboring people may have depended on the dispensing of favors.

The spread of Yayoi. As the Yayoi "culture" continued to advance up the Japanese islands from the Kansai, it lost much of its momentum and some of its cultural trappings. Reaping knives and bronze are largely unknown in the north. Iron is rare. One iron harpoon was found in a shell-mound in Matsushima Bay. The seemingly coordinated front crumbled in the face of the greater Jōmon population, until Yayoi culture became little more than rice cultivation supplementing the old Jōmon way of existence.

There are many Yayoi shell-mounds, rather few jar burials, and fewer polished tools, except for such notable sites as Tenjinzawa in Fukushima. Cord-marking is more prominent on pottery north of Toro, and the characteristic Yayoi shapes, such as seen in the Yayoi-chō pottery of Tokyo, were Jōmonized north of the Kantō. The zoned cord-marking on pots in the Tōhoku could hardly be more in the Jōmon tradition.

Yayoi people are still regarded as racially mixed, with a tendency for those who occupied the southwest and used bronze weapons to have longer skulls, but for those who occupied the east and used bronze bells to have rounder skulls.

To sum up, the slow mixing during the Yayoi period and the steady diet of nourishing food culminated in the first significantly measurable changes in physical features by the time the period was over. The second time such significant changes occurred was with the generation born after World War II. This remarkable increase in stature and overall size is attributable to the addition of proteins to the diet, more variety and the quantity of food consumed. In this case it has been accompanied by correspondingly greater longevity. Since the latter has obviously taken place without any new racial infusions, those who believe that Yayoi changes were caused by internal factors have a strong argument in their favor.

The rise of the Yamato state. The idea that the first mounded tombs were built in the Yamato region by local chieftains had not been questioned until the square-

ditched, mounded Yayoi graves were found a few years ago. But no clear connection has yet been found between the two. One similarity is that the receptacle for the dead is merely a trench sunk a few feet below the surface. Nevertheless, the large tumuli were initially erected in the Kinki and the keyhole-shaped mounds spread from there. The appearance of these mounds sometime before 300 AD marks the beginning of this period, which may be divided into pre-5th-century, 5th-century and post-5th-century stages.

The great majority of the thousands of tombs that dot the countryside are simply circular mounds, but a particularly distinctive and Japanese shape is a circular mound with squarish extension, shaped much like an old-style keyhole. Earlier mounds have a higher knoll, a lower and narrow projection; middle-stage mounds have both sections of about equal height; late-stage mounds tend to distort the square part into rounded corners or simply give it up altogether. This projection may have been a platform for ceremonies that changed with the passage of time and were eventually held on the flat surface around.

By Late Yayoi it may be assumed that the Yamato tribe had dominated the Kansai region. They formed a loose federation of tribes by the 4th century AD, spreading their trademark – the keyhole-shaped tomb – as they cemented this relationship. A further possibility, as suggested by Yukio Kobayashi, is that the diffusion of Japanese-made bronze mirrors, many of which were cast in the same molds and widely distributed, was part of the recognition of their joining the Yamato confederation. Mirrors were used as political gifts, symbolizing expected allegiance.

After the 4th century Yamato power developed

Opposite: a Middle to Late Yayoi skeleton, probably the village chief, excavated in 1959 at Hirota on Tanegashima island of Kagoshima prefecture. It was richly adorned with stylized dragons and costume ornaments, buttons and beads of shell, the patterns borrowed from traditional Chinese jade and bronze sources.

Below: distribution of tomb mounds between the 4th and 7th centuries AD.

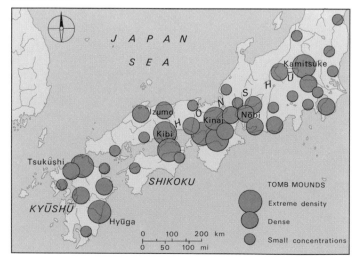

dramatically. The 5th-century "Naniwa dynasty" of emperors – Ōjin, Nintoku and Richū – appears to have reaped the profits of successful wars over access to natural resources in Korea. The *Nihon Shoki* claims the abject submission of Korean kings and boatloads of tribute arriving in Japan. Whatever the truth of this, economic dependence on Korea was considerable at this stage, while Yamato power seems never to have been greater in the Kinki. The mounted warriors, in power by the end of the 5th century, organized the labor force into Korean-style occupational groups, introduced a system of ranking the chief families, developed horse-breeding and diversified agriculture by adding vegetable crops. The economy of local areas improved greatly, even to the extent of eroding Yamato authority.

The major power centers at this time are indicated by the number, and sometimes size, of the mounded tombs: in southeast Kyushu, north Kyushu, the middle Inland Sea area, the Yamato Plain and the northern Kantō Plain. Only the Kibi region of Okayama in the middle Inland Sea came close to matching the size of tombs in the Yamato Plain, but other areas frequently outdid Yamato tombs in both quantity and quality of grave-goods.

Early burial practices. Early tombs were sometimes simply shaped out of the ends of hills. It was not until the 5th century that the immense mounds built up on the plains present a picture of marshaled manpower moving baskets of earth year after year until the job was completed. The *Nihon Shoki* says that Emperor Nintoku started his tomb in the 67th year of his reign. He was on the throne another 20 years, so the chronicles say, allowing ample time for the construction of his enormous tomb. Covering 80 acres, including its present three moats, it is the largest ever built in Japan. A reference to the death of Emperor Chūai obliquely describes the disposition of manpower. Since the country was at war, the records say, it was impossible to bury the emperor.

Burial did not follow death immediately. As the literature implies, the nobles were placed in a "shrine of temporary interment," and formally buried later, following a practice that had a long history in Japan and added greater ceremony to the rites.

The chronology of the tumuli was first established through the discovery of several Chinese mirrors in tombs in the Kinki bearing dates corresponding to 239 and 240 AD. Eventually, archaeologists found that by looking at a combination of several features of the tombs they could arrive at a satisfactory date for each: the external shape of the mound, the kind of terrain selected for the tomb, the form of the burial trench or chamber, and the variety of grave-goods.

The earliest tombs have a trench or two for one or more burials near the top of a mound or a roughly built stone cubicle to house a wooden coffin which had to be lowered in from above. Placed with the dead were great quantities of stone replicas of shell bracelets and small knives in sheaths. There are also some small stone copies of bronze mirrors, iron and bronze tools, weapons, stone vats, clay cups, metal spindles and wooden clogs. A small number of stone batons have been found that are regarded as shamanistic symbols, and many little lidded stone boxes with short legs, obviously used for some specially prized object or liquid, quite possibly the preserved umbilical cord.

Tomb period archaeology. In recent years the numerous suburban developments, often those conducted under government programs of making "dormitory towns" for commuters to the big cities, have opened a whole new field of Tomb period archaeology. Using pottery typology, archaeologists recognize the Early, Middle and Late stages in the remains of houses through the presence of Goryo, Izumi, and the Onitaka and Mama types of domestic pottery known as Haji.

Raised buildings and surface residences existed. *Haniwa* models and reliefs on bronze mirrors are adequate evidence, but archaeologically they are much more difficult to find than pit-dwellings. A preference for fireplaces lessened the desirability of raised structures, which had to do without, and surface dwellings lacked the sturdiness of houses with posts sunk into the ground.

As groups of people spread out looking for suitable farm land, the number of communities grew and the size of each shrank. The houses were clustered close together, built in rectangular shapes with rounded corners, with four postholes or none.

The Goryo type site in Saitama prefecture lies on the Matsuyama plateau and faces the Yoshimi Hyakketsu tunnel tombs across ricefields cut by a river. The village covered 12 acres and included 134 houses of this early stage. Four early houses formed a semicircle, and several houses were arranged in a circle around an open area for working space and community affairs. The size of the house varies more than that of the recovered objects, so one suspects that the house size reflects family needs and not social status. Later Goryo houses are even smaller, and all have fireplaces and some have storage pits. Iron was used extensively, but practically none was found. Many whetstones are deeply worn from the sharpening of tools, especially in later houses, indicating rather longer occupation for these. But the tools were carefully husbanded and carried along when the population moved on.

The remarkable Tōdaijiyama tomb (late 4th century) on the edge of Tenri city, Nara prefecture, had a central burial trench about 5 m long (*above*), with coffins packed around with clay and lined with stones, and about 35 iron swords in two side trenches. The third from the right sword (*below*) is Chinese with a gold inlaid inscription of an era dated 184–89 AD, 120 cm in length. Sixteen short, two-edged weapons may be spearheads. Many little stone cups of talc (*opposite*) c. 3 to 4 cm in height were found in the tomb.

Shaman-chieftains in the 5th century. Narrative in the old records begins to take its proper place at the time of Emperor Chūai, especially when foreign interests added a new dimension to Yamato politics. Chūai was more concerned with religious than with military activities and, according to the literature, was unwilling to pursue a strong foreign policy toward Korea. The *kami* snuffed out his life for failing to obey their will. The noted female shaman Empress Jingū then carried out the invasion of Korea. But she found herself to be pregnant just prior to departure, so tied a stone across her abdomen to delay the birth of the child, carried the banner, assembled the ships, attacked Korea and subdued the Korean kings. She then arranged to keep the tribute coming from Silla and Paikche and returned to give birth to a son, later Emperor Ōjin.

This rather preposterous story is taken by some as a face-saving way to disguise an invasion from Korea. Ōjin made space for incoming people, presumably his supporters, and they in turn maintained him as their shaman-chieftain and built a colossal tomb for him. In fact, intense religious activity was more likely to inspire the construction of immense tombs than simply the accumulation of wealth and control of manpower.

The Japanese kept this buffer zone in Korea called Mimana and appointed its governor. Paikche in the southwest enjoyed the presence of Mimana as a shield against Silla on the southeast and maintained close relationships with Japan for a long time, though largely through prior kin connections. This relationship was all important for the future development of Japan, but it deteriorated with succeeding generations, until Mimana was eventually lost to Silla and Paikche was later overwhelmed.

Tombs of this period were not haphazardly laid out and piled up, but were carefully calculated in length and breadth, especially when they were constructed on the open plain. In terms of a Korean *shaku* unit, c. 30 centimeters in length, they were measured off in round numbers. Beginning with the first of the imperial keyhole tombs, Sujin's was 1,000 *shaku*, Suinin's 950, Keiko's 1,300 and Seimu's 900. The irregular numbers of meters in which they are recorded today are completely misleading. For the Naniwa emperors the pattern was simply magnified: Chūai's is 1,000 *shaku*, Ōjin's 1,800, Nintoku's 2,000 and Richū's 1,500.

The irregular orientation of the tombs on the plains is unexpected, considering the now recognized precision of the plan, but the corpse receptacle was generally built for the dead to have his head toward the south and a little east. Having once cut the tombs out of hillsides with no control over their direction, the builders can never have regarded the external orientation as having any importance.

Stone sarcophagi were put in the largest tombs, the

simple chamber being designed to accommodate up to about four bodies. Japanese-style bronze mirrors, long single-edged iron swords, slat-iron body armor, helmets and a few personal ornaments make up the grave-goods. There are also iron tools in the tombs, a fact which points up the concern with domestic business and farming. The mounds were ringed with cylindrical *haniwa*, and capped by an occasional house model and other ceremonial objects.

The residential settlements of the 5th century were spread out, to allow for individual families raising their own food. The Izumi type site in Tokyo lies between two rivers at the western end of the Musashino plateau and occupies an area of roughly 100 square meters at an altitude of about 20 meters. About 15 houses of more or less equal size were loosely lined up. The houses had internal storage pits and off-center fireplaces in the one-room plan.

Opposite: a bronze mirror from the 5th-century Takarazuka tomb in Kita-katsuragi county, Nara prefecture. Diameter 23 cm.

Below right: a complete suit of iron armor from the late 5th-century Nagamochiyama tomb at Dōmyōji in Osaka prefecture.

Below: the plain before the Tanzawa hills is dotted with 42 tombs. This 6th-century site is in Hatano city, Kanagawa prefecture.

Horse-riding nobles. The chaos that preceded the accession of Keitai in 507 AD resulted in a total preoccupation with Korean problems during the 24 years of his reign. Internal affairs received short shrift. This is best explained through Keitai's heritage, which should be Korean if he was in fact related to Ōjin and actually had a father who came from a family which had settled in the Shiga area near Lake Biwa. The inability of the Yamato chieftains to reach a consensus allowed a distant relative to come in or be brought in to rule the Home Provinces.

This preoccupation with Korea is better understood against the archaeology of the end of the 5th and the beginning of the 6th century. Horse-riding warriors had entered from Korea and were approaching the heart of Yamato power. Keitai's accession no doubt represented a formal recognition of this irresistible force and the official installation of the group. Their mobility, fighting techniques, organizational powers, economic support system and cultural and material standards made their rise to power inevitable. Although Paikche rulers were equestrians, the economic and social institutions and the archaeology point much more toward Silla as the origin of most of these mounted warriors.

So far horse bones have not been found in 4th-century tombs, but they do appear occasionally in later 5th- and

6th-century tombs, and horse sacrifice probably took place, since the Taika Reform regulations of 646 proscribe it. Grave-goods are fewer in number in the small round mounds of these nobles, with prime emphasis on personal possessions, such as beads, crowns and swords, but in particular the equipment for horse riding. Iron armor is rare; mirrors are few and poor in quality except for the jingle-bell type. The horse trappings are quite comparable to Silla bridle-bits, saddle pieces, strap ornaments and stirrups. Most are of gilt bronze and occasionally inlaid with silver. The stirrups, the bit itself and the reinforcing metal plates for the ornaments are usually of iron and often largely rusted away.

The iron in the tombs is almost exclusively swords. The cultivating, carpentering and domestic tools had virtually disappeared from the inventory of grave-goods during the 5th century, partly because central controls were tightened on iron production. Earlier iron was forged. Much of the later iron in the tombs is cast.

The internal structure of the tombs introduced by the mounted warriors consisted of a stone passageway and one or two stone chambers. These were first built in north Kyushu, then elsewhere in the country. Often made of well-cut and shaped stones and constructed with remarkable precision, they were ordinarily covered by a simple circular or gourd-shaped mound, and later by a square mound with low round knoll on top. By far the longest passageway and chamber are in the Mise-no-Maruyama tomb in Asuka, which could in fact be the tomb in which Emperor Kimmei was buried. Together they measure 26·2 meters in length. Stone sarcophagi were still frequently used.

Social and economic organization. Japan may owe its economic base and life style to the Yayoi cultivators as some anthropologists believe, but the political structure and way of achieving power were set when the tribes were federated under the Yamato, and the other tribes recognized the Yamato's right to rule. This became an article of national faith when the right to rule was validated in the *Kojiki* and *Nihon Shoki*.

The Yamato were skilled in holding the delicate balance between rival tribes. They did it by socially grading the aristocracy and so restricting their ambitions, and by selected intermarriage and exploitation of family ties and loyalties. It was to the advantage of the competing families to maintain Yamato transcendency. In Japanese history, families rose, supplied wives, ruled and fell, but the Yamato Sun line reigned throughout.

No less important was a comparable grading of sacerdotal activities. In fact, the right to rule was won through the right to perform the national religious ceremonies. The Yamato priest-chiefs worshiped the Sun Goddess on behalf of the country as a whole, as a fundamental part of the national heritage. Others worshiped at their tribal shrines and elsewhere. Some-

Above: Yoshimi Hyakketsu at Higashi-matsuyama in Saitama prefecture is a tufa hill with about 230 tombs dug into its sides. The interior is cut to resemble regular tombs with passageway and chamber.

Opposite: Sue pottery was introduced from Korea in the 5th century. The largest pot known came from the Mino tomb in Okayama prefecture and stands 110 cm high.

where along the line the Izumo people received special local rights for conducting ceremonies outside Yamato jurisdiction.

The tribes or clans were called *uji*, the chiefs *kimi* or *ōkimi* (Great Chieftains). The 8th-century literature does not say what the Yamato called their tribal leaders before that time, but an inscribed mirror and inscribed sword of the 5th century, both with implications of imperial names, use the title *daio* or, another reading, *ōkimi*. The term *tennō*, translated equally as emperor or empress, was used from about the time that Empress Suiko was on the throne in the early 7th century as a Yamato device to elevate their chieftains over those of associated tribes. After the Taika Reform of 645–46 AD the chieftain was *uji-no-kami*, literally head man, a title that appeared in 663, the third year of Tenchi's reign.

The Yamato *uji* was then the chief tribe, and clustered around were other *uji*, some great names in early Japanese history like the Soga, Mononobe and Otomo. The *uji* were then ranked as Omi and Muraji and two lower levels. The Omi were possibly early settlers who in most cases had a prior claim on early ancestry. It is no coincidence that they were largely administrators at the court and have place names like Soga and Kasuga. The Muraji claimed imperial ancestry from about the time of Kōgen and were largely the chiefs of occupations as their names indicate, such as Haji, Nakatomi and Mononobe. There was also the Tomo-no-miyatsuko (attendant families), trained largely in the crafts and connected with the imperial court, and the Kuni-no-miyatsuko (territorial families), the local leaders of a tribal "state" or group of "states." Further subdivision existed in some parts of the country.

Before the Taika Reform administrators sometimes received the title of Ōomi and Ōmuraji (Great Omi and Great Muraji), but the Reform centralized the system directly under the emperor. At that time the *kuni* became more or less the later traditional provinces, and the *agata* (districts) more or less the *gun*, best called counties. When the Chinese records spoke of the Country of Wa as composed of 100 countries or kingdoms, they referred conventionally to the *kuni*.

The head of the *uji*, the *ujigami*, had several known duties. He managed the tribal community including the attached slaves (*yatsuko*), he was the legal arbiter and he conducted the ceremonies at the home shrine.

Affiliated with the *uji* were the *be*, occupational groups of artisans and workers who had been organized to meet the demands of the aristocracy for specialized products and were forcibly maintained in a virtual state of servitude. There were some native roots for the *be* system in the groups of socially respected craftsmen called *tomo* by at least the end of the Yayoi period. In the Yamato social and economic organization they were given the Chinese name *be* and downgraded to one notch above the slaves. The *be* were probably officially established by the late 5th century and were simply fitted into the increasing social stratification.

Some crafts were not exclusively the work of *be*, especially where common people needed the goods, such as the weaving of cloth; but most *be* existed purely for the aristocracy and some had to be formed of immigrants for lack of locally known techniques. This was especially true of equestrian needs, and included the horsekeepers and

A 6th-century *haniwa koto* player, with five-stringed lyre on his lap, from a tomb on the edge of Maebashi city in Gumma prefecture. Height 72·6 cm.

saddle makers. The former are described in grisly terms in the reign of Richū as branded on the face with unhealed, reeking sores.

Many *be* communities were also farmers, if the geography and type of occupation would permit, just as the "pottery villages" have been in recent times. A *be* with 50 households in the province of Yamashiro (Kyoto) was exempt from taxes – usually rice and cloth – when producing paper for the court, so it is clear that some sort of exchange had to take place for the services they rendered.

Yamato art. The *haniwa* were invented in the Kinki and are clearly the most Japanese of the arts of the period. Most however were made for tombs in the Kantō, where traditions were less restricting and a freer rein was possible. Cylinders came first, and were soon followed by house models; then things such as quivers, swords, boats and armor, and finally birds, animals and human figures.

The human figures represent shamans, funeral attendants, farmers and soldiers. The male shamans are usually in suits of armor, the female shamans in formal dress. The funeral attendants include both male and female entertainers, singers and dancers and an occasional offering bearer. The farmers are identified by their sickles and scythes, while the warriors bear light arms to full armor and military gear, wearing the tunic and trousers of cavalrymen.

A local plague in the Yamato region in the 470s (the *Nihon Shoki* says 463) caused Emperor Yūryaku to move the instructors of four *be* to a safer place. These men had been sent over from Paikche and were not expendable.

Each was highly skilled: a potter, saddler, brocade weaver and painter. They were transferred along with an interpreter.

The cultural contributions of the potters, saddlers and weavers from Korea are well known, but it is still uncertain what inroads were made by the painting instructor. The preserved paintings of this time are the wall decorations in the tombs in Kyushu but, unlike the Sue pottery, horse trappings, gold crowns, belt ornaments, ear pendants and some of the jewelry which retain obvious Korean connections, there is next to nothing in the tomb paintings that can be associated with Korea. The Japanese tomb paintings were applied directly on the stone wall, and consist mostly of collections of concentric circles, triangles, rows of shields and swords and similar things all done in an unprofessional and crude way, mostly in red, yellow, green and black. Only in later tombs is there an introduction of human and animal figures and these are in disjointed compositions of arbitrary scale. There is hardly a standardized "primitiveness" that is arrived at through tradition. The chief exception to this is the Takehara tomb, where the painting is exclusively in black and red and shows a man, horse and boat between ceremonial fans, in a surprisingly sophisticated effort to organize the composition.

The paintings were probably done by the local shaman and his helpers. Since only one among numerous tombs in the area may be painted, his practice was quite limited. Many of the symbols in the tombs were shamanistic. Horn-like motifs, boats, birds, horses, simulated mirrors, and possibly even the straight and curved pattern known as *chokkomon*, can in the case of all but the last be associated with shamanistic elements widely referred to in the mythological literature.

Ornaments from the 5th-century Eta-Funayama tomb in Kumamoto.

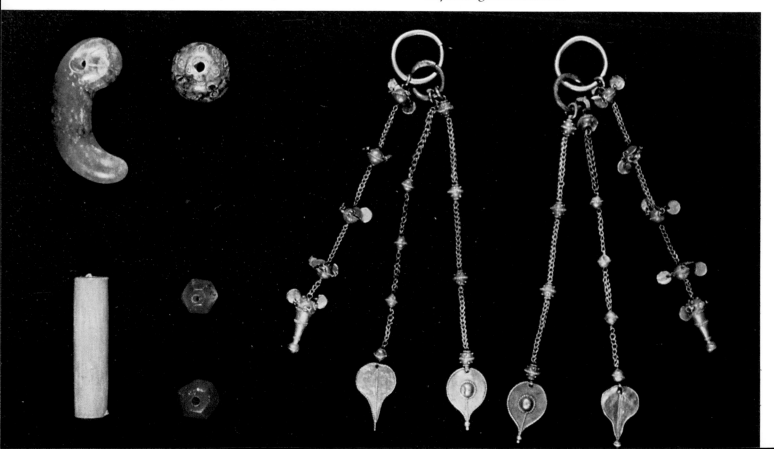

Shinto Shrines and Ritual

Shinto is rooted in animistic practices traceable to the Jōmon period, but its major ceremonies were motivated by the agricultural needs of Yayoi times and later, and it is by its ceremonies that it is known today. The most important are the *Kinen* and *Niiname*, which have probably changed little over the centuries. Prayers are offered for good crops in the spring and thanks are given for the harvest in the fall. The autumn feast becomes the union between the male forces of heaven and female forces of earth.

Shinto is still a vital social force. Communities participate in seasonal ceremonies designed to ensure an abundance of food, fertility, health and the good life in general. They coax the *kami* for such occasions from their customary habitats in the sky or from the earth or near unusual land, rock or water formations, and shrines and individuals are purified and made worthy for their visit on earth.

The *kami* defy definition – the current definitions are far from descriptive: anything that is worshiped or anything that requires ceremonies for its recognition – but are higher spirits in the range of eight million which can be prayed to by individuals and their will interpreted by diviners.

The *Nihon Shoki* says the *kami* were worshiped in Emperor Sujin's palace and he built special buildings for them, that is to say, he built separate structures rather than using the shaman's own house. The shrine building accommodated the *shintai*, the form of the *kami*, a special symbol like a mirror, into which the *kami* entered at ceremonial times. Sujin was also said to have separated and graded the *kami* and so was able to achieve spiritual peace and harmony – a clear reflection of the pattern of ranking then being established among the tribes.

In earliest times the entire group practiced fixed periods of abstention to remove impurities and allow the *kami* to appear for the ceremonies; then families or individuals did this. From the 8th century the *Nakatomi*, as hereditary priests, conducted national ceremonies of purification at the court on the last days of the 6th and 12th months.

The native religion lacked a descriptive term until well after Buddhism was introduced. To distinguish it, the term Shinto was applied, the Way of the Gods, or as later Japanese pronounced it, Kami-no-michi, using a title that seems to have been borrowed from the Chinese Tao, The Way.

Since Shinto is designed to make this world better for its inhabitants and is scarcely other-worldly in its nature, it takes a totally different view of life than Buddhism. But the two complement each other rather than conflict, and each has borrowed ceremonies from the other. The annual Buddhist *Obon* practice of inviting the souls of the dead back for a visit is the Shinto idea of offering them a periodic return to a superior world. There is no better life imaginable. On the other hand, Buddhists hope to escape from this world. Japanese live comfortably with these fundamental contradictions. It is sometimes pointed out that families built Buddhist temples, but communities built Shinto shrines. People are buried at Buddhist temples, but are married at Shinto shrines. The gloomy interiors of temple buildings, with their endless monotonous chants, have no counterpart in Shinto. Activities are outdoors; dancing and merry-making go on in shrine grounds.

Previous page: the space to be occupied by the *kami* or made hallowed by them at shrines is clearly marked by an entrance gate called *torii*. An arched red bridge in the direct line of approach is opened on special ceremonial occasions at the few shrines which have them or may be open to the public in smaller shrines.

Left: the shrines of Ise in Mie prefecture are the most sacred in Japan. Just off the coast are Futami-ga-ura, a pair of "wedded rocks," identified with the original deities Izanagi and Izanami. A *torii* has been built on one and a straw rope unites the two, paralleling the union of the sky and earth deities of the Inner and Outer shrines. The rope is replaced annually on the 5th day of the 1st month.

Above: the Outer Shrine at Ise is said to have been built here in 478 A D during the reign of Emperor Yūryaku. It is reconstructed at great expense and with much ceremony every 20 years.

Right: this small shrine is on the outskirts of Okayama city. Typical features exclusive to Shinto architecture are the extensions of the gables and the ridge-pole weights.

Opposite: tradition says that Mt Miwa north of Sakurai in Nara prefecture is the oldest "shrine," called Omiwa shrine; but the mountain itself is the object of worship and the shrine has no main hall, although it has a sacred gate and worship hall. Several rocks on the mountain called *iwakura* are the "seats of the *kami*."

Above: Inari shrines for rice-growing ceremonies are numerous all over the country and are recognized by the foxes, the messengers of the shrines. This fox is in the Yoshida shrine on the east side of Kyoto. Like others, it holds the scroll of "ultimate truth" in its mouth.

Left: according to legend, the Sumiyoshi shrine in the suburbs of Osaka was founded by or at the time of Empress Jingū. It is a raised prehistoric type but picked up its coloring from Buddhist architecture.

Left: shrines are dedicated to warriors, statesmen and rulers worthy of deification, as Emperor Meiji was, the builder of modern Japan who died in 1912. This shrine was completed in 1920 in a prominent place in Tokyo and special celebrations are held there for the family, ancestors and the state on the occasion of the emperor's birthday, 3 November.

Just within the entrance to a Shinto shrine or Buddhist temple is a water basin with long-handled wooden ladles (*below*) to be used for ceremonial ablutions – usually washing out the mouth (*below right*), thus purifying the person so that the *kami* will approach him. Buddhist temples took over the practice from Shinto. The fountain may be elegantly carved or cast as a dragon (*above*), the benign water spirit. The worshiper then steps up to the main shrine building and claps his hands to attract the *kami* and says a prayer.

Right: an exorcist, at a small shrine for people dealing with salt production in Shiogama in Miyagi prefecture, rids the shrine of evil spirits to make it habitable for the *kami* in ceremonies scheduled for the month of August.

Left: small painted wooden plaques (*ema*) used as votive gifts get their name from the horses commonly painted on them (also shrine messengers), but they include bulls, birds and other subjects depending on the creature associated with the shrine. Special buildings were sometimes erected just to hold the *ema*, but most shrines and temples manage merely with special boards or walls of buildings. These hang on the entrance gate to Kūkai's temple northeast of Kyoto, the Enryaku-ji.

Right: small fortune-prayers (*omikuji*) printed on paper can be bought for a nominal sum – still 20 yen in some shrines – often facilitated by a coin machine. The papers are read and then tied to a bush, tree, wire or fence to seek fulfillment if auspicious and reversal if not.

Below: offerings are left at a little spring: food and miniature models of frogs (a water symbol and a Zen symbol in Buddhist thought of gaining wisdom through acting foolish) in a remote corner of Hōzan-ji, a temple dedicated to Fudō in Nara prefecture.

Opposite: the Inner Shrine at Ise, dedicated to the Sun Goddess. Every Japanese hopes to visit Ise once in a 60-year period, and many offerings are made, such as the *sake* jars shown here.

Left: a ceremonial dance at Yasaka shrine is part of the elaborate Gion festival held in Kyoto annually from 10 to 28 July, with large floats being hauled through the city on the 17th and 20th. The ceremonies date to 876 when processions of shrine cars were used to alleviate a serious plague, and the floats are the successors to those cars. They are washed at the beginning of the procession and again at the end.

Below left: for several hundred years the Japanese have taken their children at the ages of three, five and seven to shrines on the 15th day of the 11th month to offer their appreciation to the *kami* for allowing them to reach these ages safely and to ask for protection and blessings on them in the years to come. Called *Shichi-go-san* (literally 7-5-3), the children are dolled up in traditional colorful kimonos, have their pictures taken and never look prettier, as here at Meiji shrine in Tokyo.

Below center: visiting shrines on New Year's Eve after the ringing of the midnight bell and on New Year's Day is done with the family to receive blessings for the forthcoming year. It would not be complete without tasting the food and drinks, buying the charms and jostling with the crowds. On New Year's Day the finest clean clothes are sported and arrows are bought at the shrines for protection throughout the year.

4. Early Buddhism to the Taika Reform

The first Buddhists. Deep in the Nara Basin lies the small district of Asuka. Emperors and empresses lived there for most of the 7th century. Occasionally a residence was maintained in Naniwa, the listening post for the continent.

The Japanese had kept close ties with Paikche, especially since Paikche had sent two horses to Emperor Ōjin, the groom of which turned out to be able to read the Chinese classics. Other specialists came at different intervals, in the fields of weaving, medicine, calendars and divination, and later in herbs, music, and Buddhist teachings and the arts. The cultural link was the one valued by Japan, from which reciprocation in military aid was usually expected. The relationship was not one of deep mutual trust: both sides held hostages. The countries adjoining Silla were banded together through common fear of their neighbor, envious of the iron ore in the eastern mountains and apprehensive of the open arable land of Paikche eyed by Silla. Japan wanted to hold its beachhead colony of Mimana, while Silla felt it had an old score to settle since the time Empress Jingū is thought to have humiliated their rulers.

The 6th-century records in the *Nihon Shoki* are saturated with activities involving Korea. On the occasion of a Silla attack on the north and west of Paikche in 552, the Korean king sent envoys to the Japanese court bearing

Previous page: 7th-century painting on paper of Prince Shōtoku, crown prince and regent under Empress Suiko, with two young men, perhaps his sons.

Below: palaces and capital cities moved progressively northward from the 7th century: Asuka, Fujiwara, Heijō, Nagaoka and Heian.

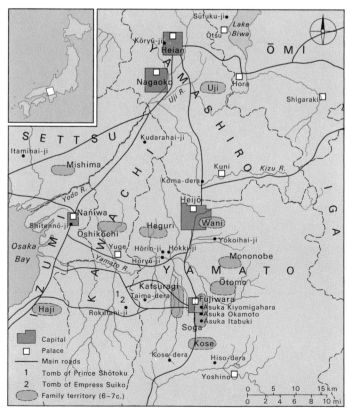

gifts of several Buddhist banners, sutras (teachings of the Buddha), and at least one gilt bronze statuette. These were accompanied by an articulate spokesman to explain their value and meaning. The king of Paikche had found them capable of satisfying a man's prayers and giving him a sense of higher wisdom, so he recommended their use. Emperor Kimmei reacted dramatically and leaped with joy, exhilarated by this discovery. But among his three top advisers, the heads of the Soga, Mononobe and Nakatomi clans, only Soga-no-Iname shared his enthusiasm. The others objected on the grounds of offending the 180 native *kami* of earth and crops and of upsetting the cycle of ceremonies. Nevertheless, Kimmei handed the articles to Iname with directions to give them a try.

Response from the local deities came in quick order. A plague reached a violent level of intensity within the year. The cause was attributed to the new deities and the house that had been used as a simple temple for the statuette was burned and the little Buddhist figure thrown into the Naniwa Canal. The plague wore itself out, but some people thought that the unexplained destruction of a main hall of the palace by fire might be construed as the Buddhist deities getting in the last word.

Paikche lost more territory to Silla and in 562 Silla destroyed the governor of Mimana. Internal difficulties in Japan added to the frustration. Family rivalry and local hostility in Kyushu to the idea of mounting operations against Silla made it impossible to send aid. Commanders were selected and some marshaled troops, but only once could they be dispatched across the strait. Paikche needed manpower, bows and horses, but received little more than accusations from Japan for not providing better protection for Mimana.

Kimmei's successor is described as not being a Buddhist, as though Kimmei himself had become a believer during the 20 years after his first contact with the new religion. Buddhism needed imperial support in order to take root, and this did come with the accession of Yōmei in 585; but even before then, monks, nuns, an image maker and a temple architect, an ascetic and a reciter had arrived with various Buddhist articles in hand from Paikche in 577, altogether a team quite large enough and able to start the building of a temple and furnish its staff.

The turning point came when Bidatsu and the people were stricken with a disease. After a short persecution of practicing Buddhists, enough sympathy was rallied for their cause to ascribe the disease in this case to the wrath of the Buddhist deities. Later rulers were all Buddhist, and, one might add, also heads of the Shinto state.

Buddhism at that stage had magical attributes: its priests were miracle workers and its practices included divination and chanting. While the outward trappings looked very different from Shinto, its practices had a great deal in common during the decades it was getting its foothold. The philosophical element was not injected until Prince Shōtoku, as regent for Empress Suiko from 594, studied the sutras with the aid of a Korean monk and by life and work exemplified the devotional side of the teachings.

Suiko took the throne only under great pressure after her predecessor Sushun had been assassinated by Soga-no-Umako. She may have installed her nephew as regent and heir apparent to balance the ever-increasing power of Umako. This was a wise move; the Soga sponsorship of Buddhism and its successful outcome at the court, and their control of the tax system, had left them firmly in the saddle and virtually unassailable.

The prince appears on the historical scene as a young man, only distantly involved in a battle between the Soga and Mononobe in 587 for court power, but in which the future of Buddhism was at stake. He vowed to build a temple to the Four Heavenly Kings should the Soga win, as did Umako, who invoked the aid of the Buddha. The tide turned and the Mononobe were defeated and remnants of the family made slaves. In fulfillment of the vow, the prince later erected a temple called Shitennō-ji in Osaka, while Umako built the Hōkō-ji or Asuka-dera in Asuka.

Temple building. A year later Umako welcomed more monks and relics from Korea, in this case perhaps from north Korea, but most important were two carpenters, a metalworker, four potters for the manufacture of roof

The Shitennō-ji in Osaka, the first temple built by Prince Shōtoku. Destroyed in World War II, it has been reconstructed in concrete, each part simulating wood and painted accordingly.

tiles, and a painter. These were no novices in Korea; the Japanese referred to them respectfully as doctors. One brought along a model of a building.

When the Chinese had adopted Buddhism and needed a form for a temple they used the basic palace plan and put the pagoda near the entrance, aligned with the other buildings on the major north-south axis. The Koreans used the same plan and brought it over when they were asked to initiate temple building in Japan. There was a central complex of buildings within a rectangular cloistered block, known in Japan by a corrupted Sanskrit word, *garan*. That and other buildings outside it were all surrounded by a bank or wall and accessible from the south through the south gate. The unit of measurement used throughout had come from north Korea. It was a foot unit called a *shaku* (about 30 centimeters), and distinguished from other units by its place of origin, the *komajaku*.

A middle gate led through the cloister into the *garan*. Immediately ahead stood the pagoda, designed as a repository for a relic of the Buddha. Sometimes a bit of bone, this and other objects were stored in a hole in the stone which supported the center pole of the building. Respects were paid to these symbols of the Buddha by worshipers through walking around, climbing, and dropping flowers, and donations of objects of value to the temple. The pagoda's *raison d'être* justified its prominent position, especially at the time when the magical character of the treasures was emphasized.

Stones to support the wooden columns of major

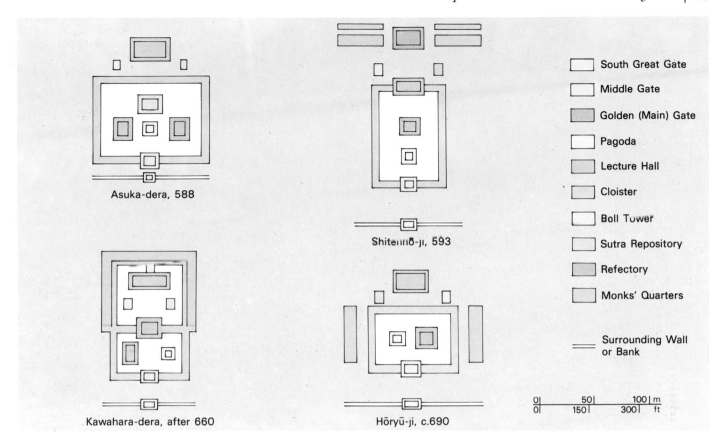

Asuka-dera, 588

Shitennō-ji, 593

Kawahara-dera, after 660

Hōryū-ji, c.690

	South Great Gate
	Middle Gate
	Golden (Main) Gate
	Pagoda
	Lecture Hall
	Cloister
	Bell Tower
	Sutra Repository
	Refectory
	Monks' Quarters
	Surrounding Wall or Bank

Above: the first Buddhist temples built in Japan followed perfectly symmetrical plans.

Opposite: the Hōryū-ji, the Japanese descendant of Prince Shōtoku's Korean-style Ikaruga-dera which was gutted by fire in 670.

buildings were often large and heavy and were frequently never moved once buildings were abandoned. This is particularly true of the stone for the center pole of the pagoda which in some cases is really enormous. Pagoda stones also enjoyed a taboo that moving them brought bad luck. Not all remain by any means, but the shape and depth of those that do, tell a lot about the date of the pagoda, if not the entire temple. Eight feet below the floor of the pagoda was not an unusual depth for the earliest temples, and it is possible that the builders were not thinking exclusively of burying the relics deep for protection, but were also trying to plant the pole firmly in place. In any case, this was highly impractical for Japan's damp soils, and within a century the pole had been systematically brought up to floor level, where it stood on a stone base on the surface, quite out of touch with the ground.

Behind the pagoda stood the golden hall (*kondō* in Japanese), the building that becomes the main hall of a temple. At this time it had almost square proportions. The chief images of the temple were placed on a central platform in this building, a symbol of the Buddhist holy mountain and protected at the corners by the Four Heavenly Kings. The platform occupied the space within the columns formed by the ambulatory, the latter lending itself ideally to the worshiper who entered on the east, circumambulated by way of the south, and left through the door by which he had come.

The last major building in the *garan* was usually a lecture hall. Some temples did without, but those that had one probably got double service from it as a refectory. As a social meeting place, the monks read and studied the sutras here. With the passage of time, as a temple inevitably acquired more images, these went into the lecture hall.

Lecture halls were not as pretentious as main halls. They had lower roof lines, a less complicated structure and an earthen floor. They were not as deep – often seven by four bays – with proportionally more southern exposure that made them somewhat more comfortable places for long hours of occupation in the winter months. As the Japanese came to realize they were no longer using the main hall as a centerpiece, they changed its proportions from the early five-by-four bays to conform more closely with the shape of their lecture halls.

All of these buildings including the gates are set on platforms of tamped earth faced with stone. The platform conforms in size to the overhang of the eaves, so the water will fall off into surrounding troughs. In early temples each building stands starkly in an unlandscaped setting, in a sense facadeless, to be seen equally well from every direction. The platforms enhance their visibility. Additional height is given a building in the *garan* by doubling the roof and elevating the interior to aggrandize its

The main hall of the Hōryū-ji, an exact replacement for the one lost by fire in 1949.

external appearance. Half of its space has no real internal function and is hidden by a false ceiling. Above this ceiling is the vast amount of woodwork that is necessary both to achieve the desired height and at the same time to support the roofs that help to create it. The structural system of providing more or less equidistant supports results in fixed spatial units of rectangles and squares. This gives order and system to the buildings, but also restricts variation. Doors and window openings had to be fitted between the columns. Some temples adopted the Chinese way of painting the exposed wooden parts a red color.

The structural systems, the external visible parts of which are the columns, brackets and rafters, were all introduced ultimately from China at different times between the 6th and the 13th centuries. The Japanese modified them and occasionally combined certain features, but they never seem to have invented a complete system of their own. Each style has its own gradations of space between columns, and an archaeologist finds that an abandoned temple site that contains little more than fragments of roof tiles and a few stone bases *in situ* offers enough evidence for reconstructing the appearance of the pagoda and halls, since a small number of buildings of each style still stand today.

Palaces and shrines. For a long time palace and shrine architecture hovered below the level of sophistication of Buddhist temple architecture, tenaciously retaining the native traditions. Shrines are frequently surrounded by Buddhist-style buildings, the shrine itself hidden from public view and constructed in a much simpler, earlier style.

The first palace buildings to be tiled were at Fujiwara, built some time after 694. As long as the roofs were of relatively light thatch, no stone bases were needed to support the wooden columns. Palaces borrowed the lotus pattern from temples for the circular eave-end tiles, and the decorated, connecting pantiles were added to temples about the time that palaces began to be roofed with tiles. To the Chinese this tile eave-end art was not very practical, as the roof edges could scarcely be seen from the ground in monumental buildings, but the Koreans thought better of it and came up with an art of great variety and beauty. The Japanese tried to follow suit.

The temple built at Asuka by Soga-no-Umako, formally called Hōkō-ji, was the showpiece of the capital and, like the other monuments sponsored by Umako, inflated far beyond the current need. His tomb, Ishibutai, has the most massive of all the stone passages and chambers.

The *Nihon Shoki* meticulously records each step of the

temple's construction. Work was started in 588 under the tutelage of the Korean experts. After cutting the wood and selecting a spot occupied earlier by a shaman and removing his house – and so retaining the magic – one building and the cloister went up in the tenth month of 592. The relics were deposited in the stone under the center pole of the pagoda on the 15th day of the first month of 593 and the center pole raised the following day. By the eleventh month of 596 the temple was complete and two Korean monks were installed. Embroidered wall hangings and a large bronze Buddha image were ready for dedication in the fourth month of 606.

The smooth progress, however, had been abruptly interrupted when it was discovered that the bronze Buddha image was too large to get through the door. The builders wanted to break down the door, but Kuratsukuri-no-Tori, the sculptor, ingeniously devised a way of moving it in. The empress rewarded him lavishly with rice land for his services and resourcefulness, and he in turn built the nunnery of Sakata for her from the revenue derived from the rice raised on the land. A historical marker in south Asuka today indicates the traditional site of the small Sakata-dera.

The Asuka-dera was host to numerous ceremonies distinguished by royal attendance, for which a paved road was laid to its south gate. After the capital was moved further north, the temple became too expensive to maintain. A fire in 1196 destroyed most of the buildings and the temple has since been reduced to a single hall to house Tori's damaged Buddha.

The excavations of the Asuka-dera were carried out 20 years ago. It did not have the plan expected, that had been brought by Paikche builders and was used elsewhere; rather, it followed a north Korean model in which an octagonal building stood in the middle of the cloister, with two large halls flanking it on east and west and a third standing on the north. The builders of the Asuka-dera simply replaced the octagonal building with a pagoda. The plan was unique. Perhaps suitable for the capital, it was otherwise too grandiose. It had at least one hall too many. No temple architect ever found it practical for further use.

Prince Shōtoku started his own temple in Naniwa in 593. He must have been familiar with Umako's Asuka-dera, since he was then living in Asuka. But the prince consistently followed the Paikche model, with the conventional alignment of buildings as seen in his Shitennō-ji today. This Osaka temple was the first of about a dozen temples built with this plan and is today the only survivor, although even it has had to be rebuilt after a typhoon in 1934 and again after aerial bombing in 1945.

The present Hōryū-ji in Nara prefecture is thought to retain the chief structural features of these early temples despite a later date for its plan that materialized when it was reconstructed about 20 years after the first temple in the area was destroyed by fire c. 670 AD.

Prince Shōtoku. Prince Shōtoku is the patron saint of all Japanese Buddhists. He is regarded by many as a reincarnation of the historic Buddha. He was already the object of a cult as early as the 8th century. History is mixed with myth, but he was undoubtedly a man of many talents and achievements. Coupled with this were his impressive physical stature and striking personality.

The 8th-century *Nihon Shoki* gives a thumbnail sketch of his early life. He was born in a painless birth near the imperial stables when his mother was inspecting the horses, he was able to speak at birth, and as an adult was endowed with the wisdom to judge ten lawsuits simultaneously. He could forecast the future. In fact, his reputation was sealed when an earthquake he had predicted occurred with devastating effect the following month. On the same note, he missed his forecast for the transfer of the capital to Nara by ten years, and the destruction of the Asuka-dera by about 100 years. He studied, translated and annotated the sutras. He wrote a 17-article constitution, heavily Confucian in its advice to obey the orders of the state and to maintain harmony, and in its insistence on the integrity of officials. It was also nominally Buddhist in its respect for the Buddha and the principles of the law.

Tradition claims he founded or was associated with about 300 temples. And, as if this were not enough, the later cult wove a wider web of legends, completing the cycle of his life in about 120 events, from which painters then took their choice when depicting his biography.

Most of this needs no comment, but the records and

A rock-cut 13-story pagoda, with Buddhist triad in relief and several other figures. Called Rokudani-ji, at Taishi-chō, they were carved in the 7th century. The pagoda is 5·28 m high.

Panel 6 on the west of the Hōryū-ji's main hall representing the Western Paradise of Amida.

tradition are in immediate conflict. Within a year of the prince's death in 622, Empress Suiko ordered a census of Buddhist temples. The *Nihon Shoki* says there were 46 and these were staffed by 816 monks and 569 nuns. Not all of these temples have been identified, despite the early start made by medieval monks in trying to do so. It was not until about 685 that 300 temples were in operation. Archaeologists and historians now believe that around 483 temples were built between 646 and 710, that is, from the Taika Reform to the transfer of the capital to Heijō, and another 380, including the provincial temples, after that and before the capital was moved to Heian in 794. The country had roughly 900 temples when Emperor Kammu decided he had had enough of the Nara clergy and moved the capital to Nagaoka and then Heian.

Prince Shōtoku started to build a palace in the Ikaruga area of Nara prefecture in 601 and went there for long periods of work and study after 604. Within three years he constructed a temple, popularly known by its geographical name and later called Hōryū-ji when all temples were ordered in 679 to assume a formal, Chinese-style name. This temple was in every known respect virtually identical to the Shitennō-ji, including the use of some decorated roof-end tiles produced from the same molds.

The prince was probably more active physically than he is generally pictured to be. Tradition has him traveling widely on horseback to the west side of the country, in the region of Mt Fuji, and extensively in Yamato and the Kii peninsula. On one of these trips he picked out a spot at Mt Shinaga for his tomb and later gave the local people permission to commence its construction. He sponsored the building of a major road between Asuka and Naniwa, doubtless after experiencing the difficulties of crossing the mountains which mark the boundary between Nara and Osaka prefectures today.

Using his Ikaruga palace as a base, he spent most of his last 20 years in that area rather than in Asuka. This palace is

the oldest imperial one to be identified by archaeologists. Its site was dug in 1939 when repairs were being carried out on the Dempō-dō, a long building at the north end of that area. A series of buildings were connected by galleries, but the plan does not have any obvious relationship to later plans of palaces in Japan. There was probably no fixed idea at that time as to how a palace should be constituted. Later palaces have a uniform sequence of buildings in a formal compound.

Images of the Buddha. The prince died in his palace in 622 from an unspecified disease that killed several members of the family, and was memorialized by a gilt bronze triad of Shaka Buddha and accompanying Bodhisattvas, cast by Tori and finished within 13 months of his death, according to a long inscription on the back of the aureole. Made at the same time was a large embroidery, the Mandala of Heavenly Longevity, fragments of which are now preserved in patchwork form in the neighboring Chūgū-ji. The Shaka triad was a larger version of a statue of Yakushi Buddha, said in an inscription on the back of the halo to have been made as a dedication to Emperor Yōmei in 607.

Tori worked in a style distantly related to that of Wei dynasty China, characterized by strong frontality, a rectangular face and high-set mouth, an "archaic" smile, long neck, drooping shoulders, rather large hands, and with thick drapery overlapping in parallel pleats. The robe accumulates in two layers in elegant curves and flared points below the legs of the seated figures. In trying to stress the devotional character of the image, the sculptors using this style played down the bodily form while giving greater prominence to the appearance of the costume.

Buddhas were still not clearly differentiated by hand gestures, crown details, postures, leg positions or lotus or throne base, partly because the differences were not

Opposite: the finest group of early bronze sculptures are those made (c. 696) for the Yakushi-ji. Yakushi, the Buddha of healing, sits between Bodhisattvas of the sun and moon.

Below: fragments of a large tapestry, called the Mandala of Heavenly Longevity, woven soon after Prince Shōtoku's death.

distinct in the minds of the patrons and the makers. Indeed, iconography was still far from being consistent throughout the 8th century and only became more so when the Japanese dissociated themselves from China after the 9th century. Buddhism could be called nonsectarian. Sect consciousness arose when the Chinese translations of greater numbers of sutras came to be read and some understanding of the role of each Buddha could be reached.

The Ikaruga-dera was destroyed by fire in 669 or 670 – the *Nihon Shoki* gives the earlier date for the Ikaruga-dera, the later date for the Hōryū-ji, combining two traditions. It was a total disaster. Lightning struck and all the buildings were wiped out. Monks rescued two of the statues and an assortment of miscellaneous objects, stored them away, and finally dispersed, despondent and divided over the future of the temple.

Eventually a few of the older monks drifted back and within about 20 years proceeded to construct a temple on a very different plan using an open spot 150 to 200 meters northwest of the old site. This spot, set into the rising ground and backed by a low hill, seemed eminently suited for the new east-west orientation of the *garan*. This is the temple which visitors see today.

The sole remaining mark of the first temple here is the immense stone of the pagoda's center pole sitting in an open field, but behind walls and buildings and not seen by the public. It is known to have been moved, but is now on the approximate spot of the original pagoda. The top has only a shallow depression for a pole and no hole for relics as would be expected for its date. It is now cut along one side where someone started to reduce it to smaller blocks.

Prince Shōtoku was buried with his mother and one wife in the place he is said to have selected, in an area now called Taishi-chō. Within a radius of a few miles lie the tombs of Bidatsu, Yōmei, Suiko and Kōtoku. The mound of the tomb is on the north side of the Eifuku-ji, a temple built in the Kamakura period when the cult of the prince reached its peak. Empress Suiko had ordered the erection of a temple by his tomb, but there is nothing left from such an early period.

The tomb was apparently looted and stood open, possibly for a long time. The temple records try to gloss over this fact. A report by a priest who entered surreptitiously in the 14th century describes things in remarkable order, including three large stone slabs holding dry-lacquer coffins. In the last century the Imperial Household Agency investigated the interior and issued a straightforward, descriptive report of their findings. The mound is 57 meters in diameter. The passage and chamber are built of large, finely cut stones, quite in accordance with the early 7th-century style. The passage is

Opposite: Prince Shōtoku's tomb at Taishi-chō on the Osaka side of Mt Nijō.

Left: Tori's gilt bronze Shaka Buddha, accompanied by Bodhisattvas, completed in 623. The group became the main icon of the Hōryū-ji.

Below: as Buddhism grew, diverse practices among ascetics appeared in out-of-the-way places. This stone structure, symbolizing the Buddhist holy mountain, deep in the mountains at Kumayama-chō in Okayama prefecture, was probably built by 8th-century monks as a repository for their bones.

8 meters long and high enough to stand up in, while the chamber is 6 meters deep and a meter or so higher. Small fragmentary remains of what seemed to be lacquered coffins were scattered near the stone slabs. Nothing else of significance could be found.

Problems of succession. No one was appointed to succeed the prince as heir apparent. Soga power increased with each new ruler, as they ensured their position by such devices as putting ex-consorts on the throne as empresses after the death of an emperor. They supplied many wives for emperors. Kimmei had had at least two Soga wives. One of Prince Shōtoku's four wives was a Soga.

The critical point arrived when Empress Suiko favored Prince Yamashiro-no-Ōe, the son of Prince Shōtoku and a popular choice, to succeed her. But Yamashiro's potential power and the widespread respect held for the family were a constant threat to the Soga. They played every known delaying tactic to avoid crowning him. A grandson of Bidatsu was put on the throne, the sickly and ineffectual Jomei. He died after more than 12 years of visiting hot springs and the country suffering rains, floods, droughts, famines and an absurd number of unexplained natural phenomena. The only accomplishment worth record was one victory over the hostile Emishi and that was pulled off by the wife of the general and the wives of his soldiers.

Above: tomb of Empress Suiko who died in 628 and was buried on the fringe of the Taishi-chō group of imperial tombs, choosing to be interred in the tomb of her son, Prince Takeda.

Jomei was an early sponsor of one of the largest of all temples then contemplated. Known as Daikandai-ji when built in the Fujiwara area, it was the first temple to have a pagoda of nine stories and, as later rebuilt at Heijō as the Daian-ji, it was a temple of mammoth size with two pagodas.

On Jomei's death, his wife was made ruler and she, known historically as Empress Kōgyoku, immediately reappointed Soga-no-Emishi. Emishi's son Iruka was a frightening oppressor. Historians condemned his mass conscription order for the construction of his tomb. Iruka alone conceived the idea of wiping out the family of Shōtoku and carried it out before his father could protest.

Miroku (Maitreya), later the Buddha of the Future, here a Bodhisattva. Buddhist statuettes were Japan's first introduction to the form deities should take. Height 31·7 cm. British Museum.

In 643 Iruka's troops forced Prince Yamashiro's family and followers to escape from the Ikaruga palace, which they burned and left, thinking that all the residents had been killed. Yamashiro and the others reappeared in the mountains, but not wanting to commit bloodshed, voluntarily came down to the Ikaruga temple. When Iruka's troops surrounded it, the prince and his family all committed suicide by strangling.

The national reaction to the violent end of Shōtoku's line was very great, but was offset by a profound fear of the Soga. In great secrecy, Nakatomi-no-Kamatari, a member of the family which had traditionally opposed the Soga, sought inside help from Prince Naka-no-Ōe, second son of Jomei and Empress Kōgyoku. Prince Naka was later to be Emperor Tenchi. Eventually they were able on the occasion of a reception at the Itabuki Palace to persuade the cautious Iruka to leave his sword at the door. The alerted guards were given weapons – Iruka kept everyone unarmed – but the two courtiers who had accepted the task of killing Iruka froze in their tracks and Naka-no-Ōe himself had to attack and slash him to death in front of the shocked empress and in full view of the visiting Koreans. Prince Naka retired to the Asuka-dera and boarded it up for his defense, but this proved to be unnecessary as groups of Soga followers soon abandoned all plans of counterattack. Emishi and his family were taken and executed, but before this could be done, he is said to have destroyed some valuables and the History of the Emperors. The History of the Country was rescued and turned over to Prince Naka.

This coup took place in 645 AD and signaled a major change in the direction of Japanese history. Nakatomi-no-Kamatari is described as an upright man with a reformist's disposition. He was given a new name, Fujiwara, and it was his descendants who dominated Japanese history for many centuries. The intention in the coup was to regain the power for the emperor and to create a system of just rule. The model for this was to be the T'ang codes, the civil and legal statutes of China.

The empress immediately tendered her resignation and, after protestations by Prince Naka that he was not the next in line were finally accepted, Prince Karu was designated. Karu became Emperor Kōtoku and proceeded to issue orders to provinces to rectify injustices while requiring the taking of a census. To gain more freedom of action, the capital was moved to Naniwa late in 645, a move the elderly people had anticipated when they noticed the rats migrating in that direction.

The Taika Reform edicts were issued in 646 and incorporated sweeping orders to put all land under the control of the emperor, organize the tax system, remove the *be* from their supporting role of the nobility, and reduce family spending on tombs and temples. As befitting the best intentions, the reign name was changed to Taika, Great Change.

The Horse-Riding Nobles

Horse-riding people who had been crossing from Korea began leaving their personal possessions in their tombs by the latter half of the 5th century A D. Although their own tomb style is the typical 6th-century style of stone passageway and chamber, until craftsmen could be trained to build them they deposited the trappings at first in the earlier style tombs with small stone-lined receptacles near the top of the mound.

On the whole, the earliest trappings are more practical equipment for horse-riding, while later ones are often more ornamental and larger, especially the rump and bit ornaments. Stirrups seem to outnumber other trappings, but get less notice than the fine gilt-bronze decorated pieces.

These horse-riders made major cultural contributions: they brought in the first horse paraphernalia, introduced Sue type pottery, then had workmen instructed in the buildings of the stone chamber tombs, to which they added simple decorations. They established the *be* for economic support, bolstered the economy through horse breeding and the raising of legumes, and ultimately ensured their position by socially scaling the important families, setting the precedent for the graded nobility of later times.

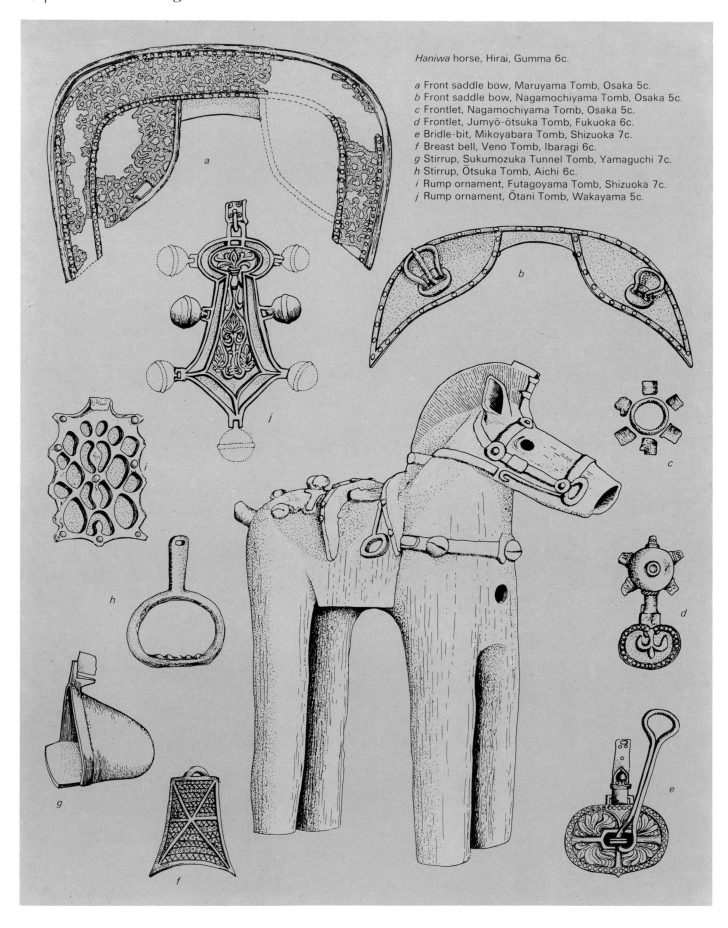

Haniwa horse, Hirai, Gumma 6c.

a Front saddle bow, Maruyama Tomb, Osaka 5c.
b Front saddle bow, Nagamochiyama Tomb, Osaka 5c.
c Frontlet, Nagamochiyama Tomb, Osaka 5c.
d Frontlet, Jumyō-ōtsuka Tomb, Fukuoka 6c.
e Bridle-bit, Mikoyabara Tomb, Shizuoka 7c.
f Breast bell, Veno Tomb, Ibaragi 6c.
g Stirrup, Sukumozuka Tunnel Tomb, Yamaguchi 7c.
h Stirrup, Ōtsuka Tomb, Aichi 6c.
i Rump ornament, Futagoyama Tomb, Shizuoka 7c.
j Rump ornament, Ōtani Tomb, Wakayama 5c.

Previous page: the Takehara tomb in Fukuoka prefecture is typical of painted tombs in Kyushu in the technique of applying the colors directly to the stone, but unusual in the advanced composition. Occupying a span of about 6 feet on the end wall, painted exclusively in black and red, the grouped objects are arranged between a pair of ceremonial fans. A horseman dressed for riding tends a horse above a boat and waves

Opposite: *haniwa* horses stood guard on the tombs. They often show how the trappings were used. A selection here illustrates different types from three centuries of use. The saddle bows and frontlet from the Maruyama and Nagamochiyama tombs in Osaka are probably the oldest horse trappings in the Yamato area, if not in all of Japan, and are undoubtedly foreign made. Style changes are not very apparent in some of the trappings, but the pocket stirrup is a late arrival.

Right: this 6th-century *haniwa* warrior, over 4 feet tall, comes from a tomb in Gumma prefecture. The tube was to be pressed into the earth of the mound. He is in full dress, probably leather, armor tied across to left. The helmet resembles a bowler hat. National Museum, Tokyo.

Below: the best-preserved horse bones found to date are those of a 12-year-old male horse associated with 5th-century pottery in a shell layer of the Kusaka site, Higashi-Osaka city. Beside it was a dog, and 11 human skeletons have been unearthed at the site since excavation started in 1939. This is a medium-sized horse of the Mongolian type, larger than the Jōmon and Yayoi horse which is closer in size to the Tokara pony.

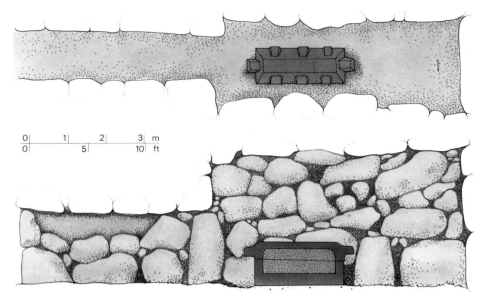

Left and below: the Kōmorizuka tomb, a large keyhole tomb, is a remarkable example of the stone passageway and chamber style of tomb the horse-riders had built for themselves. Located near both the provincial monastery and the provincial nunnery not far from Okayama city, it is made of huge well-cut stones, forming a passage 18·5 m in length, the chamber 8 m long and 3·4 m high, in a mound measuring 100 m.

Opposite: the only horse helmet found in east Asia from this period, this iron helmet was recovered from the late 5th-century keyhole Ōtani tomb in Wakayama city. It is 51·8 cm long.

Top right: Korean in manufacture, the gilt-bronze bridle-bit with jingle bells from the Ōtani tomb is one of the finest in Japan. The S-shape can be traced ultimately to Scythian sources, and the elegant floral patterns derive from 6th-century work in China.

Right: gilt-bronze strap ornament, also from the Ōtani tomb.

Bottom right: the distribution of horse trappings conforms to the distribution of late tombs, but with fewer in north Kyushu than would be expected. Local production of Sue pottery probably started in Osaka prefecture.

Below: two tombs lying side by side at Shibayama in Chiba prefecture had long lines of *haniwa* decorating their slopes. This groom stands 97·8 cm high.

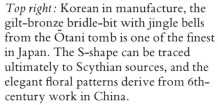

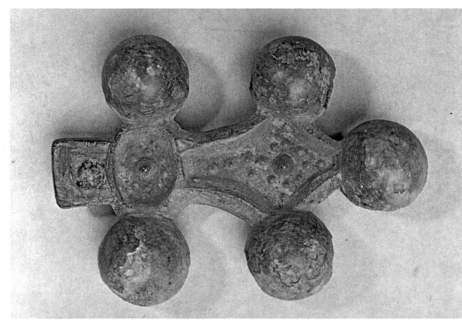

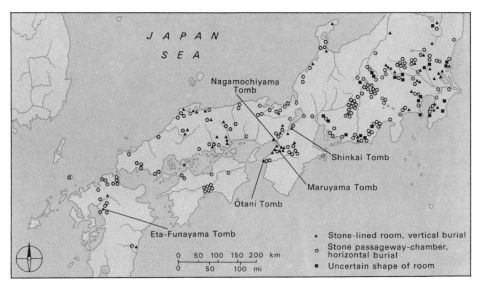

JAPAN SEA

Nagamochiyama Tomb

Shinkai Tomb

Maruyama Tomb

Ōtani Tomb

Eta-Funayama Tomb

0 50 100 150 200 km
0   50   100 mi

▲ Stone-lined room, vertical burial
○ Stone passageway-chamber, horizontal burial
■ Uncertain shape of room

Above: men shown riding horses are very rare in Tomb period art. Such little figures of people, animals, birds and boats are limited to Sue vessels in the Inland Sea area and all probably date to the 6th century. National Museum, Tokyo.

Left: low relief on the end of a clay sarcophagus from the Hirafuku tomb in Eita county, Okayama prefecture, represents a symmetrical scene of a man holding the reins of two horses with perhaps mountains overhead and a pair of knobbed posts below. The horses have high arched tails, a common feature of this period. National Museum, Tokyo.

Opposite above: rump ornaments of this sort of gilt-bronze were riveted to an iron backing plate, much or all of which usually rusts away. The heart shape with variations is a common frame for decoration. It is rather small size for a late one (diameter 92 mm) and comes from a tomb on the outskirts of Fukuoka city for which a 7th-century date might be suitable.

Left: a small silver inlaid running horse on the blade of a straight iron sword found in the Eta-Funayama tomb in Kumamoto prefecture in 1873, the oldest unquestionable representation of a horse in Japan.

Opposite below: the finest gold crown excavated in Japan, discovered in the Sammaizuka tomb in Namegata county, Ibaragi prefecture, in 1952. It had been wrapped in red dyed silk cloth and belonged to a man not quite 50 years old. Among the *haniwa* on top of the mound was one wearing a crown. Open floral work dominates the decoration of the band.

Above: from the Hōanzuka tomb in Fukuchiyama city, Kyoto prefecture, dug by Kyoto University, this 6th-century rump ornament is typically large (length 17·2 cm) for the late ones and characteristically simple. Its iron back is mostly intact.

Below: horse bells may be bell-shaped or a frame that holds jingle bells, the latter usually used over the rump. This one, from the Ōtsuka tomb, Aichi prefecture, still has little stones in four of its bells. Length 10·7 cm.

5. The Capital at Heijō

Emperor Kōtoku, who issued the Taika Reform edicts, was still not succeeded by Naka-no-Ōe, one of the framers. Saimei, his mother, the previous Empress Kōgyōku, was reinstalled on the throne. She again appointed him crown prince and was soon back and settled in Asuka. The Japanese rulers found themselves too much involved with foreign policy to devote adequate attention to the reform measures.

Foreign affairs. As Silla expanded and China put pressure on the north Korean kingdom of Kōguryō, Japan armed and sent a fleet. Saimei and Prince Naka went down to Kyushu to supervise the expedition, but she died there in 661 and did not live to see the Japanese navy of 170 ships and army of 27,000 men annihilated by the combined Chinese and Silla forces, an event which forced the withdrawal of Japan from Korea for almost 1,000 years.

It was expected that T'ang China would follow up its victory, and the Japanese rushed work on their fortifications in the south, aided by many refugees who had escaped from Korea. The southern capital of Dazaifu was built in Fukuoka as the headquarters for these defenses. Dazaifu became a military and political city of considerable importance, second only to Heijō in the 8th century.

China had no reason to fear Japan and soon offered diplomatic relations. The Japanese appointed special envoys and sent many official missions. Along with these were many monks traveling to the continent. They could be depended upon to seek out the literate people of other Asian countries and give intelligible accounts of their experiences and recent events. On their return to Japan they pioneered cultural developments in the temples.

Naka-no-Ōe became Emperor Tenchi and reigned from 661 to 672, living in a palace near Lake Biwa. He witnessed the foreign disaster in 663, but it is to his credit that he followed up the Chinese initiation of diplomatic relations only three years later.

It was during Tenchi's reign that the Hōryū-ji was destroyed. As the Japanese had been breaking up the strict symmetry of the *garan* and responding to the developing interest in the images of the main hall by giving it more prominence, they were faced with the problem of finding ways of balancing the pagoda against the dominant horizontality of the other buildings.

Experiments with less formal arrangements were already underway in the 660s, starting with the Kawahara-dera in Asuka, but the most satisfactory relationship was arrived at by around 690 when the Hōryū-ji was rebuilt. The main hall and pagoda were placed side by side, the main hall to the east, the pagoda to the west. An extra bay of cloister was allowed on the east for greater spaciousness, and the pagoda was proportioned to be twice the height of the main hall but the volume of space occupied by the two to be much the same. The middle gate was given only two open bays, perhaps in order to frame the views of the buildings as the worshiper entered.

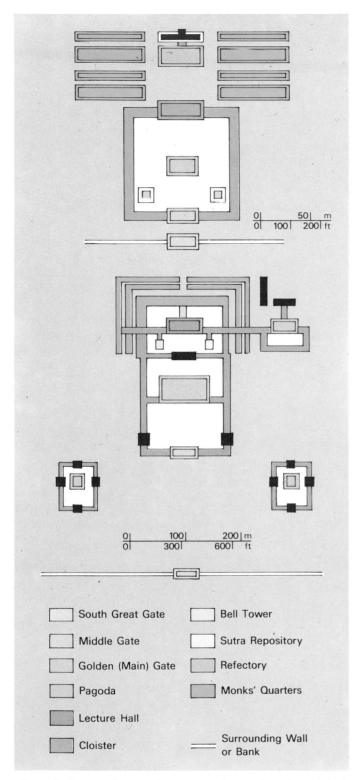

South Great Gate		Bell Tower	
Middle Gate		Sutra Repository	
Golden (Main) Gate		Refectory	
Pagoda		Monks' Quarters	
Lecture Hall			
Cloister		Surrounding Wall or Bank	

Above: the first temple to receive two pagodas was the Yakushi-ji (*top*), begun by Emperor Temmu, completed c. 695. The Tōdai-ji (*below*) was completed c. 743.

Page 91: the Roshana (Vairocana) Buddha, made by Chinese monks for the Tōshōdai-ji, is the largest seated dry-lacquer image in Japan (3·03 m).

Opposite: the Yakushi-ji was moved from Fujiwara to Heijō in 718. The main hall has recently been replaced by a reconstruction of a late 7th-century building, conforming in style to the east pagoda.

Chinese styles. Even while this was going on, word was being received from China that the most fashionable temple was now furnished with two pagodas. The temple known as Yakushi-ji, ordered by Emperor Temmu in 680 when his wife was ill, though not finished until near the end of the century, was the first to be built with a pair of pagodas and thus marked a sharp reversal of the Japanese trend toward asymmetrical plans. It may be that the Hōryū-ji was reerected by older monks who knew the early temple and out of respect for the prince and his era built it in an archaic structural style. But they did so in the most advanced and successful Japanese plan up to that time.

Because of the patently early style of the buildings, the lack of any documentation on the rebuilding of the Hōryū-ji and the feeling that the plan embodied a special genius – that of the prince – there arose a strange "no-fire theory." One can thank this bizarre controversy for the formal initiation of temple archaeology. Digging at the Hōryū-ji was decided upon to settle the argument once and for all.

When repairs were made in 1939, trenches were cut across the north side of the present cloister to look for evidence of a conflagration. The fact that none was found was a blow to those who took the literary references to a fire at face value, but they soon came to realize that this was not the temple that had been burned, and excavations in recent years in the right spot have cut through charred soil and revealed the outlines of the main hall and pagoda platforms. The middle gate and lecture hall, if the latter existed, stood under existing walls and buildings. Fragments of an exceptionally simple lotus decoration on the roof tiles are evidence for the early date of the temple on this site.

Now it is known that the Ikaruga-dera and the present Hōryū-ji had much more in common than the structural style. The buildings were the same size. All of the 28 stone bases for the wooden pillars of the first main hall were used for the present main hall. Among these, four show red and black surfaces from the 670 fire. Undamaged ones were placed in the same way, damaged ones were simply turned over. Fifteen of the stones are natural and unworked. Some have a slightly shaped circular rise, six of which had been chiseled off.

Probably the relics were supplemented or changed when the second temple was built. As a young man and still outside the inner circles of archaeologists, Professor Mosaku Ishida, whose memoirs are a remarkable record of three decades of Buddhist temple archaeology, describes his incredulity at a rumor that the base of the 32·5-meter pole of the Hōryū-ji pagoda was rotted out when repairs were underway in 1927. Such work was not then publicized. It was breaking the sanctity of the temple and a disrespect to the Buddha. But he had to see for himself, so armed with a flashlight, he crept in one night and, to his amazement, found it was in fact true. The center pole was dangling in place. How long had it hung there? Ten years or a hundred? Fifty years or five hundred?

This fact soon led to a complete reassessment of the use of this pole. It did not hold up the building; if anything, the building held it up. It has no real structural function. It stands as a mast to support the ceremonial umbrellas and other ornaments on top, as a traditional symbol of the center of the Buddhist universe and, in many early temples, to seal the relics in the stone beneath it.

During the 1944 repairs of the temple the relics were removed from the hole, facsimiles were made and the relics replaced. Their arrangement at that time was not as orderly as would be expected, so they were probably tampered with in 1927 or at some earlier time. They consist of a Chinese lion and grape mirror, a globular bronze vessel, a copper bowl, egg-shaped gold and silver containers, the smaller one made to fit inside the larger, a glass bottle, gold plaque, pearl shell, 627 pearls, 272 glass beads and other small objects like pieces of crystal, amber, calcite and incense wood. The glass bottle intended to hold the actual relic was empty.

Temple archaeology has since that time had the advantage of becoming public and, under general inspection and with considerable experience, becoming greatly refined. Temples can be dated by the minor changes in the decoration on roof tiles. A smaller temple than the present Hōryū-ji, the Hokki-ji, lies only a short distance across the fields to the northeast. Near it is the Hōrin-ji, a temple of equally small size. These two lack a full complement of buildings today, but it can be seen from the remains that the latter had a plan identical to the

Below right: the 8th-century Gankōji pagoda site at Nara city.
Below: late 7th-century roof-end tile with lotus decoration from the Yukino-dera site in Gamō county, Shiga prefecture.

Hōryū-ji while the former had the main hall and pagoda in a reversed relationship. Among the 25 temples in this general plan, with the two buildings lying side by side, the difference in roof tiles shows that the Hokki-ji arrangement was more popular as temples were being erected further out in the provinces.

Empress Jitō succeeded Temmu until Mommu was of age to take the throne. She took the major step of building the palace and laying out the capital city of Fujiwara. The stability offered by such a city was a necessity if the bureaucratic system of government was going to succeed.

The capital moves to Heijō. Mommu took the throne, but died inconveniently at the age of 25 in 707. His wife was then put on the throne since the emperor-to-be Shōmu was then only seven. Empress Gemmyō received copper, gold and silver at the court, but she is best known for transferring the capital to Heijō, now called Nara, in 710 after two years of preparation.

This move created an enormous amount of activity. Within the year temples in the south had begun to dismantle their buildings in expectation of moving to Heijō if they could be assured of a good location. Large segments of the population were transferred to keep the land more evenly occupied and ensure a smooth transmission of the taxes. To get the most out of the country's manpower, greater pressures were applied toward the conscription and forced labor requirements of the young men, along with the submission of all the assessed taxes.

Empress Gemmyō abdicated at the age of 36 when Shōmu was still only 16 and put her daughter, later called Empress Genshō, on the throne. Shōmu finally became emperor in 724 at the age of 24. He ruled for 25 years and

The Yumedono (Dream Hall), built after 739 as a memorial to Prince Shōtoku. Preserved in a box in this building is the Yumedono Kannon, illustrated on page 2.

abdicated, the first emperor to do so, apparently in order to devote his last years to Buddhist affairs. He died eight years later. He lived through very difficult times and from being a carefree young man grew into the imperial role. He found in Buddhism a way to regain a national purpose after the devastating plague that decimated the Fujiwara family and the fearful earthquakes that followed.

Emperor Shōmu's paramount concern seems to have been with the arts. Bureaus of craftsmen were established. Whole projects were taken on by workshops, resulting, in the case of sculpture for instance, in a remarkable uniformity in style. Less is preserved in painting. Whether in bronze, clay, wood or dry lacquer there is a stylistic consistency throughout, quite unlike the individual stamp of Tori's time or the regional features that characterize the art later.

As a patron, it was not only through the medium of Buddhism that Shōmu approached the arts. Some understanding of the quality of secular production can be gained from his personal possessions which his wife gave to the state on the occasion of the memorial service after his death. He had apparently been the recipient of fine gifts

from far and wide when the Great Buddha was dedicated. Preserved since 756 in the Shōsō-in, a wooden storehouse behind the Tōdai-ji, the personal property of Emperor Shōmu provides unique evidence for palace life in 8th-century Japan when Chinese influence was at its peak. Its contents number in the thousands and have an extraordinary range, including many musical instruments, pieces of Chinese furniture, textiles, bronze mirrors and drugs.

Empress Kōken, Shōmu's daughter, succeeded him at the age of 33. All went well while her father was still alive, but she later came under the spell of a priest named Dōkyō. She abdicated and installed Junnin, but rivalry between Dōkyō and her chief advisor Fujiwara Nakamaro, whose name was changed to Emi-no-Oshikatsu, prompted her to exert herself and have Junnin removed. He was exiled to Awaji Island where he died the following year in mysterious circumstances. She was reinstated as ruler, this time known as Empress Shōtoku.

Her affair with Dōkyō was unique in its extent, but had the advantage of putting to the test the legitimacy of the imperial succession system. He was promoted to all but emperor, and a messenger was sent to the Usa Hachiman Shrine in Kyushu to ask whether that too was possible. It was not; the line was preserved. Shōtoku died in office at

The Shōsō-in (*above*), built to house the personal effects of Emperor Shōmu after his death in 756. The collection is remarkable for its diversity. There are over 600 scrolls, more than 60,000 gems, swords, armor, screens, wearing apparel, lacquered cases and containers, such as this mother-of-pearl inlaid box (*below*).

the age of 52 and Dōkyō was removed to a temple in the Kantō. Japan had had one empress too many and forbade a repetition of that unhappy experience.

At the time of Oshikatsu's rebellion Shōtoku had ordered the making of one million little wooden stupas. These were ready six years later and were distributed in lots of 100,000 to ten temples. Each stupa had a small prayer printed on paper in its hollow interior, making these the oldest known printing in Japan. The Hōryū-ji claims still to have thousands of them, with about a hundred exhibited in its treasure hall.

Succession problems always abounded and the heir

apparent did not always reach the throne. The aged Emperor Kōnin did little but issue orders to control prices and receive reports of military losses in the north. During his stop-gap reign Kammu was appointed crown prince, and when Kammu came to the throne in 781, eight years later, the country had the strongest and most independent ruler of the century.

Emperor Kammu planned to move the capital, putting the management of the transfer in the hands of Fujiwara Tanetsugu. Nagaoka was selected and the buildings went up in great haste as the taxes were brought directly to the construction site. Kammu and the court moved in 784, although the "gates of Heijō" were not transferred until 791.

Nagaoka did not seem to have the right balances. The worst event was the assassination of Tanetsugu. The spirits were signaling their displeasure, so a new site was sought.

A more suitable place could hardly have been found, marked by three mountains and between two rivers; and with the approval of the local *kami*, construction got underway in 792. Two years later Kammu and his court went up to Heian (City of Peace), the largest of the checkerboard cities, today called Kyoto.

Social organization. The old family *uji* system was unsuited to the new bureaucratic government, so a series of court ranks was organized by Emperor Temmu (672–86), to which many later modifications were made. Known as *kabane*, like hereditary titles, the plan eliminated automatic succession and made a smaller number of persons directly responsible to the emperor. It could not have been forced on a large body of disgruntled ex-nobles, so it amounted to considerable juggling of the existing hierarchy and compensating with titles that commanded respect, costumes and colors that distinguished rank, special headgear, and assured ways of acquiring wealth. How the new hierarchy related to the standing of the earlier *uji* leaders is not entirely clear, but the once-powerful Omi and Muraji who had brought the Yamato state into being were in the lower grades in the new system.

The upper four ranks were imperially related, while the eight below were drawn from subject families. The levels within these ranks amounted to 30 grades. The top appointed official was the Grand Minister, and below him were the Minister of the Left and the Minister of the Right. Each of the eight ministries was supervised by an executive officer.

The exclusive top ranks had duties involving national policy. Perhaps around 300 persons occupied those ranks at any one time in the 8th century. Appointments were usually for four years, but sometimes six, and could result in long terms and slow promotion, especially since the evaluation process was notoriously sluggish.

Advantages lay in rights to possess land, own supporting household fiefs and claim exemptions from certain taxes. The economic range was exceedingly great. Lower officials were barred entirely from having fiefs. At the top, Prince Takechi, the Grand Minister under Empress Jitō and quite possibly the owner of the Takamatsuzuka painted tomb in Asuka, had support from 3,000 household fiefs in 691 and received another 2,000 the following year.

The three large categories into which the families of note were classified were, first, those with ancestry traced to the imperial line; second, those with ancestry traced to the deities (which, in fact, also included the imperial family); and third, those with ancestry known to be immigrant or foreign.

In a list of more than 1,000 families at the court at this time, the immigrants amounted to over 30 per cent, with Koreans outnumbering Chinese by a smaller margin than one would expect. Interestingly enough, descent from the *kami* did not qualify a woman to be an empress. Only those with imperial family connections were acceptable. In the early families of prominence this included the Soga and Tachibana, for instance, but did not include the Mononobe and Nakatomi (who later changed their name to Fujiwara). When Shōmu made his wife Kōmyō empress in 729 after he had been on the throne five years, he had to break the lineage barrier since she was a Fujiwara. He cited as precedent the empress of Emperor Nintoku from the Katsuragi family. While this shows how strictly the lineage system had been honored, it is a strange example since the Katsuragi themselves were supposed to be of imperial descent.

Cap ranks were also used. They were made on a more personal level and determined on the basis of merit. Prince Shōtoku is said to have introduced them with 12 grades, but they had increased to 26 grades by 664.

As the structure of the officials' ranks and duties was settling into place in the first century of application, there were innumerable regulations and endless changes. The clothing regulations of 681 contained 92 articles. Etiquette, language and ceremonies at the court were formulated. Dress was eventually put under a court dress and cap regulating office in 700, which then took care of the trivia.

Few areas of life were left unaffected, from princes down. Women were told how to ride a horse. The Chinese had said that only barbarians tied their clothes right over left, so an order in 719 required that clothes be tied left over right. Slaves were finding ways to appear like free people and receive equal treatment. Their clothes were to be black; commoners' were to be yellow.

Penal reform. A legal system had to follow the Taika Reform edicts in order to spell out what was acceptable behavior and what would be the punishment for any infringements. The Japanese wrote several of these *ritsuryō* (civil and penal codes) in the late 7th and 8th centuries. Scholars studied the legal system of T'ang China and the Japanese borrowed all they needed, often in the penal codes, but frequently not at all.

Emperor Tenchi issued a set from Ōmi near Lake Biwa in 662, one of the drafters of which was Fujiwara Kamatari, the architect of the Taika Reform. It was revised in 689. The main body of statutes was embodied in the Taihō codes which Mommu had drawn up in 701 and which stayed in use until 757 after revision in 718 when the Yōrō civil and penal codes were presented to the court. They were apparently not applied until 758, perhaps because the Taihō codes were generally adequate. Unfortunately, no text of the Taihō codes exists today, but the Yōrō codes are known in the form of later Heian period commentaries on legal interpretations.

The Japanese wrote their codes to avoid some of the problems they knew had resulted from the T'ang system, such as the creation of an unassailable bureaucracy. They were woefully lacking in the Confucian experience upon which the Chinese statutes were based, but they did profit by the many revisions and interpretations the Chinese had made. They were willing to accept the underlying principle that the codes were designed to produce social stability. They quite happily accepted such other principles as these: responsibility rested with the family for the errors of the individual; confession and repentance brought about a reduction of the punishment; the degree of punishment was tailored to the crime; and punishment could be given for a social wrong even if the wrong was not covered by a law.

Literary sources. The first of Japan's national histories were compiled at this time. The *Kojiki*, the Records of Ancient Matters, given to the court in 712, has as its primary concern the genealogy of the imperial line. The *Nihon Shoki* or *Nihongi*, Chronicles of Japan, so often referred to here, is a much fuller account, taken from many sources, some of which were written, and offered to the court in 720. Starting with the Age of the Gods and describing the physical formation of the country, it traces the activities of the "emperors" and the development of the Yamato state through the reign of Empress Jitō in 697 AD. Its sequel is the *Shoku Nihongi*, to 792, and that is followed by others until 887, making a total of six consecutive histories. All of these were commissioned by Yamato rulers and took as their premise the divine origins of the clan and its early claim to the throne.

Other sources of information are the preserved sections of the *Fudoki*, the gazetteers. The provinces were ordered in 713 to describe their traditions, natural resources, topographical features and whatever else seemed important. These began to arrive at the court about 20 years later. Probably not all were actually finished, but only one is preserved complete today, the *Izumo Fudoki*, and sections of four others are extant. Part of their value is that they did not go through the hands of Yamato editors; but in those preserved, an inordinate amount of space is devoted to the exploits of Yamato-takeru, an early hero who "pacified barbarians" in the reign of Emperor Keikō and an important figure in the regular Yamato cycle.

Also preserved is the *Man'yōshū*, a remarkable collection of over 4,000 poems compiled after 759. They are the work of numerous poets from the time of Emperor Nintoku, written in already well-established verse patterns.

Distribution of land. After land was placed under imperial authority by the edicts of the Taika Reform, it was then allotted to families according to the number of able-bodied persons, with larger shares going to males. These allotments were in multiples of a *tan* unit, or 30 by 12 paces. The annual tax on this plot of land was a little over two sheaves of rice.

Vast plains and lowlands were marked out in the simplest way, with a north-south orientation, as was the case with the plan of the cities. In some places, where the topography was too irregular or a river bank was to be the guide, other orientations were acceptable. Measured in units of east to west and north to south as *jō* and *ri*, the land allotments became known as the *jōri* system.

Jōri have left their physical mark in many parts of the country and can still be seen today in the patterns of ricefields. Some regions, however, seem to have been unaffected, although only one was officially so. A report came to the court from south Kyushu in 730 saying that the system had never been applied down there and requesting formal exemption for the region. What was meant was that the continuing hostility of the people in the area made it not worth the effort, and this is just one more instance of the difficulties the central government faced.

City planning. As early as the 660s the Kawahara-dera in Asuka was laid out to conform with the new orientation, and the most graphic example was the plan of the city of Fujiwara, where Empress Jitō set up residence in 694, modeled after the Chinese capital of Ch'ang-an, including its rectangular blocks. Later Japanese cities had square blocks. Called *jōbō* in cities, the east-west blocks were in even numbers, the north-south blocks in odd, in order to agree with the Chinese *yin-yang* principle of natural law. One found the house of a friend in the city by block numbers, not by street numbers, on the right or left side, as determined by the position of the emperor as he looked out over the city from his throne.

Many questions are left unanswered about Fujiwara, not the least of which is its exact size; but it was Japan's first grid-plan city and the country roads there can still be seen today to follow the original lines.

The palace lay to the north, surrounded by a colonnaded cloister. Emperor Temmu may have built the first formal palace at Kiyomigahara in Asuka, but a fully complete palace cannot exist without an accompanying city to support it, and archaeology has revealed little of Temmu's palace so far. At Fujiwara and again at Heijō, Naniwa and Heian, the principles followed were the same with small variations. A walled front court included a pair of buildings facing each other, the imperial assembly halls. Beyond this was the administration palace consisting of a second court with the halls of the Eight Ministries. Four buildings were lined up on either side, their main entrances opposite each other. In later palaces extra buildings were added at the south end of this court. The major receptions, installations and other ceremonies were held here. Behind

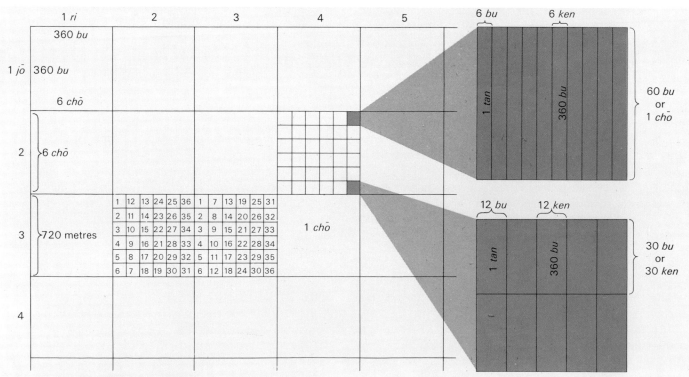

Under more stable political conditions in Heijō, expansion into new territory was extensive and much new land was developed in this way, marked out in regular fields called *jōri*, usually oriented with the cardinal directions (*opposite*). Old maps, place-names and even modern aerial views reveal their presence (*above*), here seen south of Lake Biwa.

this was a smaller, cloistered and more secluded area, the imperial council hall, where the emperor conducted business. His actual residence was in a separate section, usually to the east.

It was while the Fujiwara palace was in use that the transition from the old 60-year cyclical dating to the *nengō* (era name) took place. Recently discovered wooden tallies for goods brought into the palace are dated by both methods.

Fujiwara saw only 16 years of service and could hardly have fulfilled its grand plan. It looks in retrospect like a trial run. Its 30,000 or more inhabitants followed Empress Gemmyō to Heijō in 710 after two years spent in marking out the new city and constructing the palaces.

Heijō lies not far to the west of the present city of Nara, mostly in flat open ricefields. The area had been inhabited for a long time and many tombs had to be leveled when the capital was built. The Akishino and Sahō rivers flow

through and meet approximately where the main street led up to the palaces. It was planned as 36 by 32 *chō*, each *chō* measuring 120 meters. Its nine *jō* blocks run north-south, while its eight *bō* blocks run east-west. Each of these blocks is subdivided into 16 smaller ones. Families of commoners got about 30 by 30 meters on an inside street, nobles somewhat more and on a main street. The city's measurements were about 4·5 by 4 kilometers, and it is thought to have accommodated a population that rose to roughly 200,000 by the end of the 8th century.

Proportionately less space was assigned with each succeeding capital, including Naniwa, as population pressures mounted, more soldiers were garrisoned in the city, and country people drifted in to escape rural taxes. Complaints that life was better in the provinces were common.

The city had an appointed city master, chief masters for units of four blocks and masters for single blocks. To provide open space for the market places on either side of the city, smaller blocks toward the south edge were apparently just not built up. The Chinese had designed the plan to enable them to control the labor force and have an effective conscription system. The Japanese undoubtedly made use of it in much the same way; but without the

walls that slowly grew up around Chinese cities, a Japanese city never gave the impression of being a massively defended fortress. It always appeared open and accessible.

New styles of temple architecture. The major temples of Fujiwara were dismantled and reassembled at Heijō. The Yakushi-ji and Daikandai-ji, renamed Daian-ji, received ideal sites, similar to those they had enjoyed in Fujiwara, except that the Daian-ji in this case had to put up with a keyhole-shaped tomb on their property, removal of which was by that time illegal. Each temple had two pagodas, the Yakushi-ji following its earlier plan, but the Daian-ji built in a new style with the pagodas well out in front and within their own cloisters. It may have been the intention to separate the pagodas from the *garan*, and so protect the other buildings from the fires (caused by lightning) that usually started at a pagoda. One probably held relics; the other was ornamental; but two were doubly dangerous to the temple.

Several families erected private temples, but only those with a great deal of influence could do so. The Chinese

Above and opposite above: Heijō or old Nara was planned ideally on the principle of square blocks, each 120 meters to a side, that is 10 times 1 *jo* or 40 *shaku*. Two wide streets acted as main thoroughfares, one running due north to the palace, the other crossing east-west in front of the palace.

Opposite below: the lecture hall of the Tōshōdai-ji, erected in 759 after being moved from the imperial palace.

priest Ganjin was given a choice piece of land by an imperial prince in 759 after he had ordained monks at the Tōdai-ji. His temple, Tōshōdai-ji, was built after he received an imperial assembly hall as a gift from the empress. This building was modified into a lecture hall. When it was recently taken down for repairs, it was found to have east-west assembly marks on the beams as a guide to erection along one side of the main courtyard of the palace.

The Nara period had its Six Sects of the Southern Capital, as they were called. Three of these sects of Buddhism have disappeared with hardly a trace, but Hossō, Kegon and

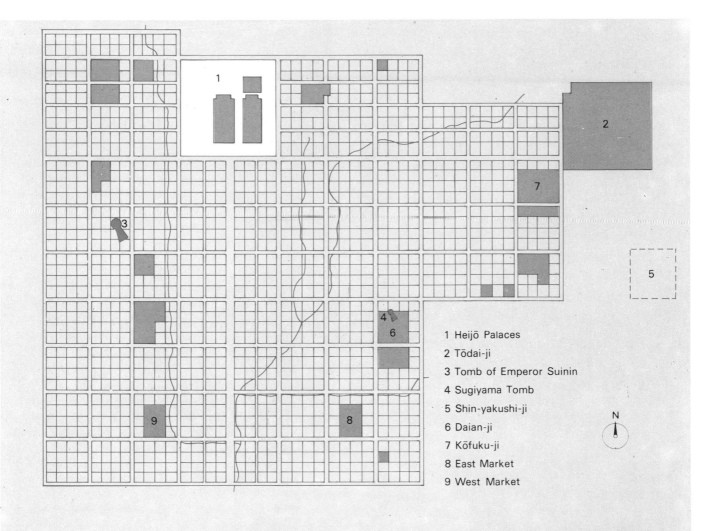

1 Heijō Palaces

2 Tōdai-ji

3 Tomb of Emperor Suinin

4 Sugiyama Tomb

5 Shin-yakushi-ji

6 Daian-ji

7 Kōfuku-ji

8 East Market

9 West Market

N

Ritsu are still thriving despite popular interest later swinging toward Zen philosophy and practices. The Hōryū-ji was Hossō by the Nara period and only recently declared itself a Shōtoku sect. The Tōdai-ji is the head Kegon (Garland) temple. The Tōshōdai-ji is Ritsu (Rules), and has about two dozen allied temples. It was an unusual college of learning in the 8th century, a center of Chinese Buddhist studies and uniquely influential.

The court had a school, and a minister of education was periodically appointed, but his efforts were directed toward medicine, managing the awkward calendar and reading the Chinese classics. At least after the time of Emperor Shōmu, instruction also went on through the provincial offices.

In times of emergency and when notable donations were made, the temples show their rank in the eyes of the court. In the early 700s the Shidaiji (Four Great Temples) were Gankō-ji, Gūfuku-ji, Daian-ji and Yakushi-ji, all still in Fujiwara, but three of them making plans to move to Heijō. There they were the Asuka-dera, Kawahara-dera, Daikandai-ji and Yakushi-ji, which must have left enough of an establishment in Fujiwara when it moved to be called the Moto-yakushi-ji, Original Yakushi-ji. When the country was crippled by constant earthquakes in 745, the four great temples which bore the load of the prayer services were the Yakushi-ji, Gankō-ji, Kōfuku-ji and Daian-ji, all of course in Heijō.

Above: a dry-lacquer statue of Priest Gyōshin (died 750) in the Yumedono of the Hōryū-ji.

Opposite: the Great Buddha Hall of the Tōdai-ji in Nara.

Left: at the corners of the Buddha platform in the main hall of the Tōshōdai-ji stand the Four Heavenly Kings. On the SE corner Jikoku-ten, king of the east, wields his sword menacingly. Height 2·05 m.

New interpretations of Buddhism. As a way of making Buddhism more understandable to the rank and file, Priest Gyōgi, a Korean by birth and a Hossō adherent, began propagating a philosophy that came to be called Ryōbu-Shinto, that is Dual-Aspect Shinto, in which it was claimed that Shinto deities could be identified with Buddhist counterparts. This signalizes the merging of the two, best known through the esoteric doctrines of later centuries.

By 699 there had been built a Jingū-ji, a Buddhist temple near the Ise Shrine. The priests sometimes held each other's services. The *kami* of Shinto shrines came to be the tutelary deities of Buddhist temples, one of the most historically significant being the Usa Hachiman Shrine of Ōita in Kyushu which became allied with the Tōdai-ji in Heijō. This happened as the female shaman of the Usa Hachiman felt compelled by the *kami* to go up to Heijō to pay her respects to the Great Buddha when it was completed in 749. She arrived with many attendants, was welcomed by

the court, and became a Buddhist novice before she worshiped the Great Buddha and entered the temple. Starting a practice that became common later, a Shinto shrine was built in a protective location near the temple. The Tamukeyama Hachiman Shrine on the hill in the Tōdai-ji precincts commemorates this event.

Mergers were taking place at the highest levels of religious activity. Another major step was Empress Shōtoku's insistence that Buddhist priests should join in conducting her coronation ceremony called Daijō-e which up to that time had been the exclusive duty of Shinto priests.

The appearance of stability at Heijō in the 8th century is no more than a mirage. The capital twice came within a hairsbreadth of being moved by Shōmu, and was saved only by warnings from the spirits of nature.

Shōmu was dissatisfied with the factionalism and the constant jockeying for position at Heijō and moved to Kuni in 741. He even had the market places transferred later in the same year. He apparently also visited Naniwa and seriously considered living there. A straw vote taken among his nobles at the court on the two sites showed Kuni just ahead of Naniwa, and the shopkeepers along the streets were almost unanimously in favor of Kuni, the closer of the two. Shōmu decided he wanted to be further away – Kuni was less than 10 kilometers – and he chose Naniwa. Plans were made to transfer the capital, and the palace was "swept out" and prepared for his arrival.

In the next year he had a "detached" palace built at Shigaraki, about 35 kilometers northeast of Heijō. It being a detached palace, he would have had no intention of making the place a "capital," but he went so far as to order workmen to start on a colossal bronze image of a Buddha and to build a temple to accommodate it. The remoteness of Shigaraki put the stamp of an almost totally private undertaking on this project and when the efforts of the craftsmen met with failure after two years of trial and error, Shōmu began to sense that the *kami* were trying to tell him something.

Earthquakes rocked the country day and night in the summer of 745. Better counsel was sought and the priests at the Four Great Temples were asked for a recommendation. They could hardly be said to compose an impartial court. Their answer was, in effect, that the spirits of Heijō were chafing at their desertion by the emperor.

Monuments of the later 8th century. Back at Heijō, Shōmu settled down to see a new team of craftsmen realize his dream of an immense Universal Buddha. He needed far more space than was then available for his ambitious temple, so he leveled off a huge expanse directly east of the city, employing tens of thousands of laborers and skilled workers for more than 20 years. He put "all the copper resources of the country," as the temple archives say, into the making of the Great Buddha.

The Great Buddha Hall is still the largest wooden building in the world, despite a reduction of two bays at either end when it was rebuilt in the 12th century after the

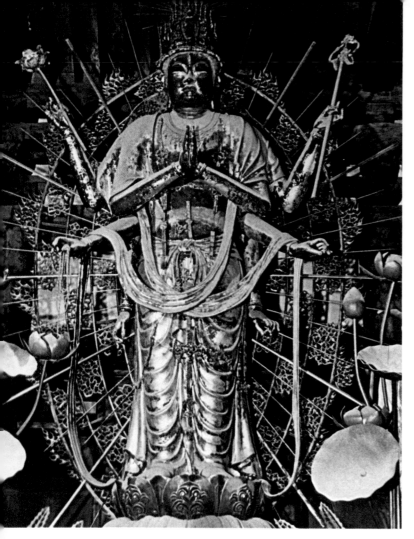

civil war. A large cloister that surrounded the forecourt was colonnaded both inside and out. Two nine-storied pagodas stood 100 meters high and well out in front, enclosed within their own cloisters. They failed to survive many storms and were soon destroyed. Even the base stones for their wooden pillars are now gone.

The Bureau for Construction of Konkōmyō-ji, probably the planning agency for the provincial temples, was changed to Bureau for Construction of the Tōdai-ji, and remained in the service of later rulers. The great monuments of the latter half of the century were temples of staggering magnitude and decorative beauty, each with a pair of large pagodas: the Shinyakushi-ji, built by Empress Kōmyō when Shōmu was sick in 747; the Saidai-ji, built by Empress Shōtoku in 765; and the Akishino-dera, built by Emperors Kōnin and Kammu around 780. The Saidai-ji was the most distinguished, attracting the praise of early writers. As the West Great Temple, it was Empress Shōtoku's effort to match her father's East Great Temple which dominated the eastern edge of the city.

These temples had such strong personal ties with the imperial family they could not survive the vicissitudes of imperial rule in the more distant city of Heian, and are all only pathetic reminders now of their former greatness.

Left: the Fukūkenjaku Kannon, the multiarmed hunter and fisher for souls, at Nara. Height 3·6 m.

Below: reconstruction of the 8th-century Rikuzen Provincial Temple, Sendai.

Provincial reorganization. Emperor Shōmu wanted to tighten government controls in the provinces. Provinces and their boundaries had often been reorganized. He ordered all of the provinces to submit a map to the court in 739 and in the following year he reduced the number of provincial officials, thereby cutting expenses and threatening any others suspected of diverting taxes intended for Heijō.

Sutra reading in the provinces had often been ordered before Shōmu's time. After barely surviving the plague, each province was told to build a seven-storied pagoda, to make statues and to copy the Konkōmyō-kyō, the realm-protecting sutra, which was to be placed in the pagoda. A year later, in 741, the provinces were ordered to build an entire temple, a Kokubun-ji, a provincial monastery, and a Kokubunni-ji, a provincial nunnery. The former should have 20 monks, the latter 10 nuns, and each would have a specified amount of land, number of ceremonial objects and so forth.

There was no end of orders in sight, but the government was alleviating the burden by assigning rice lands, and the officials in the provinces were told to release government stores of rice for the workers constructing these temples. In 745 they were to make seven statues of Yakushi, and two years later were ordered to get the temples finished. More rice land was donated.

There may have been some coordination with the completion of the Great Buddha in Heijō and the construction of the Tōdai-ji. The ultimate deadline was set for 750 and the "eye-opening" ceremony for the Great Buddha was held in early 752. Perhaps that was also a national celebration for the opening of the provincial temples.

Administrators for these temples were sent from Heijō and civil officials sometimes used them as lodging places. Regional resistance had been lessened by offering private ownership of land to local lords if they would cooperate. The similarity between roof tiles of provincial temples and neighboring private temples may mean that the government had relaxed its restrictions on the construction of private temples – restrictions because patrons often used the building of a temple as a pretext for the acquisition of more land – modifying its principles to get this work done. Then again, it may mean that the local lord, when he saw the provincial temple being built, siphoned off a set of roof tiles for his own project.

More than 60 of the provincial temples were put up and an equal number of nunneries. The latter were to be within earshot of the monastery's bell. But all were destroyed, in some cases by arson, and few were rebuilt. Many remain as open sites today, others as small temples with a hall or two, occasionally holding an image as old as the Kamakura period. Some of the temples were resurrected and renamed at that time.

It would be expected that somewhere within the mass of orders the provinces received there would be blueprints

Above: a piece of three-color ware found in the palace at Heijō.

Below: there were several wells and drainage devices in the grounds of the palace which have been rich sources of disposed objects, especially wooden tallies documenting palace business, painted wooden figures, wooden tools and broken pottery.

for an ideal temple, showing the precise size and plan. Yet the plans are varied, some even being like the Hōryū-ji. Most had the pagoda in isolation to the east and within its own cloister, and the other buildings aligned on a north-south axis. In all instances, where enough base stones are in place, it seems the provinces did in fact build a seven-storied pagoda as directed. It may well be that temples already under construction were converted to provincial temples and the plans – if any were dispatched from Heijō – were ignored in the interest of seeing the projects through. When all were finished they were sent a "map." But this unexplained item would seem to be ten years too late. In 767 the temples were ordered to make repairs, so there is little question but that they were all in good working order by that time.

The large temple which lies in the Deer Park of Nara today, the Kōfuku-ji, was moved into an extended eastern section of the city by the Fujiwara in the 730s. Perhaps never intended to have more than one large pagoda, it may have set the plan used for the provincial temples a few years later. It introduced the style of three main halls, which several other temples accepted. Its fortunes fluctuated greatly, and its militant monks, who were trying to get their way in Kyoto politics in the 12th and 13th centuries, were literally playing with fire. The large five-story pagoda is only the last of many to stand on the spot.

One record says that by 864 the buildings and roads of the Heijō palaces had disappeared and reverted to fields. The modern city of Nara grew up on the more picturesque eastern hillside, but archaeologists have excavated for many years at Heijō and have now fully exposed the site of the more easterly of the two palaces which lay side by side. It is preserved as a large park, with the locations of the main palace buildings maintained as grassy plots. More excavations are projected over the years, including the western palace which is now thought to have been the more frequently occupied of the two.

Much pottery and many wooden items have been recovered from the palace site. Some interesting three-color-ware pieces are glazed in a style learned from China. There are many "ink-stones" and pots with curiously painted faces. The kilns where the roof tiles were made have been discovered in the neighboring hills.

Wooden objects have been found in wells and drainage ditches. Thousands of inscribed wooden tallies are dated between 709 and 782 and record the arrival at the palace of many goods, telling where they came from and their quantity. They give a remarkable insight into the workings of the tax system.

Taxation and coinage. The palace and the city depended on a steady flow of taxes into the city. To ensure this, land controls had to be effective, new land had to be opened up and uniformly apportioned as the population expanded, roads had to be improved, canals and irrigation ditches dug, posting stations and local headquarters established

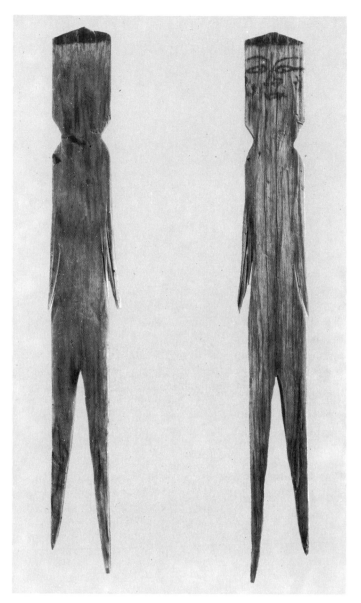

and inspectors periodically dispatched. Transportation time was calculated in days of travel from the capital and in the south from Dazaifu. The total population was probably somewhere in the neighborhood of six million people in the late 8th century.

Taxes were primarily in the form of rice and cloth, and the government often improved its vested interest in the local products by sending weavers to teach more efficient techniques.

To facilitate the payment of taxes and make transactions more flexible, the government instituted its own minting of coins in 708, basing the first issue on a type used in China since 621 but with a different set of characters. On this date the Japanese commemorated the discovery of copper by changing the name of the era to Wadō (708–15), meaning either Japanese Copper or Refined Copper. Since thousands of pieces of this T'ang dynasty coin have been found in Japan – many of which may be local copies – it is assumed that the Japanese were already finding ways of using coins

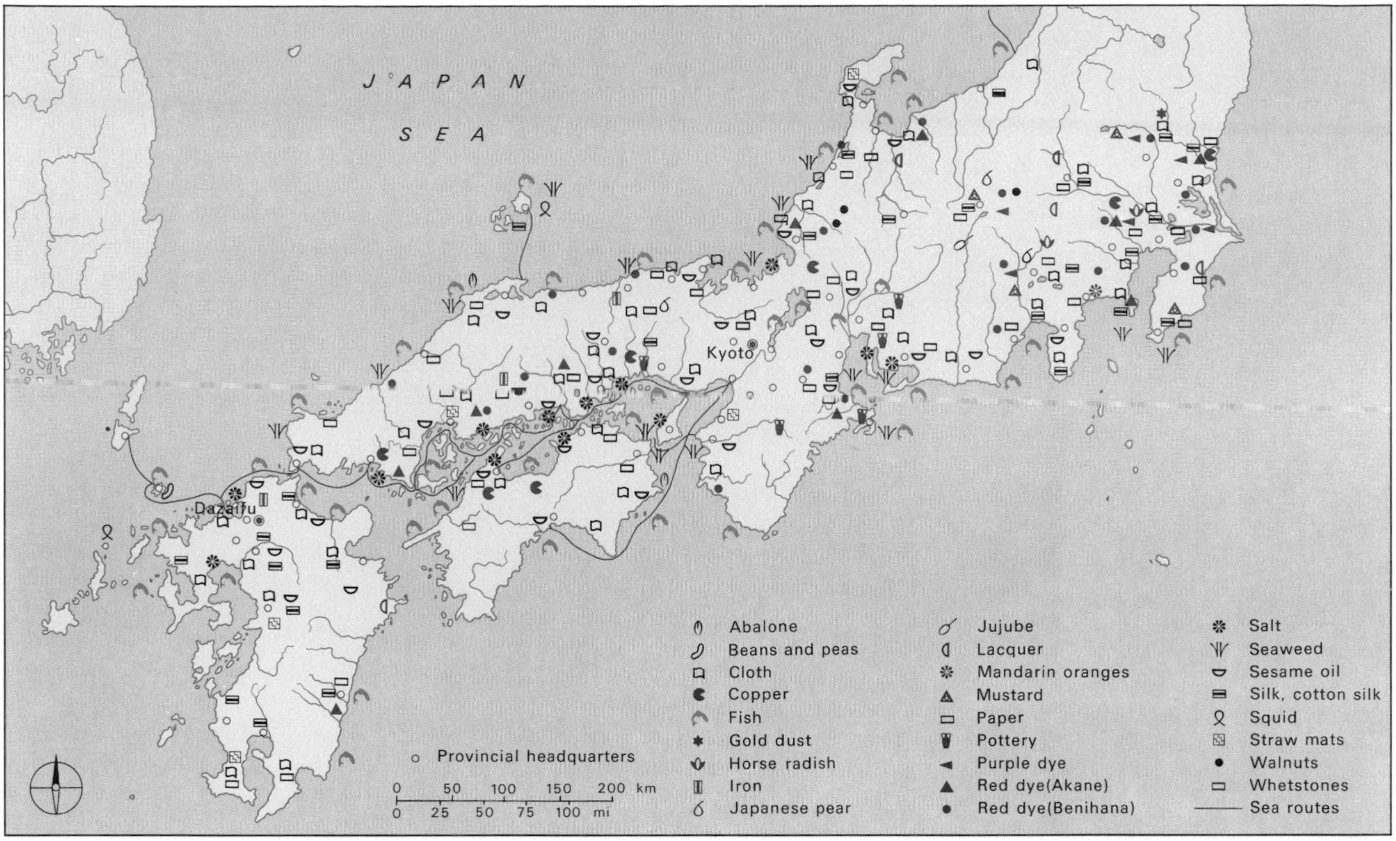
JAPAN
SEA
Kyoto
Dazaifu
Provincial headquarters
0 50 100 150 200 km
0 25 50 75 100 mi
Abalone
Beans and peas
Cloth
Copper
Fish
Gold dust
Horse radish
Iron
Japanese pear
Jujube
Lacquer
Mandarin oranges
Mustard
Paper
Pottery
Purple dye
Red dye(Akane)
Red dye(Benihana)
Salt
Seaweed
Sesame oil
Silk, cotton silk
Squid
Straw mats
Walnuts
Whetstones
Sea routes

Above: transportation, production and produce. New information has been provided by the discovery of thousands of inscribed wooden tallies, some of which are legible and record the arrival of every kind of produce. Goods came by fixed land and sea tax routes, all calculated in the number of days required for travel from Heijō.

Opposite: figures from the palace at Hiejō include puppets, subjects for effigy magic and others, usually about 15 cm high.

prior to minting their own. Indeed, Temmu had told his people to use coins in 683. The way had been paved for their own issue when in 702 orders to standardize all weights and measures were sent out.

Called Wadō-kaichin or Wadō-kaihō, copper cash with a square hole was minted in several places in the country, as the discovery of production sites has shown. Strangely enough, counterfeiting was actually encouraged by the government in its zeal to get its money into circulation. Ranks were offered to people who would acquire and use coins, and the range within this type implies that forgery was a thriving business.

Other issues followed, including several silver and gold denominations. Normally, when a new issue was contemplated, efforts were made to withdraw most of the earlier coins. These were then melted down and reissued in smaller sizes with proportionally less copper and at a devalued rate. Altogether 12 copper types were minted between 708 and 958, at which juncture the Japanese finally gave up and resorted to the barter system and the use of Chinese coins exclusively. The Wadō-kaichin were always highly prized, and discoveries of them in sites, sometimes in hoards, far outnumber other recovered coins. In later years people complained that the casting was often so bad that they could not read the characters on the coins.

The frequent issue of cheaper money was demoralizing and damaging to the economy. Land prices were frozen in 773. Farmers had been recommended to plant barley and wheat and more greens. The long-grained Indica rice had been introduced from Korea and gave a little variety to the diet in parts of the country. The Heijō palace tallies point up the diversity of products. For Heijō, salt, seaweed, fish and shellfish came from the coastal areas to the north, east and west of the Home Provinces and sometimes from more distant points, rice was brought in from many directions, iron was sent from the Inland Sea and cotton-silk from north Kyushu. Ores and raw goods were preferred in Heijō to finished products as they could be utilized by the city's craftsmen for local needs.

Burial practices. The Taika Reform edicts outlined rules by which to live and rules by which to be buried. The section dealing with tombs was introduced by the complaint that "the poverty of our people is absolutely owing to the construction of tombs." Temporary interment and grave goods were prohibited; mounds were to be built only within designated cemeteries.

The size of the tomb, and the number of laborers allowed for fixed lengths of time were specified for each rank, and all forbidden to commoners. Other prohibitions read like a list of shamanistic practices: strangling of people at the time of the funeral, sacrifice of horses, cutting the hair and stabbing the thighs, and eulogies on the dead by frenzied attendants.

For all of this, there have yet to be found tombs belonging to the second half of the 7th century which conform to these prescribed dimensions. They seem not to have been taken literally, although there was a continuing reduction of the number of tumuli built, fewer grave-goods and a tendency to make small mounds on the tops of low hills.

Rarely could a family afford to lavish its riches on both tombs and temples, but along with government coercion was the slow adoption of cremation by the court and its eventual spread. This was incompatible with large mounded tombs.

As the first ruler to be cremated, Empress Jitō gave the practice considerable respectability in 701. Yet there is no explanation for the delay of one year after her death as there is in so many other cases of delay. Whether it was a protracted argument or the preference for a desiccated corpse can hardly be known, but it is the case that the Shinto cult of the rulers finally won out. Otherwise only Emperor Mommu and Empresses Gemmyō and Genshō were cremated, all rather closely related and perhaps all Hossō-inclined. The imperial family has usually abstained.

Tomb looters seem to have confirmed the fact that Empress Jitō was cremated. Her ashes were buried in the tomb with her husband Temmu in Asuka, and a report, compiled after the pilferage was discovered, tells of a gilt bronze bowl holding a silver ash container, placed at the end of the emperor's dry-lacquer coffin.

Cremation is traditionally said to have originated in Japan with Priest Dōshō, the founder of the Hossō sect, but archaeological evidence now indicates that some forms of cremation were being practiced a century or more before. Dōshō requested that his remains be cremated after his death. This was done by his disciples in 700. They fought each other for his ashes which were, mercifully, dispersed by a high wind. Cremation was not required by law and is still only an accepted practice.

Examples of cinerary urns of bronze, pottery and stone have been recovered from small mounds, along with a few grave-goods. Earlier urns are sometimes elaborately inscribed with biographical information or have an accompanying epitaph plate. After the 8th century, in more outlying areas, the urns are usually of pottery as the practice was adopted by people lower in the social scale who were less likely to be literate.

Chinese coins imported into Japan, ranging in date from 621 to 1260. Apart from a short period, Japan relied to a great extent on China for her currency.

The Capital Area of Asuka

Asuka has been an archaeologist's dream. A small spot well down in Nara prefecture, until recently rather little known, it is set off by the Yamato Sanzan (Three Mountains) in the north, rising hills in the south and cut through obliquely by the Asuka river (*below*). This little hollow was the capital of the country throughout most of the 7th century. The area was abandoned, caretakers manned dilapidated temples, ricefields encroached on the remains, and few people thought the place worth disturbing. Remains of palaces, temples and houses lay just below the surface, and even a few still unlooted tombs crowned the hilltops, all just waiting for the archaeologists' spade.

Uncovering these remains had been going on leisurely for about two decades with interesting but not sensational public notices until the discovery of the painted Takamatsuzuka tomb by Professor Masao Suenaga on 21 March 1972. Asuka sprang to life.

Empress Suiko built the Toyura palace in 592; it was here that Prince Shōtoku was born; and Emperors Kimmei, Mommu. Temmu and Empress Jitō are thought to be buried in Asuka.

Above: on the western (right) edge of the aerial view can just be made out the outlines of a once colossal keyhole tomb, known officially as Mise-no-Maruyama. This could be the tomb of Emperor Kimmei.

Right: a rare, rather overlooked stage in Japanese art is seen in the many carved stones at Asuka. The Sakafuneishi (Rice-wine-boat-stone) lies just at the top of the hill, southeast of the Asuka-dera. Length 5·45 m.

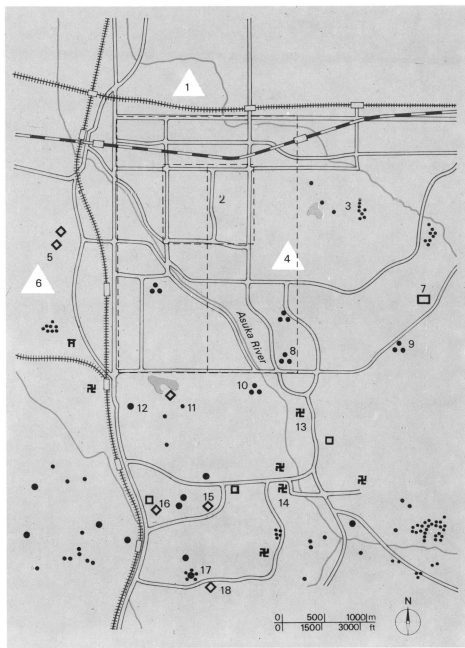

Above: Asuka in the 6th–7th century A D. 1 Mt Miminashi, 2 Fujiwara Palace, 3 Ikenoshi Tombs, 4 Mt Amenokagu, 5 Tomb of Emperor Jimmu, 6 Mt Unebi, 7 Museum, 8 Kiyomigahara Palace, 9 Yamada-dera, 10 Toyura Palace, 11 Tomb of Emperor Kōgen, 12 Mise-no-Maruyama Tomb, 13 Asuka-dera, 14 Tachibana-dera, 15 Tomb of Emperor Temmu and Empress Jitō, 16 Tomb of Emperor Kimmei, 17 Takamatsuzuka Tomb, 18 Tomb of Emperor Mommu.

Top right: this stone was probably a roadside guardian and a fertility symbol for the fields.

Bottom right: the Buddhist holy mountain, Mt Meru, which the Japanese call Shumisen, seems to be represented in this three-piece structure of granite with relief mountains as decoration. Made as rings, it may have been used like a fountain in the garden of the Kiyomigahara palace. Empress Saimei erected one before entertaining foreign visitors in 657. This and the paired figures are now displayed in the new Asuka Museum. Height 2·34 m.

Right: known as Monkey Stones, averaging about 1 meter in height, this is one of four which sit in front of a small tomb after being moved from the open fields because they seemed embarrassingly close to Emperor Kimmei's tomb. These were probably road or field guardians, arranged in male and female pairs. Their crudity and nudity offended the Japanese in the 19th century.

Below right: sitting out in the open a little west of the Tachibana-dera, the 4-meter-long Turtle Stone has been traditionally called a boundary marker, perhaps placed or carved there after the Taika Reform when the land was formally marked off in the first land survey. Recent exposure of the full stone shows its features are almost complete.

Below: Among the enigmatic monuments of Asuka is this large hollowed-out stone, 3.9 m in length, most likely the lower part of a stone sarcophagus. Across the road and above it lies a flat stone that is close enough in size to be its lid. Its popular Japanese name translates as Devil's Toilet.

Above: Ishibutai or Stone Stage is the largest exposed stone passageway and chamber in Japan. It is assumed that Soga-no-Umako, prime minister under Suiko and other rulers, built this tomb and was buried in it in 626.

Located in the southern part of Asuka, the Takamatsuzuka tomb (*below*) is the only one so far discovered to have plastered and painted walls in the Chinese and Korean technique. The women (*left*) wear "Korean" costumes, but quite possibly these were formal wear at the Japanese court. The paintings follow Chinese cosmic symbolism in using the tutelary deities of the cardinal directions: the Azure Dragon is on the east, seen here (*below left*), under a sun.

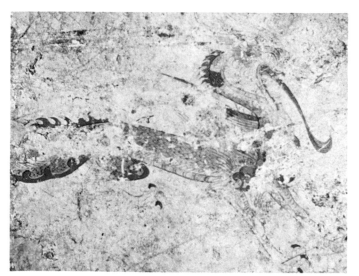

Opposite: the Yamada-dera contained a remarkable bronze Buddha triad of large dimensions finished in 685 after the death of the temple's patron. Priests from the Kōfuku-ji forcibly removed it in 1184 and installed it in Nara, but after a fire in 1411 it disappeared from sight, only for the head to reappear in 1937 during digging under the altar of the west main hall. The head is 42·2 cm high and is in the early T'ang dynasty style of China reflected at this stage in Japan.

Above: the site of the temple of the capital, Asuka-dera, formally called Hōkō-ji, built by Soga-no-Umako in the late 6th century, is now only a few base stones and a single building of a much later date that houses the large Buddha by Tori (*right*). The sculptor Tori cast this monumental bronze in 606 by request of Empress Suiko for the Asuka-dera; it proved to be so large that it required considerable ingenuity to get it into the building. It suffered later in a serious fire and was clumsily repaired, leaving a figure too deformed to allow fair judgment of Tori's early work. As a seated figure, 2·75 m high, it is evidence, however, that large-scale casting was done from the very beginning of Buddhist art in Japan.

Above: archaeologists have recently exposed and "restored" the plan of what they believe to be the remains of the Itabuki palace occupied by Empress Kōgyoku from 642 until its destruction in 655. The well was working until recent restoration of the site, since the photograph was taken, and was probably where the wine was made in the palace.

Below: the Oka-dera, formally the Ryūgai-ji, built by the founder of the Hossō sect Priest Gien in 703, is the major active temple in Asuka today, comfortably nestled on the southeastern hillside, surviving the neglect that befell the exposed temples below.

Above: Prince Shōtoku built the Tachibana-dera on the edge of the hillside traditionally in 606. The temple deteriorated in recent centuries. Now exposed for public view is the base stone for the center pole of the pagoda. The projecting arcs are for reinforcing engaged columns. The hole is 90 cm in diameter and 8 cm deep.

5. Heian and the Fujiwara Aristocracy

The Kasuga shrine on the hillside of Nara was a strategically placed tutelary shrine of the Fujiwara family, founded here after Heijō became the capital.

Warfare in the 9th century. Military preparedness had been a great economic drain in the 8th century. Hope of recovering lost Korean land was still alive a hundred years after Japan had been defeated by Silla and the government was training young people in the study of the Silla language, pressing conscription and reinforcing its defenses in the south. Emperor Junnin could review 40,700 troops and a fleet of 394 vessels in 761.

Most debilitating, however, was the demoralizing, century-old war in the north against the Emishi or Ezo (Ainu). This region, then called Mutsu or Dewa, represented more ricefields and the potential route to the gold mines. The randomly conscripted troops were of poor quality and badly trained. They had been commanded by political appointees from Heijō. One man in four between the ages of 20 and 59 was drafted to serve four years. One of these might be on guard duty in the capital, but three might be on the southern defenses or in the front lines to the north.

These troops were no match for the well-dug-in Ezo, who were desperately defending their slowly diminishing territory. Disaster followed disaster. Large losses were reported to the capital, investigations took place, and little by little the Japanese learned that only by shortening their supply lines would they be able to win. The shifting front has been identified archaeologically by the earthworks and pit-dwellings the Ezo built, and the transfer of Japanese stockades and "castles" to more northern positions.

The Japanese headquarters was located at Taga-jō in Miyagi prefecture. It has been excavated for years and is now a major archaeological site preserved as it existed around 790. It was a protected low hilltop with defensive earthen banks running one kilometer north-south and 800 meters east-west. A wall surrounded a smaller area on the top, within which was the major office. The base stones of the central building give the the impression that it looked much like a lecture hall of a temple. Hundreds of bags of broken tiles have been collected on the site, along with some Sue and Haji pottery and a little later Sanage ware that may have come from the Aichi area. A full temple site is very well preserved below the hill.

Emperor Kammu (781–806) was successful in ending the war with the Ezo once the policy of conscripting local recruits starting in 792 had begun to take effect and Sakanoue Tamuramaro was appointed field commander in 797. Some additional battles still had to be fought after his victories and the Ezo were still very much alive as late as 878 when they destroyed the chief northern fort of Akita-jō, but the captives had been displaced to different parts of the country and their periodic rebellions were of only minor consequence. The Japanese respected them as fighters and used them later against the Silla pirates, rating each Ezo as a thousand times better than a Japanese soldier.

It is from Kammu's time that the emperors were given the posthumous names by which they are known today. He rubbed salt into the wounds of the Nara clergy by appointing a chief investigator to look into their behavior, defrocked priests with children and those living with nuns, and assigned supervisors to reside in the temples in the home provinces and the capital and preside over their morals.

Kammu ordered the enforcement of the allotment system and curbs on the expansion of the untaxed private estates. Perhaps more effective, he terminated the hereditary local offices, but those who were expected to apply the laws were themselves profiting from the laxity and uninterested in reverting to the established legal practice.

These manor estates (*shōen*) grew in size and power and, as the war in the north wound down, leaving a residue of experienced soldiers, and lawlessness spread throughout

Below the nucleus of the site of Taga-jō on the hilltop is the preserved plan of a large temple, the base stones and platform outlines all intact.

the country, they took on security guards and began to produce a class of professional fighting men (*bushi*) who later served under the banners of prominent families. In fact, it was not uncommon for a man to attach himself to what looked like a promising venture, since life for the ordinary person under government controls was almost unbearable. The government provided tax-free loans, but the average man working *jōri* lands paid interest on private loans up to 30 per cent in 795 and that was allowed to rise to 50 per cent by 819. The Home Provinces made no allotments in the 50 years following 828, and the central government finally admitted defeat when the land allocation system was turned over to local provincial governors and, in Yamashiro, the province of the capital, to the wealthy families to administer. This sealed the fate of the system.

Kammu ruled for 23 years, at the peak of imperial power, not to be equaled until Emperor Meiji of modern times. Saga (809–23) established a bureau of archivists (*Kurōdo-dokoro*), reinforced the adviser (*sangi*) system and formed the Office of Imperial Police (*Kebiishi*), thereby circumventing the traditional administrative procedure and keeping the power of making decisions in the hands of a small number of chosen advisers. This was eminently successful for the emperor until the Fujiwara moved into this inner circle.

The police organization was the best yet devised and, while it could never fully control the lawlessness in the capital, despite the use of night patrols and the intimidating effect of selected six-foot guards from remote corners of the country, it was on occasion good enough to dispatch to the provinces when help was needed.

Piracy grew out of hand along the coasts and especially in the Inland Sea. Marauding gangs terrorized the circuit roads. The governor of Chikugo (now part of Fukuoka) was killed by a band of 100 robbers in 883. People armed themselves, as did institutions. One astonishing outcome was the appearance of bands of armed monks who eventually imposed themselves on the politics of Kyoto in a highly destructive way. The acts of arson and the pitched street battles between monks of the Kōfuku-ji in Nara and the Enryaku-ji on Mt Hiei and their subsidiaries left many homeless victims and Kyoto residents living in dread of the night sallies into the city.

When Fujiwara Yorifusa was made unofficial regent on the accession of his nine-year-old grandson Emperor Seiwa in 858, Japan entered the Fujiwara Age. Less than 40 years later (894) Japan officially ended all formal contacts with China.

The imperial line. The Fujiwara had ousted other branches of the vast family, forced the Tomo and Tachibana out of the government, and were left with few competitors. Glimpses of palace life in this period can be seen in the remarkable literature of the time, the most celebrated example of which is the *Tales of Genji* (*Genji*

Monogatari), stories of court romance by Lady Murasaki written around the year 1000. These come graphically to life in the scenes that were painted in narrative scrolls of about 100 years later. The rise of such popular forms of literature was encouraged because women wrote in the vernacular, although men were still expected to follow the traditional Chinese styles of writing.

Older forms of literature were still required by the court. The *Engishiki* was material presented to the emperor in 927 in the Engi era, and is composed of detailed descriptions of ceremonies at the court, events and customs in other parts of the country. The numerous volumes are today a rich store of information on the shrines and cult practices of the time that would be otherwise unknown.

The regent (*Sesshō*) system was tailor-made by the Fujiwara and was the way they kept their power. The position later became official and remained so until modern times. The regent was appointed while the emperor was still too young to rule, then appointed administrator (*Kampaku*) when the emperor became of age, and then finally prime minister and head of the Supreme Council. Fujiwara Tadahira by the 10th century was the chief minister and his two sons the Minister of the Left and the Minister of the Right. The latter half of the century was dominated by three brothers who succeeded each other directly, Michitaka, Michikane and Michinaga (966–1027), the last marking the peak of Fujiwara power. He was able to look back on a 30-year rule and on having installed seven of his immediate relatives on the imperial throne. Short reigns were in order, after which the emperor abdicated, often little above the age of 30. A morass of ceremony hampered the emperor's other activities and restricted his attention to political affairs.

The Fujiwara kept the imperial position intact, since it was more to their advantage to make emperors than to be emperors. Marrying Fujiwara wives was an old practice. Emperor Kammu had had at least two, but on rare occasions the Fujiwara women failed to produce sons, and it was an independent-minded emperor and his successor who exploited the situation, using their inherent powers.

Emperor Go-sanjō (1068–72) (Go means Sanjō II) lacked a Fujiwara mother, but no respectable person could be found who had one. He took a strong attitude toward the immense estates and compelled the owners to show the legitimacy of their titles. His son, Emperor Shirakawa, pursued his policy for exerting imperial power and, after his abdication in 1086, maintained a secretariat in the monastery to which he retired, as did some other ex-emperors, thus producing this peculiarly Japanese situation of *insei* ("cloister rule"). Thus the real machinery for running the government passed into the hands of the ex-emperor. Shirakawa ensured his position and the income for his office and the later building of temples by selling governorships, first for a four-year period and later extended to life. When they became hereditary, the feudal

The *Tales of Genji*, a prince at the Fujiwara court, were illustrated by court painters as a series of scrolls.

system took shape. It need hardly be said that there inevitably arose a three-way race between the ex-emperor, the emperor and the Fujiwara regent.

The Kyoto Fujiwara had relied on the established provincial families to keep order, shifting their alliances when the power balance changed. Many of the local lords had imperial blood, and the great names in later Japanese history, such as Minamoto, Ashikaga and Tokugawa, were all descendants of a son of Emperor Seiwa. The Taira family (other pronunciation: Heishi) traced their genesis ultimately to a son of Emperor Kammu as did, for instance, the Hōjō family which held the reins of government in the Kamakura period.

The Fujiwara position was clearly becoming untenable when they were no longer able to keep peace among the regional families. Eventually the Kyoto Fujiwara looked on helplessly and were caught in the destruction. Several rebellions had been resolved, but from the time of the Hōgen War (era name: 1156–59) of 1156, the conflicts increased in intensity and brutality as the power of the government declined. Capital punishment was once again introduced for the losers – it had not been a Fujiwara policy – and the climax was heralded by the Heiji War (era name: 1159–60) in which the Taira won against a combination of Fujiwara and Minamoto. Taira rule, however, was relatively short-lived. It reached its pinnacle under Kiyomori who died in 1181, shortly after the Gempei (Gen = Minamoto, Pei = Taira in Chinese-style pronunciation) War got under way. One of the many tragedies was the destruction of the Tōdai-ji and the Kōfuku-ji by Taira Shigehira in 1180. In five years of fighting, Minamoto Yoritomo emerged the victor, and with family land in the eastern Kantō, he moved his military capital to Kamakura.

These events marked a profound break with the traditions of Heian Kyoto and with its prevailing interest in Buddhist movements of thought and cult. The country entered a new stage with the development of a hereditary feudal system and the rise of the samurai class of warrior clans. But Japan continued until the 19th century under the rule of a succession of Shōguns who maintained their control by military and bureaucratic power vested in a dominant family.

The city of Heian. The site chosen for the capital of Heian proved to be far superior to earlier selections. Lake Biwa and the large Uji river were not far away. The city could be laid out almost entirely west of the Kamo river and east of the Katsura river if an area no larger than 5·312 kilometers north-south and 4·570 east-west was desired. The Takano river joins the Kamo in the northeast corner and together they flow along the eastern edge. The Ōi changes its name to Katsura and flows past the southwest corner. The two meet at some distance from the city but almost due south of the old main street. The site was protected by mountains on three sides, was open to the south and had numerous springs feeding the rivers.

Several little rivers divided the blocks on the west side, but, except for the Hori, the spaces were easily managed on the east side. Because of this and for other reasons, in particular the natural routes coming up from the populated southern regions and the unsurpassed beauty of the hills, the east side was always favored. Even as early as 842 the eastern half was more prosperous. The eastern and

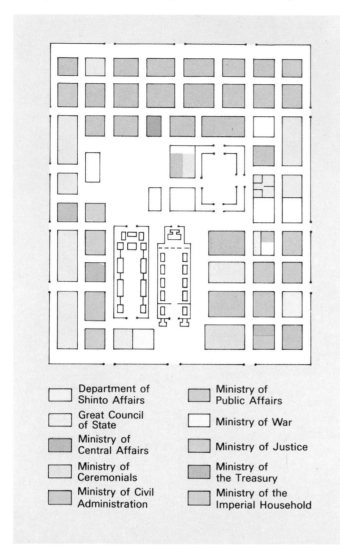

Department of Shinto Affairs

Great Council of State

Ministry of Central Affairs

Ministry of Ceremonials

Ministry of Civil Administration

Ministry of Public Affairs

Ministry of War

Ministry of Justice

Ministry of the Treasury

Ministry of the Imperial Household

Left: the main street of Kyoto led directly to the imperial palace. Scores of blocks crammed with buildings, all teeming with bureaucrats and clerks, surrounded the courtyard that accommodated the halls of the Eight Ministries and the public ceremonies.

Below: aerial view of Kyoto.

western markets fought with each other over the distribution and sale of incoming supplies. The eastern market perpetually needed more than its half.

Unlike Kammu, most later emperors had no objection to the erection of temples in the capital, and many rulers and lesser figures built them. They usually preferred the eastern ridges. The city drifted across the river and into the Higashiyama hills as residences and scores of temples were built around the outskirts of the city. Some larger Zen temples and temples of other sects occupied major city blocks.

Heian's main street, Sujaku-ōji, led directly to the primary imperial palace. It had the unusual width of 85 meters, making it a highly practical fire-break. Certain east-west streets were widened in World War II to prepare for a similar threat of fires from aerial bombing, but Kyoto was fortunately spared as being of little military value.

Four major blocks and two half-blocks were devoted to the entire palace complex in the north. The main palace faced the gate of the Sujaku-ōji, while a secondary palace stood to the west of it. Surrounding them were numerous blocks of buildings that grew up in rather haphazard fashion, each collection of buildings providing offices and quarters for various ministries, their officials, clerks, workmen and caretakers. Many changes occurred over the centuries in the form and use of these blocks of buildings. This Administration Palace was enclosed by a wall with three gates on the north and south and four gates on the east and west.

The Imperial Residence lay a little north and east of the Administration Palace. It was a walled area with a forecourt, but contained many buildings in regular sequence that allowed little other space in the block.

Two temples were planned to stand sentinel at Rashōmon, the southern gate of the city. These were the Tō-ji and Sai-ji, but nothing at all remains of the latter today if, indeed, it was built. Priest Kūkai was made chief priest of the Tō-ji in 823, at which time it became a principal Shingon center.

Most of the major buildings of the Tō-ji lasted until 1486 when they were burned in the local wars, after which they were slowly rebuilt. The large landmark on the southern edge of the old city, the five-story pagoda, was first put up by the priest in 826, but was lost successively five times and is now a building of 1643.

In land assignments in the city, a noble family did roughly as well as it had in earlier cities, with a space of about 120 by 120 meters, but a commoner family was reduced to lots half the size it had enjoyed in Nara.

Without intending to do so, Emperor Kammu had curtailed the welfare services by excluding the temples, and at a time when the government was not prepared to take up the slack. The number of temples was proportionally too small for the population. People left their aged and ill by the roadside to die. The remains of thousands of poorly buried dead near the Kamo river were

recovered and cremated in 842. There were disastrous years of famine, earthquakes and sweeping fires.

Nothing remains from the early centuries of Kyoto's existence because of the earthquakes, massive fires, occasional floods and civil wars. The present palace has some similarity to the former ones and can be compared with the Heian shrine which was built to reproduce the appearance of the early palace. After an opportunity arose to keep the palace in the middle of the city when it was destroyed by fire, it was moved to its present location further east in 1855. It is modeled on earlier buildings erected in 1790.

Esoteric and Shinto practices. Emperor Shōmu had used the Nara clergy and temples to his advantage and had made Buddhism a state religion and protector of the people. But Emperor Kammu dissociated the two, in effect separating church and state, and might have succeeded had not new and subtle factors linked Buddhism to Shinto, the natural and from time immemorial the "state" religion.

As a result of visiting China, two monks brought back esoteric sects and founded temples in which their doctrines were expounded. The thought and practices of these sects quickly forged a direct link with Shinto. In 788 Saichō had started a small temple on Mt Hiei, northeast of Kyoto. After his return from a year in China in 805 he introduced the composite beliefs of Tendai (Heavenly Platform) for which he won the support of the emperor. Tendai is the Middle Way, an attempt to bring together various doctrines, stressing good works. Its primary scripture is

Shinsen garden, the only remaining part of the old Heian palace grounds, now reconstructed to show its original form.

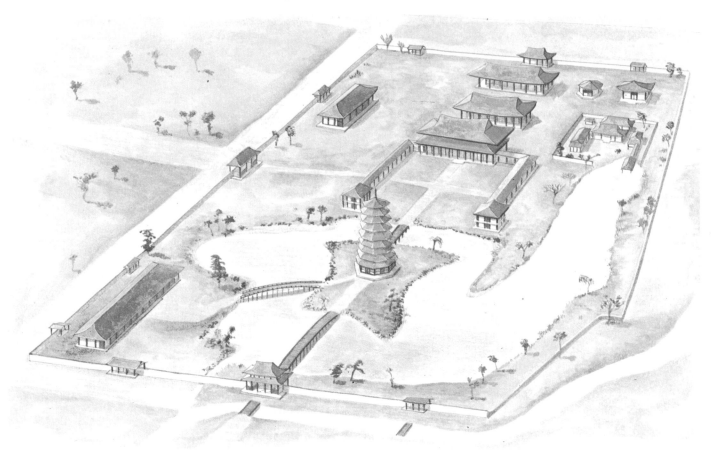

the Lotus Sutra and it was later a major supporter of "Pure Land" Amida worship.

Saichō petitioned the emperor to grant permission to build an ordination platform at his temple, a request that was bitterly fought by the Nara priests who wanted to keep their control over the ceremony and therefore over the clergy. The request was finally granted five years after Saichō's death. The temple's name was officially set as Enryaku-ji in 823, and Saichō was given the posthumous name and title of Dengyō Daishi in 866. Many great Buddhist personalities were connected with his temple over the centuries, not the least of whom was Ennin, the founder of the Chūson-ji and a noted traveler who kept an observant diary of his trip to China.

Kūkai had also gone to China in 804, but returned a year later than Saichō. Trained in the Tōdai-ji in Nara, he found on his return there little room for individuality and expansion of his doctrine, so he went down to Kii province and climbed Mt Kōya where he started a temple in 816 that came to be known as the Kongōbu-ji, the headquarters of the Shingon (True Word) sect.

Kūkai's contribution to Buddhism and Japanese culture as a whole is immeasurable. Tradition and legend of course outdo fact, but he was a man of enormous talent and receives the credit for introducing the *kana* phonetic system which, to put it simply, has helped to give the Japanese a rare degree of literacy in their part of the world. Innumerable temples claim to have been founded by him

Above: Emperor Shirakawa dedicated his Hōshō-ji in 1077, a massive temple due east of the wide Nijō street. It was later destroyed and the area is now mainly residential.

Below: individual stones mark the burials of hundreds of Shingon believers on this stupa in the vast cemetery known as Okuno-in on Mt Kōya, not far from the tomb of the saint Kōbō Daishi.

or were in some way associated with him. His powers were miraculous; rain-making was only one of many. Guides point to hosts of sculptures and paintings said to have been done by him. He founded a new type of public school. In ten volumes he outlined ten stages of spiritual development, grading other sects and culminating in Shingon.

Centered on Dainichi, the Great Shining Illuminator, the Infinite Buddha Vairocana, his spiritual omnipresence in Shingon graced a Diamond and a Matrix World, the spiritual and material worlds, while all deities and, indeed, all things in the universe are manifestations of him. The Buddha was in no distant paradise, but here in every conceivable form. Man is Buddha by his very existence, and does not reach Buddhahood through any required act of faith.

Magical formulas in diagrammatic form are singularly important in Shingon. The painted versions at first followed examples of mandalas brought from China by Kūkai. Both the buildings and the images of the Kongōbu-ji were arranged by him in the shape of a mandala. A new type of building called *tahō-tō*, rather much like a pagoda but with two roofs, reproducing in wood and plaster architecture a series of five shapes stacked on top of each other symbolizing earth, water, fire, wind and air, was built as a corresponding pair, each holding the Five Buddhas of the Diamond and Matrix Worlds. In the Kanjō Hall, a special ritual hall, two large mandalas were hung on either side behind a screen where the ceremonies took place. The element of mystery played a large part; the believer was separated from the esoteric rituals taking place behind.

Mountain retreats. The Kongōbu-ji on Mt Kōya suffered from conflagrations and much rebuilding has been necessary, including a rather modern, huge *tahō-tō*. Situated on the top of a wind-swept mountain, across which grew up one long thoroughfare, many other temples mushroomed, then spread out along side streets. Devotees desiring to be buried in the vicinity of Kūkai's grave have created one of the largest cemeteries in Japan. Much Japanese history can be read in the distinguished family names engraved on the stones crowded into plots that extend for over a kilometer.

Kūkai was made head priest of the Tō-ji in south Kyoto in 823, which then became a second Shingon headquarters and a center of much activity after he added several buildings in 826.

The lecture hall of the Tō-ji was reerected close to its original form after a fire in 1486. The light in the interior is kept to a minimum by opening up as doors only three of the nine bays on the south side. The hall is unique in that its platform holds a full complement of statues comprising the Mikkyō Mandala. Fifteen of the figures are 9th century and are attributed by the temple to Kūkai himself, said to have been carved about ten years before his death.

Three clusters of five figures each are arranged to fit the description in the chief sutra of esoteric Buddhism. The central group consists of Five Buddhas, the four esoteric Buddhas of Amida, starting in the southwest and going clockwise, Amida, Fukū, Ashuku and Hōshō, all surrounding Dainichi. At the east end are the Five Bodhisattvas, and at the west end the Five Great Power Howling Lords (*Godai-myō-ō*), in the middle of which is their chief, Fudō. Ferocious in appearance, many of these figures are multi-armed and multi-headed, and some have vehicles of animals or birds. Their ultimate origin was India. They must have come through China to reach Japan, but they left few traces on the way. The platform is protected by the Four Heavenly Kings, and the gods Bon and Taishaku, the Indian Brahma and Indra, stand at the east and west ends.

Kūkai tutored the crown prince and died in 835 at the height of his career as a top administrative Buddhist church official. He was posthumously titled Kōbō Daishi in 921.

The third great Shingon temple has a much more tenuous connection with the saint, despite its many claims. No texts before the 14th century associate him with the temple. Murō-ji was popularly called Women's Mt Kōya because women, who were forbidden to climb the

Mandalas are magical diagrams of a considerable pantheon of deities surrounding Vairocana Buddha. The oldest, like this one kept in the Tō-ji in Kyoto, are 9th century.

mountain in Wakayama, were permitted to climb Mt Murō in Nara prefecture.

The place was selected like most other esoteric centers as an older sacred natural spot from which miracles were said to have emanated. A dragon hole shrine is somewhat further up the road from the entrance to the temple and had been widely used as a place of prayer for rain. Kōbō Daishi had enhanced his reputation as a rain maker when he produced a veritable deluge in the Kyoto drought of 824.

The area maintained an exceptional and unexplained relationship to the Kōfuku-ji. Its chief priest was appointed from the ranks of the Kōfuku-ji clergy until Tokugawa times, possibly because of some unstated Fujiwara patronage. Kammu favored Murō-ji. When he was still crown prince and fell ill in 777 and 778, prayers said here were credited with his recovery.

The only two buildings of the 9th century standing today are the main hall and pagoda of the Murō-ji, but they are strangely different types. Both are small and have cypress thatch roofs, but the similarity stops there. In a kind of Nara style, the pagoda is needlessly complicated as its flat roofs create no weight. The main hall is informally simple in a nondescript way. The buildings stand on terraces cut out of the hillside reached by flights of stone

Above: the Dragon Hole shrine at Murō-ji, the original worship site of the Mt Murō water spirit.

Opposite: this Late Heian Yakushi at Ōbama is on a Shingon Buddha platform of special local type in the Myōtsu-ji.

Below: Murō-ji's attractions include little images of Jizō, the spiritual guardian of children; bibs are hung around their necks and offerings left beside them and stones piled up for good luck.

steps. Paths zigzag back and forth between the different buildings. At the top of the last 300 steps is a small hall dedicated to the "founder" of the temple and another building hanging out over the hill which offers a spectacular view of the river valley below.

The naturalization of Buddhism. Located deep in Shinto territory, the atmosphere of these mountain temples was radically different from that of the old city temples. Buddhism was undergoing a process of naturalization. Its establishments were being reduced to human scale and built and supplied with statues in local materials. In relating the buildings to the landscape in the tradition of small Shinto shrines, both the physical organization of the temple and its social organization were profoundly and irrevocably changed.

The early centuries in Kyoto saw the appearance of a peculiar belief that westerners might attribute to a social guilt complex. Known as *goryō* (spirit pacifying), it may be no coincidence that it occurred as the Fujiwara rose to power. Kyoto experienced an extraordinarily paralyzing series of earthquakes, fires and disease, all of which were blamed on the spirits of prominent scholarly officials who had been disgraced and banished. The most notable case in Kyoto was that of Sugawara Michizane (845–903), who was exiled to Kyushu in 901 on trumped-up charges. Most of the scholars and lawyers came from the Sugawara and Tachibana families as these families had given their youths the benefit of special schooling, but compared with the Fujiwara they showed up as politically quite inept. The Kitano Shrine in Kyoto was built to placate Michizane's

rambunctious spirit and he was reinstated in office posthumously. The satisfied spirit of this *tenjin* then allowed Kyoto a few years of peace. From this display it may be seen that elementary shamanism had reached a level of intellectual sophistication accepted by all social strata. Whether recognized or not, it was a Confucian belief that the spirits of the ancestors had to be assuaged for their descendants to live comfortably in this world.

The retreats deep in the mountains carved out by Saichō and Kūkai stimulated mountain worship cults which, incidentally, are still very much alive today. The *yamabushi*, the white-garbed ascetics with magical instruments, control the spirits of nature through rigorous practices and exorcise the supernatural forces of the mountains. Formally known as Shūgen-dō, and embodying a peculiar mixture of Buddhism and Shinto, it can be traced to the 9th- and 10th-century practices of placating the spirits of the dead. Practitioners of Shūgen-dō often married female shamans, and together they performed many of the rites normally conducted by Shinto priests. In fact, in some parts of the country the *yamabushi* are actually recognized as Shinto priests.

By the later Heian period the center of the cult was Mt Kumano. Ascetics from there walked to all parts of the country, making a great impact on the religious attitudes of the time. Zao Gongen is the mountain spirit often shown in image form. The chief of these Zao Gongen mountains is Kinbusen in Yoshino, far down in Nara prefecture, but there are many mountains in Japan which have shrines with close Shingon or Tendai connections. These are visited by great numbers of people today.

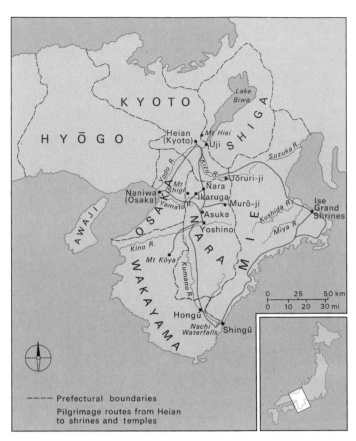

Above: pilgrimage routes from Heian. By taking the coastal route a pilgrim could include the Grand Shrines of Ise.

Left: a pilgrim praying at the temple at Kannonji in his walk around the 88 sacred sites of Shikoku.

Opposite: the temple grounds on the hill offer a particularly spectacular view of the magnificent Nachi waterfalls (*above*). Local sites have revealed mirrors, swords, beads, pottery, Chinese coins, Buddhist images and gold ornaments, such as these (*below*) of the 12th or 13th century.

Shrines and pilgrims. Not long after the capital was settled in Heian, pilgrimages to the Seven Great Temples of the Southern Capital became popular, reaching their peak in the Late Heian and Kamakura periods. At certain times of the year the roads were clogged with lines of pilgrims, referred to as "ants," many heading even further south, their destination Kumano, the mecca of all miracle seekers.

The Nara temples did all they could to encourage pilgrimages for fear of withering on the vine since Emperor Kammu had ordered a reduction in their incomes in 796. The injunction lists the temples, obviously in the order of their importance at that time: Tōdai-ji, Kōfuku-ji, Gankō-ji, Daian-ji, Yakushi-ji, Saidai-ji and Hōryū-ji.

The temples could be visited in seven days, with the Tōshōdai-ji included for good measure with little extra effort. Once in Nara, all but the Hōryū-ji were easy to see, and the temples themselves served as hostels while the pilgrimage was under way.

In the long and arduous journey to the Kumano region near the southeast coast, a distance of about 200 miles round trip, usually requiring about a month to be made on foot, the pilgrims stayed at many small shrines located along the roads. This picturesque, more direct but exceptionally difficult route over mountainous roads was ordinarily taken in Heian times, but the longer course by way of Ise and around the coast was much preferred later, coinciding with a rising interest in the shrines at Ise.

From the emperor down, everyone hoped to make the pilgrimage in his lifetime, and numerous imperial and other official trips are recorded. Ex-Emperor Uda was the first in 907. It took ex-Emperor Shirakawa 22 days, 16 of which were apparently spent bouncing along rough roads in a palanquin. He dedicated a stupa at Kumano and stopped to leave gifts at every shrine.

The pilgrim who arrived at Hongū (Main Shrine), the first and foremost of three shrines, entered a vast mandala known as Kumano Gongen or also Kumano Sanzan (Three Mountains), and was welcomed by the local *yamabushi*.

His next stop was down the river to Shingū (New Shrine), close to the coast, and then on to Nachi Shrine, where an exhilarating view of the waterfalls, the embodiment of Dainichi, climaxed the entire trip. He left offerings before the waterfalls, and some aristocrats and older priests buried sutras with accompanying articles. He was then shown the evidence of where Yatagarasu, the black three-legged crow, had lit – three holes in a large stone. The founding of the shrine supposedly dates to the time of Emperor Sujin, but the present location has been used only since 1889, when the older site was flooded out. The Shinto *kami* of the three shrines are identified in Dual-Aspect Shinto with Amida, Kannon and Seishi as their "true natures." As the sun rose over the mountains there may have been envisioned a mystic union with Dainichi and the spirit (*gongen*) of the Nachi waterfalls.

Other pilgrimages were popular, such as to the tomb of Prince Shōtoku and what came to be known as the 88 Sacred Sites of Shikoku. These were temples traditionally connected with Kōbō Daishi, to which were added others, making more than 100. The circuit was formalized by the early Edo period. The trip required up to two months and covered about 900 miles of mountain paths and coastal roads. The 1200-year anniversary of the priest's birth in 1973 saw many older people doing it on foot and younger people by car.

The Great Shrine at Izumo in Shimane prefecture remains in relative obscurity in early centuries because it was outside the scope of Yamato concern. It owed its survival within the Yamato orbit only to special dispensation. Okuninushi, the local *kami*, vowed his allegiance to the Yamato ruler, and when the Izumo governor was installed, at least as late as the Nara period, he made a trip to the Heijō court and repeated the same oath, an act not required of any other governors.

The most remarkable story is the dramatic rise of the Usa Hachiman shrine in Kyushu from a small cult center in the middle of the 6th century to the oracle that had the final word on whether Priest Dōkyō could become emperor in the late 760s. It was such a nonentity that it is never once named in the *Kojiki* or *Nihon Shoki*.

Some Yamato-Usa connections are known to have existed. There were Ōmiwa clansmen in Kyushu, probably remnants of warriors dispatched from Yamato to put down disturbances, and the shrine had aided in the suppression of two rebellions in the 8th century.

After the *kami* rebuffed Dōkyō and the subsequent death of the empress, Usa Hachiman's eclipse paralleled his; but an effort was made later to get back into court circles when, in 859, a *kami* from Usa was said to have come to Kyoto. A shrine had to be built and this is the Iwashimizu Hachiman shrine at Otokoyama.

In 798 Emperor Kammu designated certain shrines as national shrines and others as provincial shrines. The former enjoyed special privileges and received appropriate government support. For instance, shrines of great prominence still, Katori in Chiba, Kashima in Ibaragi and Sumiyoshi in Osaka petitioned to be allowed to rebuild every 20 years. Their request was granted in 812.

Private family shrines, like Kasuga in Nara, have a special tutelary function, though broad enough for the public to feel it could also benefit from their supernatural powers. Established in 768 by the Fujiwara family and dedicated to four *kami,* two of which were their own ancestors, it was placed in a protective position on the hillside east of their temple. Known to every visitor to Nara for the splendid rows of stone lanterns lining its roads and the metal ones gracing its eaves and the Buddhist style buildings, the four connected, narrow shrine buildings are actually entirely hidden from public view. They represent certain developments in shrine architecture of the 9th century in which the cypress thatch roof extends over a steep flight of steps, either in a continuous unbroken line or in broken lines as here at Kasuga.

Worship of Amida. Amida, the Buddha of the Western Paradise, was worshiped by the 7th century in Japan, but his glorification as the Buddha of the Pure Land of Eternal Bliss through whom one achieved eternal life did not come until rather late in the 10th century and was made a special cult only in the 12th.

Outside the domain of the orthodox Nara monasteries, native magical elements found far greater range. Amida worshipers picked up the *nembutsu,* the prayer for Buddha, through popular usage, first employed as a magical incantation to counteract evil spirits. It became associated specifically with Amidism after the Tendai priest Kūya explained its relevance in the 10th century. It was sufficient conscientiously to repeat the name of the Buddha as much as 70,000 times daily.

Amida worship was frequently referred to as the "easy path" because of the meager intellectual and social requirements. For the effort involved, its promises were enormous, but the *nembutsu* led to an incredible degeneration of Buddhist ideals and was as much as any thing responsible for the strong reform movements that arose by the 13th century, aimed at a return to conventional beliefs.

Amida worship entered a new stage after the articulation of the Pure Land (Jōdō) doctrine by Priest Genshin (or Eshin Sōzu) in his *Ōjō-yōshū* in 985. In this treatise he praised the value of the *nembutsu* and described the descent of the Buddha to welcome the soul of the deceased in optimistic and hopeful terms; yet he also foresaw a period of great degeneration resulting in a waning of the power of the Buddha, a loss of the scriptures and ultimately of the civilization on which they were based. Known as the End of the Law (Mappō) and anticipated for 1052 AD (or 2,000 years after it was said Gautama had been born), this depressing forecast led to greater reliance on magic to transcend the critical period.

The practice of burying sutras in the ground in an effort to tide the scriptures over this juncture was rationalized for this purpose, although it had been started by a Tendai priest in the 9th century after his return from China. Sutras were placed in a metal tube or clay vessel, and other articles such as swords, mirrors and little Chinese celadon bowls with lids, were buried together in small mounds, usually in mountains beside old Shinto sacred sites. The practice spread from the Yamato region to other parts of the country and lasted until a few hundred years ago, carried out as a matter of form and for a variety of reasons after Mappō proved to be of no consequence.

Some sutra containers bear inscriptions and many of these are dated, making sutra-mound archaeology an important aspect of historical archaeology. There is now an elaborate chronology for sutra-mound containers and related items which has been especially useful for tracing the development of the metallic arts through these centuries. The oldest sutra-mound so far found with a precise date is one made by Fujiwara Dōchō on Kinbusen in Nara prefecture in 1007.

Amida worship was made sectarian by Genkū, better known as Hōnen Shōnin and posthumously called Enkō Daishi. He read Genshin's exposition on salvation, abandoned his Tendai training and founded the Jōdō (Pure Land) sect in 1175. The monks of Tendai persuaded the

Opposite: the Jōruri-ji is a rather small temple today located in a remote corner of Kyoto prefecture. Nine gilt wooden Buddhas sit in a simple 11-bay, ceilingless building facing east.

Below: 12th-century frontispiece of the Lotus Sutra, the most popular of all the scriptures, translated into Chinese at an early date.

ruler to exile him to Shikoku, which was done in 1206, but he returned to Kyoto four years later and built the Chion-in, one of Kyoto's major eastside temples. Genkū defined more sharply the practices and blessings and formalized these into a sect which, in the course of time, took many temples under its wing. In simple terms, his preaching centered on gaining salvation into the Pure Land of Eternal Bliss through the medium of prayer. One way was by repeating the *nembutsu* up to 60,000 times daily.

Amida temples. The first Amida halls were built at the Tōdai-ji and Kōfuku-ji in the Nara period, but they had no distinctive features and it was not until Amida worship developed special characteristics that the shape of the halls responded to ritual needs. Circumambulation was important. Saichō's pupil Ennin seems to have built the prototype in 852 at the Enryaku-ji. It was a five-by-five-bay building, covered with a cypress bark roof. A Buddha and four Bodhisattvas were seated on a central platform, while the walls carried scenes of the Western Paradise called the Nine States of Pure Land.

The form came to be standardized as three by three bays with raised wooden floor and a surrounding porch. They were family, not public, worship halls and often lavishly

decorated on the interior. Many were oriented toward the east, since in the Shin sect this enabled the worshiper to look toward the Western Paradise as he prayed to the Buddha, for the same reason that the Christian worships facing Jerusalem.

The setting, to get the atmosphere of the palace in paradise, was advancing along the lines of the *shinden* style of nobleman's residence. It had a south-oriented central building with a pond and island in front, and was connected with flanking buildings by galleries. The heavenly ideal, in other words, was being reproduced on earth and the transformation from villa to temple architecture, like most transformations between the secular and the religious in Japan, was not difficult.

In the 11th century a special kind of Amida hall evolved under Fujiwara patronage. Representing the Nine States of Amida, a long narrow structure was designed to hold nine images of Buddha, all seated on a one-bay-deep altar platform. The number nine had several connotations, among which were the nine versions of the way Amida descended to receive pious souls, and the three births of three degrees in paradise. The highest of these was as saints, the middle as virtuous men and the lowest as sinners, especially those who had caught fish, had stolen canopies of temples and had killed people

Michinaga built the first of these long Amida halls in 1020 as part of his Hōjō-ji, a huge temple located northeast of the original outlines of Kyoto city. While he needed a retirement temple, it may be no coincidence that an epidemic of smallpox was raging through the city that year which even the emperor had contracted but survived.

Inside the immense blocked-out area was built a rectangular cloistered courtyard within which was a pond and Middle Island, reached by three bridges. The Amida hall was placed on the west side, its nine Buddhas all facing east. The doors were painted with the Nine States of Amida Paradise.

Michinaga had a special prayer seat made on which he sat with a ribbon reaching the main Amida and draped in both directions through the hands of the other eight. There he could repeat his *nembutsu* each morning.

The Hōjō-ji was destroyed by a great fire in 1058. Michinaga's family made some effort to rebuild it in 1065 and the two pagodas erected in 1079 were said to have come from the Yakushi-ji. Perhaps they were replacements that had been put up at the old temple down in Fujiwara. The 12th century witnessed many fires and the temple was allowed to disintegrate by the end of the 14th century.

Emperor Shirakawa revised this plan when he built the Hōshō-ji in 1075 along what would be an eastward extension of Nijō-ōji, the Second Block, on the Higashiyama side where he could draw water from the Shira river.

The usual single pagoda of these temples was magnified in this case to nine stories, the Amidist magical number, made in an octagonal shape and placed on the Middle Island, thus creating an axially aligned pagoda, main hall, lecture hall and Yakushi hall from the south entrance. Galleries reached out from the main hall to the belfry and sutra repository on the edge of the pond. The Amida hall was located in the southwest corner of the enormous square.

All of these Amidist temples had halls for other deities and uses. There was a hall for the esoteric deities and one where the Lotus Sutra was read.

Within a span of a century, this region east of Kyoto was the setting for the erection of more than 20 temples, the ones under imperial sponsorship usually of grand size and lavish detail. It is one of history's great losses that none remains today, especially since they embodied the major architectural and iconographic advances at the time. Nevertheless, by piecing together the Byōdō-in at Uji, the Jōruri-ji in Kyoto prefecture and the Mōtsu-ji in Hiraizumi one gets a complete picture of the way the paradise concept was given its terrestrial form.

Yorimichi and the Phoenix Hall. Michinaga's successor, Yorimichi, inherited the Byōdō-in at Uji, a villa marked for conversion to a temple upon his retirement or death, whichever came first. Yorimichi used it off and on until he retired there in 1068 at the age of 77 and died six years later. He had actually had it changed to a temple in 1053. The Phoenix Hall (Hōō-dō) has two phoenixes on its roof, the symbols of resurrection, and the building itself preserves its original character as a palace.

Yorimichi digressed from normal practice by building a Hondō (main hall) first, dedicated to Dainichi. A year later the Phoenix Hall was put up to the south of it, also facing east, more directly related to the pond. The nucleus of the hall is a three-by-two-bay space, with a porch projecting from three sides. The wings of the fabulous bird extend in either direction as galleries, while its tail reaches across the back of the pond. These galleries originally projected well forward, but a fire in 1325 destroyed about 20 of the bays, and the river bank and the pond were reshaped in the early 17th century. The river Uji is no longer visible from the porch of the hall.

At the turn of this century the Phoenix Hall was in pathetic condition as no one was concerned about its upkeep. Finally major repairs were made and between 1950 and 1957 it was dismantled and the deteriorated parts were replaced. But the damage had already been done when it was stripped of its gold and nacre inlay work and its paintings were allowed to fade through neglect.

Despite what is missing today, a complete iconographical scheme can be recognized. The central image of the Buddha, the many little relief Bodhisattvas on the walls, the paintings on the five large wooden doors and the large screen behind the Buddha, together with the architecture and the idyllic landscape, weave together a grand concept known as *raigō*, the descent of Amida to receive the soul of the deceased, as Eshin had described the event. The paintings are seasonal on four sides and depict nine versions or states of the way Amida accepts the spirit of the dead. Bodhisattvas descend on the clouds. One detail shows a galleried building like the Phoenix Hall itself in a comparable landscape.

The paintings are credited to Takuma Tamenari, but this is frequently discounted. His "school" introduced landscape elements into Buddhist paintings and, significantly, these have Japanese-style soft rolling hills and spatial relationships and gently modulated colors, thereby putting the event into a Japanese setting. Buddhist salvation could now be fully identified with Japan, a point that the Dainichi doctrines had been making in other ways.

The little wooden figures on the walls number 52 instead of the canonical 25, but it was not until later that the rendition was done literally. In two different kinds of costumes, they are heavenly musicians and attendants, many with instruments in their hands.

The sculpture of Jōchō. The sculptor employed by Yorimichi is one of the great names in the history of this art in Japan. Known as Jōchō, he had had long experience working for the Fujiwara in Kyoto, but this is the only statue that can be definitely attributed to him. He is still known to have had one commission after this Amida, before his death in 1057.

Jōchō was descended from royalty five generations earlier, and had social status not usual for sculptors. His workshop was in Kyoto and he was forced to devise a way to do most of the work there and install the image in Uji.

Right: a drawing from the *Choju-giga*, one of Japan's national treasures (12th century). The animals are thought to represent satirical comment on political or religious leaders.

Below: the Hōō-dō, known in English as the Phoenix Hall after the bronze birds on its roof, is the main hall of the Byōdō-in, a temple in Uji southeast of Kyoto, dedicated in 1053.

His workshop invented the technique of joining small wooden blocks to make a statue and he organized it in such a way that each apprentice was a specialist in one stage of the production. Various methods had been used to avoid the problem of splitting wood – hollowing out the interior, splitting and wedging the wood – but with nominal success. This practical solution opened up new vistas in Buddhist sculpture and paved the way for a renaissance of the art in the Kamakura period.

More than this, Jōchō carved an Amida which incorporated the best of the Japanese modifications of the basic Chinese style, and a canon of proportions that was to stand for several centuries. In other words, he abandoned the heavy monumentality of the Chinese and eliminated the mannerisms of the Japanese that had been creeping in since the 9th century. The Amida is rather flat and linear, and his relatively thin legs extend in such a way as to give a firm base for a triangular shape. The openwork mandala and canopy, all of wood and fully gilt, are also from his workshop.

The Jōruri-ji takes a special place of importance in Amidist temples today because it is the sole survivor. Moreover, the Amida hall, garden, island and pagoda all retain their original Heian character and relationship by the sheer good fortune of the temple's distance from civil disorders.

The Amida hall was put in its present place in 1157 and the pagoda was brought from a temple that was being dismantled in Kyoto in 1178. They were both spared in the temple fire of 1348.

The large central and eight smaller Amidas have occasionally been associated with Jōchō and his workshop, but they are most likely a generation or more later. The chief Buddha makes the hand gesture of appeasement, the others clasp both hands together signifying meditation. The pagoda holds a Yakushi image that may well be the temple's oldest statue, and its doors, pillars, beams, ceiling and walls are painted on the inside with the Eight Aspects of Buddha and the 16 Arhats, disciples of the Buddha.

Opposite: the large painted triptych of the *raigō* on silk, attributed to Genshin, the priest who described the transition from this world to the next for the devout Amidist.

Below: the gilt wooden image at the Byōdō-in is the work of Jōchō, and is a major landmark in the history of Japanese sculpture. Height 2·95 m.

Provincial styles. The achievements of the Fujiwara are not complete without looking at what their country cousins did in the north. This was a fascinating relationship that annoyed the Kyoto rulers and had the northern Fujiwara running to keep up. A distantly related offshoot of the Fujiwara family, commonly referred to as the Ōu or Ōshu Fujiwara from the old geographical name of the north, they had carved out a dynasty with their headquarters at Hiraizumi in Iwate prefecture, just out of Kyoto's reach. This had come about after the refusal of the locally ensconced Abe family to pay their taxes, and the ineffectual efforts of the government to quell their rebellion. When it was finally settled, Fujiwara Kiyohira received recognition from Kyoto as the ruler of the region. The Abe were regarded as Ainu and Kiyohira had an Abe mother.

Three generations spaced themselves out over a century. Kiyohira died in 1126, his son Motohira in 1157, and his grandson Hidehira in 1187. But great-grandson Yasuhira lost the territory to Minamoto Yoritomo and was assassinated by one of his own soldiers in the northern campaigns of the wars that destroyed the Taira family and brought the Heian age to a close. These Fujiwara constructed many large temples, invited artists up from Kyoto or ordered their paintings and sculptures in Kyoto, and furnished their temples with exotic objects and precious materials.

Kiyohira rebuilt the Chūson-ji into a temple of great size and grandeur, only fragments of which remain today. Nevertheless, it is the only major remaining temple at Hiraizumi. From the hilltop, where it ranges across a wide plateau, one has a spectacular view of the unfolding Kitakami plain and river. A fire in 1337 left only the belfry and a mausoleum. Several lost buildings were eventually replaced. The early descriptions were so effusive that archaeologists hoped to verify them. Excavations in recent years have located the position of the main hall and a pagoda, and the outlines of gardens and other features.

The building in which the Ōu Fujiwara were entombed is the Konjiki-dō (Gold-colored Hall), erected in 1124. It is only a small Amida hall about 6 by 6 meters, but was gorgeously decorated and seemed so worth preserving that another building was constructed over it about 150 years later. The visitor could then see the Konjiki-dō only through this outer building, but recently both were dismantled, the Konjiki-dō taken to Tokyo and repaired and then reassembled back at Hiraizumi. The outer building has been put up not far away on the hillside and can be entered, and the Konjiki-dō is where it once stood but in a huge glass case within a new building, looking like a large museum display. Nevertheless, its doors stand open and the altars, statues and luxurious ornamentation can now be seen at their best.

On the central altar, arranged in a trim and orderly fashion, is the Amida Buddha, his two Bodhisattvas, the Four Heavenly Kings at the corners and six Jizō figures in two rows; the last deity favors children and was particularly popular with the Fujiwara. Much of the interior surface decoration is now missing. It was first lacquered, then a variety of paints, metals and inlays were applied. The pillars are of a hard wood, like teak, brought to Japan from the south Pacific. The railings have thin decorative strips of sandalwood, also foreign. The pillars carry gold medallions of the Twelve Light Buddhas, the Twelve Aspects of Amida, with floral patterns done in shell inlay, while the foot of each column bears plaques in gilt bronze. The platforms are decorated with thin, gilt bronze sheets engraved in flower patterns. Jewels were once embedded at key points. The peacock is a popular subject, seen in bronze repoussé panels along the lower line of the platform, as is the *karyōbinga*, a human-headed bird of Indian origin, appreciated for its gift of song.

The remains of these Fujiwara rulers were put in gold and lacquered boxes and placed under the altars: Kiyohira and his wife under the main altar, and his son and grandson under the two side altars. The bodies are still well preserved, but it is not known whether mummification was intentional or not since no embalming materials have been identified.

They were opened up in 1699 and taken out and examined in 1931. Some of the burial articles can be seen in a room of the exhibition hall. Interestingly, they have some Ainu features, although the head is a little longer than the Ainu. They averaged a little less than 158 centimeters in height, and Hidehira had three cavities, which are rarely seen in Ainu teeth.

Motohira and Kiyohira each contributed sections to the spacious Mōtsu-ji on the lower, level ground in Hiraizumi in the early 12th century. Hidehira had put up a similar temple not far away, the Muryōkō-in, and all may have followed the plan of the Hōshō-ji built by Emperor Shirakawa in Kyoto.

The Mōtsu-ji had two separate sets of central halls and extended galleries lying side by side, the larger of the two lined up with the pond and south gate on a north-south axis. Everything was on a larger scale than the Byōdō-in at Uji. The site is well cared for today and makes a worthwhile visit since it is the only place where the full plan of such halls with galleries and pond can be seen in their 12th-century form, unlike the sadly truncated landscape of the Phoenix Hall.

Pottery and glass. The remarkable lacquering still visible in some of these buildings represents a highly developed art, although rather few cups, bowls, trays and other utensils have been found for these centuries in other sites. Nevertheless, it seems that the popularity of lacquer at the court reduced the demand for more sophisticated pottery and may have inhibited any latent desires to develop blown glass.

The glass receptacles for relics found in temples are thought to be of foreign manufacture. The Japanese made

Above: the Konjiki-dō, the family mausoleum of the Ōu Fujiwara in their temple called Chūson-ji in Hiraizumi, Iwate prefecture. The building measures only 5·5 m to a side.

Opposite: the pagoda of the Jōruri-ji, founded in 1047.

Below: in the Konjiki-dō all the bodies remained mysteriously preserved. That of the grandson Hidehira who died in 1187 is here being examined by Dr Hisashi Suzuki. All have features relating them to the Ainu.

only molded glass, such as the beads recovered from the mounded tombs, the glass in the Shōsō-in, or on Buddhist images and occasionally elsewhere. The cups from tombs and in the Shōsō-in are likely to be Iranian, but one or two pieces may be Chinese.

The appearance and disappearance of the three-color pottery ware so closely parallels that of the glass cups as to suggest some similar reasons. The use of lead glazing was introduced in the Nara period. The three-color ware – green, brown and white are the most usual – deriving from the similar type of Chinese T'ang dynasty wares, is closely identified with court circles and temples with court connections. It is very rarely found in other sites. Even in

Above: trails leading through the mountains behind Kasuga in Nara pass many rock faces with carved stone Buddhist images. This group, called Kasugayama Stone Buddhas, is dated to 1157.

Below: a large temple known as Mōtsu-ji, built by Fujiwara Kiyohira and Motohira in the early 12th century. This view is from across the remains of the South Gate.

the Shōsō-in, where one might expect more, among its 57 pieces that fall into this broad category, only five are three-colored; most are green and white. On the other hand, green glazed monochrome pottery has been recovered from scores of sites. It was obviously the poor man's three-color ware.

The three-color ware found in Japan is unquestionably locally made, unlike the complicated glass shapes. The glass was imported when the Nara court enjoyed exotic novelties. Why the three-color ware virtually ceased to be produced around the end of the Nara period is a mystery. Either its materials were largely imported and the source dried up, or it was so directly connected with imperial business that diminished imperial interest or power also meant less three-color ware.

While the table might be set with lacquer "dishes," domestic and ritual pottery was manufactured in and distributed from several large centers. As the building of tombs was phased out, the widely proliferated kilns were pulled back to concentrate in areas of especially good clays and turned to commercial production of the highly practical Sue ware.

Kyoto and Nara received much of their pottery from the Mt Sanage area on the border between the old provinces of Owari and Mikawa, that is, northeast of present Nagoya city. Sanage wares were sent to the Kantō, and some seem to have been carried as far north as Taga-jō. Many years of excavations in scores of abandoned Sanage kiln sites revealed that ash glazes were common on bottles by the late 8th century and green lead glazes were being applied to Sue pottery in the 11th century. Incised floral patterns on pots, bowls and plates were characteristic of the products of the 11th and 12th centuries. Over a thousand kilns were in operation there at different times until around the 15th century, when the potters left the area for a better one.

Further Reading

Aston, William G. (tr.), *Nihongi* (Tuttle, Tokyo and Rutland, Vt., 1972).

Batchelor, John, *The Ainu of Japan* (Religious Tract Society, London, 1892).

Befu, Harumi, *Japan: An Anthropological Introduction* (Chandler, San Francisco, Calif., 1971).

Benedict, Ruth, *The Chrysanthemum and the Sword* (Houghton Mifflin, Boston, Mass., 1946).

Bleed, Peter, "The Yayoi Culture of Japan: An Interpretive Summary," *Arctic Anthropology*, vol. 9, no. 2, 1972.

Bock, Felicia G. (tr.), *Engi-shiki: Procedures of the Engi Era* (Sophia University, Tokyo, 1970).

Brown, Delmer M., *Money Economy in Medieval Japan: A Study in the Use of Coins* (Institute of Far Eastern Languages, New Haven, Conn., 1951).

Chamberlain, Basil H. (tr.), *Kojiki* (J. L. Thompson, Kobe, 1932).

Egami, Namio, *The Beginnings of Japanese Art* (Weatherhill/Heibonsha, Tokyo, 1973).

Eliseeff, Vadime, *Japan* (Ancient Civilizations) (Barrie and Jenkins, London, 1974).

Hall, John W., *Japan, from Prehistory to Modern Times* (Tuttle, Tokyo and Rutland, Vt., 1971).

Hall, John W., and Richard K. Beardsley, *Twelve Doors to Japan* (McGraw-Hill, New York, 1965).

Hayashi, Ryoichi, *The Silk Road and the Shoso-in* (Weatherhill/Heibonsha, Tokyo, 1975).

Hori, Ichiro, *Folk Religion in Japan: Continuity and Change* (University of Tokyo Press, Tokyo, 1968).

—— "Shamanism in Japan," *Japanese Journal of Religious Studies*, vol. 2, no. 4, 1975, pp. 231–87.

Ishida, Eiichirō, *Japanese Culture: A Study of Origins and Characteristics* (University of Tokyo Press, Tokyo, 1974).

Kageyama, Haruki, *The Arts of Shinto* (Weatherhill/Shibundō, New York and Tokyo, 1973).

Kamstra, J. H., *Encounter or Syncretism: The Initial Growth of Japanese Buddhism* (E. J. Brill, Leiden, 1967).

Kidder, J. Edward, *Japan Before Buddhism* (Thames & Hudson, Praeger, London and New York, 1966).

—— *Early Buddhist Japan* (Thames & Hudson, Praeger, London and New York, 1972).

Kiley, Cornelius J., "State and Dynasty in Archaic Yamato," *Journal of Asian Studies*, vol. 33, no. 1, 1973, pp. 25–49.

Kitagawa, Joseph, *Religion in Japanese History* (Columbia University Press, New York, 1966).

Kobayashi, Takeshi, *Nara Buddhist Art: Todai-ji* (Weatherhill/Heibonsha, Tokyo, 1975).

Ledyard, Gari, "Galloping Along with the Horseriders: Looking for the Founders of Japan," *Journal of Japanese Studies*, vol. 1, no. 2, 1975, pp. 217–54.

Miki, Fumio, *Haniwa* (Weatherhill/Shibundo, New York and Tokyo, 1974).

Miller, Richard J., *Ancient Japanese Nobility: The Kabane Ranking System* (University of California Press, Berkeley, Calif., 1974).

Miller, Roy A., *The Japanese Language* (Chicago University Press, Chicago, Ill., 1967).

Mizuno, Yu, *Origins of the Japanese People* (Understanding Japan, no. 22) (Tokyo, 1968).

Morris, Ivan I., *The World of the Shining Prince: Court Life in Ancient Japan* (Knopf, New York, 1964).

Muraoka, Tsunetsugu, *Studies in Shinto Thought* (Japanese Committee for UNESCO, Tokyo, 1964).

Nakamura, Hajime, Ichiro Hori and Seiroku Noma, *Japan and Buddhism* (The Association of the Buddha Jayanti, Tokyo, 1959).

Ono, S., *Shinto, The Kami Way* (Bridgeway Press, Tokyo, 1962).

Ooka, Minoru, *Temples of Nara and Their Art* (Weatherhill/Heibonsha, Tokyo, 1973).

Ponsonby-Fane, Richard A. B., *Ancient Capitals and Palaces of Japan* (Transactions of the Japan Society of London, vol. 20, 1923).

—— *Studies in Shinto and Shrines* (Ponsonby Memorial Society, Kyoto, 1953).

—— *Kyoto: The Old Capital of Japan* (Ponsonby Memorial Society, Kyoto, 1956).

Reischauer, Robert K., *Early Japanese History* (Princeton University Press, Princeton, N.J., 1937).

Sansom, George, *A History of Japan to 1334* (Stanford University Press, Stanford, Calif., 1958).

Saunders, E. Dale, *Buddhism in Japan* (University of Pennsylvania Press, Philadelphia, Pa., 1964).

Snellen, J. B. (tr.), "Shoku Nihongi," *Transactions of the Asiatic Society of Japan*, 2nd series, vol. 11, 1934, pp. 151–239; vol. 14, 1937, pp. 209–78.

Soper, Alexander C., *The Evolution of Buddhist Architecture in Japan* (Princeton University Press, Princeton, N.J., 1942).

Tsunoda, Ryūsaku and L. Carrington Goodrich, *Japan in the Chinese Dynastic Histories* (Perkins, South Pasadena, Calif., 1951).

Varley, H. Paul, *Japanese Culture: A Short History* (Praeger, New York, 1973).

Visser, M. W., De, *Ancient Buddhism in Japan*, 2 vols. (E. J. Brill, Leiden, 1935).

Waley, Arthur (tr.), *The Tale of Genji by Lady Murasaki* (Houghton Mifflin, Boston, Mass., 1925).

Young, John, *The Location of Yamatai: A Case Study in Japanese Historiography, 720–1945* (The Johns Hopkins University, Baltimore, Md., 1957).

Acknowledgments

Unless otherwise stated all the illustrations on a given page are credited to the same source.

Aikawa Archaeology Museum; photo Kenishi Ozawa 59 right
Arts Council of Great Britain, London 16
Bijutsu Shuppan-Sha, Tokyo 60, 71, 78 bottom, 79, 80 left, 91, 96 bottom, 104 top, 114, 119, 123, 132, 133, 134 top
Bodleian Library, Oxford 18 top and bottom right
John Brennan, Oxford 84
British Museum, London 82
Errol Bryant, London 45, 104 bottom, 122 top
Werner Forman Archive, London 12 top, 96 top, 103, 117
Roger Gorringe, London 25 bottom left, 29 left, 86 top
Robert Harding Associates, London 13 top, 62, 65 top, 66 bottom, 67 bottom left, 68 center, 69, 70 bottom left, 76 top, 102 bottom
Heijo Research Institute 105, 106
A. A. M. van der Heyden, Amsterdam Jacket, 67 top left
Takayasu Higuchi, Kyoto 21 top and bottom left, 22 top, 87 top left, 94 left
Michael Holford Library, Loughton 74
Ibaragi Prefecture Art Museum; photo Kenishi Ozawa 89 top
Idojiri Archaeology Museum 41 top
Imperial Household Collection, Japan 88 bottom
Japan Map Center, Tokyo 14, 99, 100, 110 top, 120 bottom
Hiroshi Kanaseki, Tenri 53; by courtesy of Osaka Cultural Properties Center 47 bottom; by courtesy of Tenri Sarkōkan 50, 54, 55
Tadashi Katada 85 left
J. Edward Kidder, Jr. 12 bottom, 13 bottom, 22 bottom, 25 top and bottom right, 27 top and bottom right, 29 right, 30 bottom, 31, 35, 36 top, 37, 38, 39, 40 bottom, 41 bottom, 43, 46, 49, 51,

56 bottom, 58, 59 left, 64, 65 bottom, 66 top, 67 top right, 68 top and bottom, 73, 77, 80 right, 81, 86 bottom, 92, 94 right, 95, 101 bottom, 102 top, 108, 109, 110 bottom, 111 right, 112, 113 top right, 115, 116, 118, 121, 122 bottom, 124, 125, 126 left, 127 top, 131 bottom, 135, 136; by courtesy of Takayasu Higuchi, Kyoto 87 top right and center, 89 bottom, 90
Tatsuo Kobayashi; by courtesy of the Cultural Properties Commission 32
Yukio Kobayashi; by courtesy of the Department of Archaeology, Kyoto University 57 right
Shuzo Koyama 127 bottom
Lovell Johns, Oxford 10, 19, 24 left, 36 bottom, 44 left, 47 top, 52, 72, 87 bottom right, 107, 126 right
Masakatsu Morikawa 27 bottom left
Yukiko Nakatsu 24 right
Isamu Okamoto 48 bottom
Kenishi Ozawa 40 top, 42, 83, 87 bottom left
Peabody Museum, Salem 18 bottom left
Picturepoint Ltd, London 11, 70 top
Nagano Rokumeiso 115 bottom, 129
Royal Scottish Museum, Edinburgh 20
Spectrum Colour Library, London 9, 61, 67 bottom right, 70 bottom right, 131 top
Masao Suenaga 113 top left and bottom
Hitoshi Suzuki 21 bottom right, 33, 134 bottom
Tokyo National Museum 85 right; photo Kenishi Ozawa 88 top
Transart, Oxford 26, 98
John Way, London, 48 top, 75, 93, 101 top, 111 left, 120 top

The Publishers have attempted to observe the legal requirements with respect to the rights of the suppliers of photographic materials. Nevertheless, persons who have claims are invited to apply to the Publishers.

I am indebted to many people, and the agencies with which they are associated, for giving generously of their time and in supplying illustrations. Special thanks go to Mr Hideya Harunari of Okayama University, Mr Hiroshi Kanaseki of Tenri University, Mr Tatsuo Kobayashi of the Cultural Properties Commission, and Mr Masakatsu Morikawa, excavator of the Torihama shell-mound. For providing illustrations and for permission to use them, to Dr Masao Suenaga, Dr Hitoshi Suzuki, Mr Takayasu Higuchi, Mr Tadashi Katada, Mr Yasushi Egami, Mr Tadanao Yamamoto, Mr Isamu Okamoto and Mr Atsushi Oshita.

Among those who have been most closely associated with our archaeological work through the ICU Archaeology Research Center, I should like to express my appreciation to Miss Yukiko Nakatsu, Mr Shizuo Oda, Mr Charles Keally and Mr Shuzo Koyama for various services, and especially to Mrs Michiko Morii Chiura for invaluable help given in ways too countless to name. And to my wife, for her constant encouragement and arguments, I would like to add a word of thanks.

J. EDWARD KIDDER, JR.

Glossary

Ainu People with non-Japanese physical characteristics now residing in Hokkaido. Probably an ancient people of Caucasoid origin, called Emishi and Ezo (hence the island of Ezo, or Yezo, old name for Hokkaido) in the early literature, they are short, hairy people with light complexion. They had no written language, have beliefs of an animistic nature quite similar to **Shinto** (their term for *kami* is *kamui*), and lived on Honshu long enough to leave many place names. They are being rapidly assimilated, which seems to be their present desire and intention.

Amida Amitabha, Buddha of the Western Paradise, the Pure Land. The Japanese name embodies two Indian forms, Amitābha (Infinite Light) and Amitāyus (Infinite Life). Amida was only one of many Buddhas initially. He rose to prominence in the 8th century in Japan as one of the four exoteric Buddhas in the Hossō pantheon, which still visualized rebirth in Maitreya's Tusita paradise. From the 10th century Amidism was given a firm intellectual base by **Tendai** priests and Amida was rapidly popularized as the Buddha of the Pure Land into which new souls could be reborn, formalized into a sect.

Ashikaga Minamoto-related family descended from Ashikaga Yoshiyasu (1126–57) who took the name of the place where the family had lived in Tochigi prefecture. There were several branches. Ashikaga Yoshimitsu (1358–1408), builder of the Kinkaku-ji in Kyoto, was *shōgun* from 1367 to 1395. He was politically astute in dealing with the new regime of the Ming dynasty in China (1366–1644) and highly valued the Chinese art and cultural objects he could acquire.

Asuka Small area of Nara prefecture at the extreme southern edge of the Yamato Plain where the rulers were domiciled in the 7th century. Asuka was **Soga**-controlled territory. From the arrival of Empress Suiko in 592 to the construction of the palace of Fujiwara and the accompanying city by Empress Jitō in 694, Asuka was the seat of the government, with the exception of the reign of Emperor Kōtoku who moved to Naniwa to issue the **Taika Reform** (646) after the elimination of the Soga. Asuka has preserved sites of major monuments – palaces, temples and tombs – including the painted **Takamatsuzuka tomb**. Asuka period: art-historical designation for material dated between 552 and 646 AD.

Be, tomo Occupational groups of craftsmen and other workers employed for the support of the aristocracy. The *tomo* were earlier, less formal groups who for practical reasons had banded together. The *be* were formally organized by the late 5th century, composed of members living on a serf level, providing highly specialized services in many areas, such as in the metal arts, horse breeding and pottery making.

Bidatsu (538–85). The 30th emperor, reigned 572–85, second child of **Kimmei**, succeeding his father. Non-Buddhist Bidatsu witnessed the struggle between the **Soga** and **Mononobe** over Buddhism's future. Negotiations to recover Mimana led only to the murder of an adviser brought over from Paikche in 583. Temple craftsmen and builders had come from Korea in 577. Bidatsu was not buried until 591, and then in his mother's tomb at Shinaga, Taishi-chō, Osaka prefecture.

Byōdō-in Temple at Uji, converted from a villa in 1053 by Fujiwara Yorimichi of which the Hōō-dō, Phoenix Hall, is the central part. Located southeast of Kyoto city and along the Uji river, Fujiwara Michinaga had built a retreat which he gave to his son, who then proceeded to transform the grounds into a temple. Well known to tourists because of its proximity to Kyoto, the Phoenix Hall is a complex Amida hall facing east towards a lotus pond, with extended galleries and "tail" reaching across the pond at the back. The wooden Amida figure is by the sculptor **Jōchō** and the screen paintings said to be by **Takuma Tamenari**. The pond and galleries have lost much of their original form.

Calendar Japan received "calendar makers" from Korea in the middle of the 6th century and tried two or more systems before adopting the Chinese lunar calendar in 604 with 60-year cycles (10 by 12). This required the addition of a 13th month at calculated intervals. Days were in units of 12 hours. The *nengō* or era system was started from 645, but was used regularly only from the reign of Temmu. It was never planned to be coordinated exactly with the dates of a reign. Such coordination only came in with Emperor Meiji. The year 1977 is Showa 52, the 52nd year of the reign of Emperor Hirohito. Japan went on to the European Gregorian system in 1872. Conversion of dates has been very complicated, and consideration has to be given to the method of always listing a new reign as starting in the year following the death or abdication of the previous ruler. Dates often vary by a year or so in books, for which one develops a degree of tolerance.

Chūai The 14th emperor, son of Yamato-takeru and husband of regent **Jingū**, late 4th century AD. He refused to accept the recommendation to fight Silla, said to be the instigators of the Kumaso rebellion, and died. His wife, Jingū, communed with the *kami* and received the signal to proceed. The Japanese accounts claim complete submission of all the Korean kings, and she returned to give birth to the next emperor, **Ōjin**. Chūai was put in a shrine of temporary interment and buried in Osaka a year later.

Chūgoku Middle provinces, the lower part of the island of Honshu, to the north of the Inland Sea, comprising the prefectures of Yamaguchi, Shimane, Hiroshima, Tottori, Okayama and usually including Hyōgo.

Chūson-ji Chief Amida temple built at Hiraizumi in Iwate prefecture by Ōu Fujiwara Kiyohira and dedicated in 1126. The only original buildings remaining today are the Konjiki-dō, used as a mausoleum by the family, and the sutra repository, but some halls have been added since the temple was burned in 1337, and the new treasure hall contains many sculptures and possessions of the Fujiwara of considerable interest.

Daigo (885–930). The 60th ruler, reigned 897–930, the first son of Uda. He ascended the throne at the age of 13. The country was increasingly difficult to manage because of the expansion of private estates and the unreliability of provincial governors, but the arts flourished in Heian. Outstanding writers were active during this period marked by the Engi era (901–22). Emperor Daigo built the Daigo-ji in southeast Kyoto and was buried there.

Dainichi Vairocana, the supreme deity, the embodiment of all existence. Vairocana, the sun, was changed phonetically in Japan to Roshana and the meaning of this was translated as Dainichi, Great Sun, Great Illuminator. He is the chief deity of **Shingon**, which regards all things in the universe as embodied in Dainichi, the universe composed of an infinite number of worlds, each with an infinite number of Buddhas. Dainichi is shown in mandalas as the center of a large pantheon of deities.

Dazaifu Government's chief military outpost in Fukuoka, north Kyushu, and a regular grid-plan city by the 8th century. Dazaifu was started around the 660s to coordinate the building of defenses against Korea in the mountains overlooking the exposed plain. It became a southern capital, the second largest city in the country. A revolt by its governor in 740 caused a change in the administration, but the old one was shortly reinstated. The nucleus of the city is now preserved as an interesting archaeological site.

Dōkyō (?–770). Priest of Hossō sect who almost became emperor under Empress **Shōtoku**. Dōkyō attended ex-Empress **Kōken** in 761 and his prayers were seen as responsible for her recovery. He connived with her to resume the sovereignty, which she did as Empress Shōtoku in 764, raising Dōkyō to unprecedented ranks for a priest during the period of their close liaison, and even investigating with the *kami* at Usa Hachiman shrine in 768 to see whether he could be designated emperor. He outlived the empress by about a year, having been retired to a temple in Tochigi prefecture on her death.

Ennin (792–862). Tendai priest, posthumously known as Jikaku Daishi. Ennin entered the monastery on Mt Hiei at the age of 14. At 46 he went to China where he studied and traveled for nine years, noting many valuable observations in a diary that has provided valuable information on contemporary T'ang China. He was appointed chief priest of the **Tendai** sect in 854.

En-n-Ozunu (c.634–705). Mountain ascetic regarded as the first **yamabushi** and therefore the founder of Shūgen-dō. Also called En-no-Gyōja, En-no-Shōkaku and other names, he stayed in a cave on Mt Katsuragi in Nara prefecture for several decades, was exiled to Izu in 699 and freed two years later. In further travels he may have died somewhere in west Japan.

Enryaku-ji Chief **Tendai** sect temple on Mt Hiei, northeast of Kyoto, in Ōtsu city. Once Heijō was built, Emperor Kammu felt the palace needed protection in the direction from which evil spirits usually attack, and encouraged the building of a temple on Mt

Hiei. **Saichō** (767–822) erected a small one that came to be called Ichijō-shikan-in and later, after Saichō's trip to China, it grew to considerable size and received the era (782–805) name Enryaku in 823. Three sub-temples were built, but the militant monks who did much damage to Kyoto brought on their own destruction. It went up in a big conflagration in 1571. Toyotomi Hideyoshi and Tokugawa Ieyasu contributed to its rebuilding. From 6 to 15 May 1976 the temple exhibited a small statue of Yakushi for the first time in 614 years, said to have been carved by Saichō.

Esoteric sects Secret teachings, not revealed to the uninitiated. Called Mikkyō in Japanese, these are **Tendai** and **Shingon**, the latter described by Kūkai as the supreme attainment in man's quest for Buddhahood. In contrast to other sects, the mystical doctrines were largely transmitted orally and the rituals were performed behind screens and out of sight of the believers.

Four Heavenly Kings Lokapālas, in Japanese, Shitennō, or sometimes called Four Deva Kings, they are protectors of the Buddhist realm. Four images stand at the corners of the Buddha platform in many temple buildings. Deities of popular Indian origins noted for their strength, they were converted and brought into service: Bishamon of the north, with spear and stupa; Zōchō of the south, with sword and club; Jigoku of the east, with sword, gem and more rarely a musical instrument; and Kōmoku of the west, with stupa, noose and occasionally a spear. The attributes are often not consistent and rarely original.

Fudō Acala, a form of **Dainichi**, the chief of the Five Great Howling Lords, the Wisdom Kings, and other English designations. Go-dai-myō-ō entered Japan with esoteric Buddhism, and personifies the wrath of the five esoteric Buddhas against unrighteousness. He was born a slave to help others. Rural people associated Fudō with rain-making; samurai invoked him for courage. He is the Immovable One, hence his name, shown on a rock against a background of brilliant red flames, accompanied by two children symbolizing power and virtue. His sword destroys and his rope contains evil.

Fudoki See **Nihon Shoki**.

Fujiwara Name of family which traced its ancestry to the **kami**, called Nakatomi until Nakatomi-no-Kamako (614–69) was given the name Fujiwara. Kamako was instrumental in the **Taika Reform** and served Kōtoku, Saimei and Tenchi. As a reward he was given the family territorial name on his death-bed, Fujiwara Kamatari. It developed into a vast family with four branches, the northern one

becoming politically dominant when Fujiwara Yoshifusa (804–72) was appointed regent for his grandson, Emperor Seiwa, who took the throne at the age of 9. Fujiwara daughters were married to emperors, the peak of Fujiwara control coming at the time of Michinaga (966–1027) who as *kampaku*, Administrator or Chancellor, served three emperors. He and most of his family lived in the **Hōjō-ji** in his later years. Ōu Fujiwara: a dynasty of distant relatives centered at Hiraizumi, Iwate prefecture, in the 12th century, attempting to build monuments as splendid as those in Kyoto.

Ganjin (686–763). Chinese priest Chien-chên who arrived in Japan after many shipwrecks at the age of 66, ordained some 400 novitiates on a platform in the courtyard of the Tōdai-ji, and built the **Tōshōdai-ji**, the first temple of the Ritsu or Rules sects, an important collegiate institution served by Chinese monks. A life-size sculpture of him at the temple was probably done around the time of his death.

Garan Japanese abbreviations of *samgharama*, originally the place where a community of monks or nuns resided and performed their worship ceremonies. Also called *shōja* in Japan, it came to be looked on as the cloistered nucleus of a temple.

Gemmyō (662–722). Empress, the 43rd ruler, reigned 707–15, a daughter of **Tenchi** who followed her son **Mommu**. The events of her 7-year reign include the minting of the first copper coins in 708, for which the era was named Wadō, transferring the capital to **Heijō** in 710, sending weaving instructors to the provinces, receiving the *Kojiki* at the court in 712 and ordering the *Fudoki* to be written by the provinces.

Coin of Empress Gemmyō

Gempei War War between the Minamoto (Gen) family and the Taira (Pei) family between 1180 and 1185, the outcome of which brought Minamoto Yoritomo (1147–99) to power to start the **Kamakura** period (1185–1333). Early losses by Yoritomo through 1181 were overcome and, after defeating Taira Shigehira's soldiers and entering Kyoto, then disposing of Minamoto Yoshinaka, a cousin whose rule was disrupting the city, he brought his victories in southwest Japan to a climax in the battle of Dan-no-ura and the destruction of the Taira.

Genji Monogatari *Tales of Genji* (Minamoto), the classic court romance written in the early 11th century by Lady Murasaki while she was residing at the Ishiyama-dera near Lake Biwa. This voluminous work contains a great wealth of detail on court life of the late 10th century in Heian, unavailable in the official histories.

Lady Murasaki, author of the Tales of Genji

Genshin (942–1017). Also called Eshin Sōzu, a priest who studied at the Enryaku-ji and wrote the *Ōjō-yōshū* in 985 (variously translated as The Essentials of Salvation, Collection of the Praises of Amitabha, and Birth in the Land of Purity). In it Amida Buddha presides over the Pure Land (Jōdo) accompanied by bodhisattvas and an angelic host of 25, all poised to welcome the dead. The state of bliss may be reached by the "one gate of *nembutsu,*" that is, by repeating the name of the Buddha prayerfully.

Genshō (679–748). Empress, the 44th ruler, reigned 715–24, a daughter of **Gemmyō**. Genshō marked time until **Shōmu** became of age, supporting the arts and sciences. The *Nihon Shoki* was received at the court in 720, the Yōrō codes were completed the same year the Asuka-dera was moved to Heijō in 718, while other temples were in the process of moving. A rebellion in south Kuyshu was suppressed. She abdicated in 724 in order to put her nephew Shōmu on the throne.

Gyōgi (670–749). Hossō sect priest, perhaps of Korean birth, commonly called Gyōgi Bosatsu (bodhisattva), from the title awarded him by Emperor Shōmu. Known for both his practical good works and his erudition, he is usually looked on as the father of **Ryōbu-Shinto** that came to be such a useful doctrine for the spread of the esoteric sects. In actual fact, he may have only advocated greater harmony between the two religions. Shōmu used Gyōgi to get approval from the *kami* at Ise to have the Great Buddha cast.

Gyōshin (?–750). Hossō sect priest who took up residence in the Hōryū-ji and with the support of Fujiwara Fusasaki built the Tō-in in 739. Gyōshin constructed the Tō-in or Jōgū-ō-in, the eastern part of the Hōryū-ji, as a memorial to **Prince Shōtoku**, on the spot on which the palace had once stood. Fujiwara Fusasaki did not live to see it; he and his three brothers, all heads of branches of the family, died in the smallpox plague of 737.

Hachiman Traditionally called the God of War, a deification of **Emperor Ōjin**. There are many Hachiman shrines in the country, the chief of which is at Usa in Ōita prefecture, founded in the 6th century. Probably the written characters were for long pronounced Yawata. Ōjin's place of origin (Jingū is said to have given birth to him on her return from Korea) was the connection, but he was less warlike than many early emperors, and popularization came rather late, especially under the patronage of the Minamoto. Called Daibosatsu Hachiman, the Great Bodhisattva Hachiman, since the 8th century, Shinto and Buddhist elements were fused in this deity at an early date.

Haji Term used for the reddish domestic pottery of the Tomb period and for the *be* which produced it. This pottery was little different from the preceding Yayoi and is best distinguished by its context and its rounded bottoms. According to the *Nihon Shoki*, when **haniwa** were first made, Nomi-no-Sukune, the famous wrestler, was made head of the Haji-*be*, and their charge included superintending imperial burials.

Hakuhō Era name (650–54), now usually used for an art period and expanded to 645–710. The *Nihon Shoki* refers to the era as Hakuji, white pheasant, and it was probably changed later to Hakuhō, white phoenix. Late Asuka would be a better term, or Asuka-Fujiwara period, but at best it is not a stylistically coherent period because of the arrival of new styles from China. It should be subdivided into the pre-Chinese and the Chinese-influenced stages.

Hamada, Kōsaku (1881–1937). Kyoto University archaeologist and president of the university. Born in Osaka, he graduated from Tokyo Imperial University and went to Kyoto Imperial University to lecture on Japanese art and archaeology. After studying in Europe he developed the archaeology program at Kyoto, which excavated and published annual reports. His own book of 1922, *Tsūron Kōkogaku* (General Theory of Archaeology), was then an outstanding accomplishment. He died shortly after becoming president of the university in 1937.

Haniwa Literally, rings of clay, the clay cylinders, inanimate objects, animals and human figures placed on the slopes of mounded tombs in the 5th and 6th centuries A D. According to the story told at the time of Emperor Suinin in the *Nihon Shoki*, these were substitutes for live human burials. Whether true or not, they were first made in the Kansai in the 4th century and became the major native art form of the late Tomb period. Many fine examples can be seen in collections like the Tokyo National Museum.

Heian Capital of Tranquility and Peace, capital of Japan from 794 to 1869. The city, the appendage to the palace, was now recognized: the palace was Heian-jō, the Castle of Tranquility and Peace; the city, Heian-kyō. It was sometimes called Kyoto, meaning just capital, and sometimes Northern Capital, to differentiate it from the former capital of Nara. It was laid out with more deliberation and consultation than earlier capitals and, as the third experience with rectangular, square-grid cities, assumed an ideal form, 9 *jō* north and south, 8 *bō* east and west, 5 by 4½ km. Emperor **Kammu** took up residence there late in 794; Emperor Meiji moved to Tokyo in early 1869. The population in Meiji's time was around 400,000.

Heiji Insurrection Short civil war of 1159 in the Heiji era (1159–60) when Fujiwara Nobuyori (1133–59) and Minamoto Yoshitomo (1123–60) fought the Taira and died in defeat. *Heiji Monogatari* is the written account of the war and the event inspired its illustration in scrolls.

Wooden tallies from Heijō

Heijō Castle of Peace, name of the 8th-century palace and so, incidentally, the city which supported it, west of present Nara. Heijō was used from 710 by emperors and empresses Gemmyō, Genshō, Shōmu, Kōken, Junnin, Shōtoku, Kōnin and by Kammu until he transferred the capital shortly after ascending the throne in 784. Heijō was a grid-plan, rectangular city with two palaces in the north for alternative use, a pair of markets in the south and, by including the expanded blocks in the northwest and the northeast, seven major temples and nine minor or family temples. The survival of these temples made the city the prime goal of pilgrimage after the capital was moved further north.

Himiko (variously Pimiko, Himeko, etc.). Name meaning princess, a female ruler of Yamatai, the kingdom described by Chinese historians as the largest of the country of Wa (Japan). She is dated by the Chinese as coming to power around 180 AD and dying about 248. As a shaman, she was virtually unapproachable, in constant touch with the *kami*. She reached her position after much strife and upon her death was replaced by a female shaman only after an attempt to install a male leader had failed. While Himiko symbolizes female religious leaders, of which Japan had many, she seems to be too early for Jingū and might be more accurately identified with someone like Yamato-hime, a daughter of Emperor Suinin, the first *miko* of the shrine of the Sun Goddess at Ise.

Hōgen War Short civil war of 1156 in the Hōgen era (1156–59) over the successor to Emperor Konoe. Fought between Minamoto supporters of retired Emperor Sutoku and Taira supporters of Emperor Toba, the latter won and Shirakawa was enthroned, an event which greatly enhanced the position of Taira Kiyomori (1118–81).

Hōjō Family descended from the Taira, with territorial jurisdiction in the Kamakura area, the administrators of the government during the Kamakura period. Succeeding Minamoto Yoritomo (1147–99), they were technically not titled *shōguns*, more like regents (*shikken*), nine administered successively until Ashikaga Takauji (1305–58) destroyed the remnants of the family which was already disintegrating from within.

Hōjō-ji Large Amida temple built over a ten-year period by Fujiwara Michinaga in east Kyoto from 1021. The Hōjō-ji was constructed in a large block with a new arrangement of landscape, lotus pond and buildings to suit the canonical description of the Western Pure Land Paradise. The long Amida hall was set into the cloister and faced east. Seven Yakushi images sat in a hall outside the cloister on the east, facing west. The temple was destroyed by fire in 1058, somewhat rebuilt, and eventually abandoned after the 12th century.

Hōnen (1133–1212). Tendai priest, posthumously named Genkū or Enkō Daishi, the founder of the Pure Land sect (Jōdo-shū) in 1175. Hōnen preached faith, orderly life and repetition of the *nembutsu*, and organized a formal sect based on the ideas developed in the Chinese Ching-t'u of the late 4th century. The sect gained popularity rapidly, but the alienated Tendai clergy got him exiled to Shikoku in 1206. He returned to Kyoto four years later and built the Chion-in, now the head temple of the sect, with many later branches.

Hōryū-ji Successor to a temple built by **Prince Shōtoku** in 607 in Ikaruga, Nara prefecture, probably constructed late in the 7th century. At first called Ikaruga-dera and Wakakusa-dera, perhaps a favorite name the prince used, it took the Chinese-style name of Hōryū-ji when rebuilt, following the order of Emperor Temmu in 679 for all temples to do so. It was also called Hōryū-gakumon-ji. The first temple was burned in 669 or 670 and rebuilt on a different spot in a distinctively Japanese plan. It preserved many early works of art and its fundamental 7th- and 8th-century architectural characteristics.

Hōshō-ji Large temple dedicated to Amida, built by Emperor **Shirakawa** in east Kyoto in 1075. Using the newly evolving Pure Land plan, here laid out within the square city block, the Hōshō-ji had open galleries reaching forward to join the sutra repository and belfry standing beside the lotus pond, and a nine-story pagoda on the Middle Island. Other buildings lay behind, a Yakushi hall at the north end and an Amida hall in the southwest. Fires eventually destroyed the temple.

Inari *Kami* of rice, whose messenger is a fox. Inari shrines are found in great numbers all over the country, perhaps originating around the early 8th century during long periods of drought. The female **kami** of rice and food is Uga-no-Mitama, but others are Omiyama and Saruta-hiko at Inari shrines. The head Inari shrine is at Fushimi in southeast Kyoto where the main buildings now date to 1499. A festival is held for three weeks in April every year.

Ingyō The 19th emperor, fourth son of **Nintoku**, who succeeded his brother Hanzei, mid-5th century AD. During a reign traditionally claimed to be 40 years, his chief accomplishment was to separate those with honest claims to nobility from those with false claims by requiring that they plunge their arms into boiling water. It was predicted that honest claims to ancestry would be immune from suffering, whereas false claims would not. Only those with legitimate claims appeared for the trial. Ingyō's tomb is identified at Dōmyōji in Osaka prefecture.

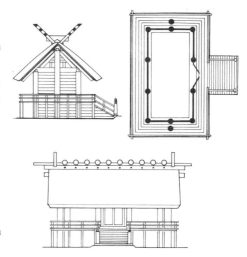

The shrine at Ise

Ise, Grand Shrines Preeminent Shinto shrines, the home of the Sun Goddess, Amaterasu-ō-mi-kami. Located in Mie prefecture near Uji-yamada, in a large evergreen forest cut by the Isuzu river, are the Inner and Outer shrines, the former enshrining the Sun Goddess since about the 4th century AD, the latter the Grain and Harvest Goddess (Toyouke) since about the 5th century. Each is traditionally rebuilt every 20 years in the same pre-Buddhist style on adjoining lots. In early centuries the chief priestess was an imperial princess.

Ishibutai Remains of the largest stone passageway and chamber in Japan, a tomb in southeast Asuka believed to be the burial place of Soga-no-Umako (?–626). The granite stones of the south-oriented passageway and chamber are fully exposed. Two cover the chamber, one 5 meters in length, the other 4. The stone structure was built on a square base with surrounding moat 8 meters wide, the banks of which are walled with boulders.

Iwajuku Site where Palaeolithic tools were first clearly identified in 1949, 1 km northwest of Iwajuku station, Gumma prefecture. A delivery boy, Tadahiro Aizawa, noticed stones eroding out of the Kantō Loam, dug more and took them to Tokyo for identification. Meiji University excavated, finding hand-axes, end and side scrapers, flakes and points in pre-Jōmon levels. Earliest Jōmon pottery was discovered in Jōmon levels not far away.

Izanagi and Izanami Creators of the Eight Island Country, 7th generation of the gods. Usually translated as the Male who Invites and the Female who Invites, they were probably just the Male of Izu and the Female of Izu. They were instructed to produce a country for the **kami** to oversee and inhabit, and formed the islands and created the *kami* of the natural

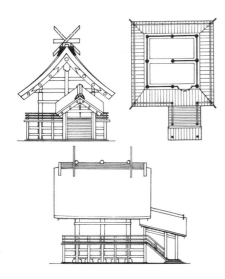

The shrine at Izumo

phenomena. Izanami died after giving birth to Kagutsuchi, the Fire God. Izanagi tried to recover her from Yomi-no-kuni, the netherworld to which she had gone, but was forced to leave and then purified himself by washing. Spontaneous generation produced three important *kami*: the Sun Goddess, her brother, Susano-o, an earth deity, and the Moon God. Izanagi retired, rarely to be heard from again.

Izumo, the Great Shrine Large, early type of shrine in Shimane prefecture dedicated to Okuninishi, *kami* of fishing, medicine, silk production and matrimony. The area was the most difficult for the Yamato people to pacify. When that was done, the Izumo *kami* agreed to a compromise and retired to a palace built for him, the first Izumo shrine. Okuninushi is a descendant of Susano-o, brother of the Sun Goddess. He goes by other names, including Ōmononushi in the Yamato area where the two cycles, the Izumo earth deity cycle and the Yamato sky deity cycle, are combined. All that *kami* congregate at the Izumo shrine in the month of October. *Izumo Fudoki*: gazetteer of the area of Izumo, written c. 730.

Jimmu Said to be the first emperor, ruling from 660 to 585 BC, perhaps the grandson of the *kami* Ninigi-no-mikoto. Jimmu is the first mortal ruler of Japanese history. In many skirmishes, he moved from southeast Kyushu through the Inland Sea, around the Kansai to Ise, then back and to Kashiwara in Nara prefecture. He built a palace, and official Japanese history began, in the year 660 BC. He is said to be buried nearby. If anything, Jimmu would have been a Yayoi chieftain of about the 1st century AD who led his tribe into the Yamato plain.

Jingū Regent after Chūai's death, from c. 380 AD. A female shaman warrior who led the

Japanese troops against the Korean kings and forced them to submit annual tribute. She remained regent, suppressing one revolt in Yamato, and was supposedly the sole ruler for 69 years, living to be 100. She was succeeded by her son **Ōjin**. The tomb associated with her is just north of old Heijō city.

Jitō (646–703). Empress, the 41st ruler, ruled 686–97 (ascended the throne in 689), a daughter of **Tenchi** and wife of **Temmu**, succeeding her husband. Empress Jitō saw to the construction of the palace at Fujiwara and the adjoining city, into which she moved in 694. She made new appointments, determined cap and costume colors for ranks and dealt with court protocol. She made 31 trips to Yoshino in an 11-year reign, where she and Temmu had hidden out before Temmu became emperor. She abdicated in favor of her 14-year-old nephew and was the first ruler to be cremated (in 704). She was buried with her husband in south Asuka.

Jizō Kshitigarbha, an all-encompassing bodhisattva of salvation. Jizō made the supreme effort to save souls by going all the way into Hell to retrieve them. Popularized in the Heian period, closely associated with Amida in temple sculptures, Jizō protects travelers, pregnant women and children and may be seen in numerous roadside stone images dressed like a monk. There are many names for Jizō, who has associated himself with the Six Classes of Creation.

Jōchō (?–1057). Most important sculptor of the Heian period, head of a workshop in Kyoto. Jōchō was a distant descendant of Emperor Kōkō (885–88) who took commissions for his workshop, among which were images for the Hōjō-ji of Fujiwara Michinaga in 1023, for the Kōfuku-ji in 1048, and the Amida Buddha for the Byōdō-in of Fujiwara Yorimichi in 1053. His wokshop developed the multiple-block technique and his style was the fashion for a century and a half. He was awarded high rank for his artistic contribution to the church.

Jōdo Pure Land, or Saihō Jōdo, Western Pure Land, the paradise of Amida Buddha. Strictly speaking, it is a general concept, but in Japan it is identified with **Amida**. The Pure Land could be entered after death through genuine efforts to believe in Amida; there one was assigned to one of nine levels relative to the degree of virtue achieved in this world. Pure Land was an old composite Indian and Chinese concept that grew in Japan under the umbrella of **Tendai**, accepted on all social levels after the creed was reduced to the *nembutsu* ritual, but given doctrinal form in the thesis by Ryōgen (912–85) in 960 – Rebirth of the Nine Classes of Believers in Amida's Paradise. Hōnen systematized it into a sect in 1175, of which Shinshū and Ji are surviving offshoots.

Jōmon Literally, cord patterns, referring initially to the cord-marking on the prehistoric pottery, then to the entire period in which it was made. The period appears to have had a duration of about 10,000 years, terminating around the 3rd century BC in Japan. It was divided into five stages by Sugao Yamanouchi, to which a sixth has recently been added at the beginning.

Jōri, jobō Terms describing the basic units of land as it was laid out in the 7th and 8th centuries in rural and city areas. *Jō* and *ri* run north-south and east-west in the country; *jō* and *bō* are terms used for a city. For instance, each large *jōbō* square at Heijō measured 1,600 **shaku** or feet either way, the original city rectangle then being 9 by 8 *jōbō* plus, presumably, the width of the streets. The purpose in rural areas was to provide equitably distributed taxable land, but it became too widely abused.

Jōruri-ji Temple in Kyoto prefecture preserving the original buildings and garden of the Western Pure Land Paradise. The temple was first called the Nishi-odawara-ji when started in 1047. It came under the wing of the Kōfuku-ji in 1150. Its Nine States of Amida hall dates to 1107 and the three-story pagoda was moved from a Kyoto temple in 1178. A fire in 1343 destroyed most of the related buildings. Among the many halls with nine Amida Buddhas built by the Fujiwara and aristocrats aping them, this is the sole survivor, and the garden retains its 12th-century form.

Kamakura City on the coast in Kanagawa prefecture from which Minamoto Yoritomo (1147–99) administered the country as *shōgun*. Kamakura was home territory for Yoritomo and was easily defended, being surrounded by hills and the sea. It grew rapidly, with a Great Buddha and numerous large Zen temples. Yoritomo was succeeded by the **Hōjō**, who were regent-*shōguns*. Kamakura period: 1185 or 1192 to 1333, the period when the military headquarters were located at Kamakura.

Kami Word used for the deities or higher spirits in Japan. The meaning is closer to top or above, and does not carry the connotations that deities and gods do in English, by which absolute qualities are usually implied and each may be individually personified. Some have lost their immortality and some humans have been given *kami* status. *Kami* have their own hierarchy, and shrines are usually built to specific ones, but most are nameless. They remain rather aloof, unless enticed to the shrines through the proper ritual.

Kammu (736–806). The 50th ruler, reigned 781–806, first son of **Kōnin**. Kammu, the most powerful figure in early Heian, attributed most of the state's problems to the clergy at Heijō and, along with numerous orders to restrict their activities, moved the capital to Nagaoka (784), and ten years later to **Heian**. Munitions were stored all over the country and the major effort against the Ezo in the north was successful. Despite greater distance from the Nara clergy, he never relaxed his pressure on them, but supported **Saichō** in the development of his Tendai monastery on Mt Hiei. Efforts were made to control the spread of manors, orders were given to sort out the genealogies, and posthumous names were assigned to rulers up to the time of Jitō.

Emperor Kammu

Kannon Avalokitesvara, Deity of Compassion and Mercy. Initially sexless, Kannon became progressively female in China, somewhat less so in Japan, hence called the Goddess of Mercy. One of the bodhisattvas in the Amida triad, Kannon is widely worshiped in eight forms and in 33 manifestations. The best-known forms show Kannon as Senjū with 1,000 arms; Jūichimen as 11-headed; Batō with three faces, a small horse in the coiffure and eight arms; Nyoirin, seated with six arms, holding a jewel. The 11-headed Kannon was a favorite in the Heian period. Pilgrimages are made by his followers to the 33 Kannon Temples of the Kansai.

Kantō Large plain along the east coast, "east of the mountains." The Kanto Plain covers about 5,000 square miles, fanned out in all directions from Tokyo, comprising the prefectures of Chiba, Ibaragi, Saitama, Tokyo and the lowlands of Tochigi and Gumma.

Kawahara-dera Temple in Asuka, built on the site of a palace, started in the 660s and embodying several new important features. It is not clear who sponsored the construction of the Kawahara-dera, but it was apparently the first major temple in Yamato to assume the due north orientation after the Taika Reform; it was probably the first to have a main hall and pagoda side by side in a forecourt (a plan that went through several stages to culminate in the Hōryū-ji), and an intercolumniation

system of its west main hall (like the Yakushi-ji, therefore probably a new structural style).

Keikō The 12th emperor, son of **Suinin**, early 4th century AD. In a long reign, it took him seven years to subdue the rebellious Kumaso in southeast Kyushu. His son Yamato-takeru, one of Japan's early heroes, championed the cause against the Kumaso, and in the north against the early Ezo, dying on his way home. Keikō is said to have had 80 children, and almost all the later aristocratic families claiming native origins trace themselves to him.

Keitai The 26th emperor, said to be fifth-generation descendant of **Ōjin**, traditional dates of reign 507–31. These dates should be fairly accurate. Buretsu left no offspring and Keitai was a compromise candidate, probably of direct Korean descent from horse-riding nobles recently settled near Lake Biwa. His father died soon after he was born and his mother took him back to her home in Fukui prefecture to raise him. Earlier emperors are sometimes mentioned as receiving the signet, the sign of regal authority, but Keitai received the full regalia, the first historical emperor to do so, and was the first to appoint his successor by imperial decree. Iwai, the governor of north Kyushu, was killed because of a revolt in 527. Keitai was the father of emperors Ankan, Senka and Kimmei. All of these reigns are taken up almost exclusively with complicated Korean relations.

Kimmei The 29th emperor, reigned 539–71 AD, succeeding his brother Senka. The *Nihon Shoki* says Kimmei was on the throne when the ruler of Paikche sent several Buddhist gifts to the court in 552. Thy loss of Mimana on the Korean peninsula in 562 resulted in a large influx of about 5,000 Korean refugee families for whom space had to be found. He occupied a palace at Sakurai in the northeast corner of the Fujiwara area, and a large keyhole tomb on the west side of Asuka is officially identified as his.

Kojiki See **Nihon Shoki**.

Kōken (716–70). The 46th ruler, reigned 749–58, abdicated, then resumed the throne 6 years later as **Shōtoku**. The daughter of Shōmu, a devout Buddhist, she ordered a prohibition on the killing of all live creatures. She was on the throne when the Great Buddha of the Tōdai-ji was consecrated in 752.

Kongōbu-ji Temple built on Mt Kōya by **Kūkai** (774–835) in 816 to be a place for Shingon worship. The temple was finished in its later form after his death, but he planned a mandala of buildings, a west *tahōtō*, a "precious tower" with two roofs, for the

Diamond World, and a larger east one for the Womb World with the residence of the priests lying between and the main hall situated in the front. Several fires have left no original buildings. The east one was rebuilt not long ago, a large *tahōtō*, often confused with a pagoda, called the Kompon Daitō, the Great Central Tower.

Kōnin (719–81). The 49th ruler, reigned 770–81, a grandson of Tenchi, succeeded **Shōtoku**. Priest Dōkyō was relegated to a temple in the Kantō and his surviving enemies reinstated. The war in the north went badly, inflation was high and new laws to control prices were ineffective. Poor conditions were ascribed by some to the prevalence of sorcery, and known sorcerers were banished. Mounded tombs were not to be destroyed under the pretext of building temples on the spot. Kōnin abdicated in favor of his son **Kammu** and died within the year.

Kōtoku (596–654). Prince Karu, 36th ruler, reigned 645–54, brother of Empress Kōgyoku. Shortly after Iruka and Emishi of the Soga family were killed, the palace was moved to Naniwa, and Kōtoku, who had been among the conspirators, announced the **Taika Reform** in 646, a series of proclamations designed to solidify power under the emperor and establish a government rather similar to the Chinese bureaucracy. Kōtoku was buried at Shinaga in Taishi-chō, Osaka prefecture.

Kūkai (774–835). Priest, posthumously known as Kōbō Daishi, founder of the esoteric **Shingon** sect in Japan. Kūkai studied in China for about two years, returning in 806. He was at the Jingo-ji in west Kyoto for several years and in 816 founded the Kongōbu-ji on Mt Kōya, the chief temple of Shingon for rural areas, and was later head priest of the Tō-ji in Kyoto, the chief temple for the city. Credited with magical powers, he invented the *hiragana*, the cursive phonetic writing, and is associated with innumerable temples. His exposition of Shingon in two treatises ranks it above all other doctrines.

Kumano Region in the southeast of the Kii peninsula, noted for three popular shrines. In the prefecture of Wakayama, a coastal area, syncretic Buddhist thought in the Late Heian and early Kamakura periods accounted for a flood of pilgrimages. Then considered to be more important than the Ise shrines, pilgrims visited Hongū, enshrining Ketsumi-no-Miko; Shingū, enshrining Hayatama-no-o; and Nachi, enshrining Izanagi and associated *kami*. Each was identified respectively with Amida and his bodhisattvas, Kannon and Seishi.

Kūya (903–72). Tendai priest, a non-conformist itinerant worker of miracles and preacher. Kūya built roads and bridges, and in 951 made his reputation by helping to alleviate the plague, then making statues for the souls of those who died in it. He explained the **nembutsu** in specifically Amidist terms, and his followers have been called the Kūya School of the **Tendai** sect. He is said to have founded the Saikō-ji in Heian in 964.

Kyōgoku (594–661). Empress and 35th ruler, reigned 642–44; and as **Saimei**, 37th ruler, 655–61. A grand-daughter of Prince Shōtoku, she succeeded her husband Jomei. During a short but critical period, Soga-no-Iruka was assassinated in the palace and his father Emishi killed, paving the way for the Taika Reform and the concentration of authority in the hands of the emperor. She lived in the Itabuki palace at Asuka, then moved to Osaka (Naniwa) after her abdication.

Lacquer Resin of the *Rhus vernicifera* tree, usually applied over pigments to get a waterproof effect. Lacquer was already in use in the Jōmon period, but a major development in its use came in the late 7th century when dry-lacquer Buddhist images were made, quite possibly in some cases with material brought from China. Heian aristocrats preferred lacquer to other materials for bowls, cups and trays, encouraging an art that has survived to this day.

Lacquered musical instrument from the Shōsō-in

Lotus Flowering water plant (*Nelumbo nucifera*), sacred to Buddhism. Its spontaneous generation was thought to signify divine birth, its whiteness the nature of purity and truth.

Amida Buddha presides over a lotus pond in his Western Paradise, and Kannon holds a lotus as a special attribute. The eight petals resemble the Wheel of the Law and are associated with the Eightfold Path. The Lotus Throne on which the Buddhas sit is a mark of their authority. The *Lotus Sutra (Hokke-kyō)* is a major Buddhist scripture extolling the merits and mercies of **Kannon**.

Tile decorated with a lotus blossom

Mandala Holy diagram, usually painted, but including magical arrangements of sacred objects, buildings and landscape. Mandala paintings brought from China were the inspiration for Japanese examples which, if used canonically, were hung as a pair facing each other in the Kanchō-dō, the ritual hall of a Shingon temple: the Kongō-kai mandala on the west, the Diamond or indestructible spiritual cycle, the Taizō-kai mandala on the east, the Womb or material cycle, both manifestations of the great progenitor Dainichi, set in geometric compositions of circles and squares filled with Buddhist figures.

Mappō End of the Law, the last of three stages of Buddhism. Buddhism was believed to pass through three stages: first, the doctrines and practices and the opportunity for enlightenment existed; second, enlightenment was no longer possible; third, the doctrine survived, but at the end even the doctrine would disappear. Various durations were given for each, but in the early 11th century in Japan the date of 1052 had been set for Mappō. It caused considerable anxiety and efforts to circumvent it, but the religious zeal generated by it exploded in mass pilgrimages later.

Meiji (1852–1912). The 122nd ruler, reigned 1868–1912. Meiji ascended the throne at the age of 16. He promoted a rapid modernization of Japan under a new constitution. Japan won the Sino-Japanese War (1894–95) and took Taiwan, and the Russo-Japanese War (1904–05), and later annexed Korea (1910). The revival of imperial power brought on a great strengthening of the nationalistic spirit, including emphasis on Shinto and ancestor worship. A shrine is dedicated to Emperor

Meiji in Tokyo. Meiji period: name given to the time in which he was emperor.

Miroku Maitreya, the Buddha of the Future. Presiding over the Tusita paradise, he is prepared to descend when the power of Shaka wanes. Miroku was first shown as a bodhisattva in Japan, but as a Buddha by the late 7th century, without fixed iconographic form. During the 8th century he was slowly replaced by **Amida**, slightly revived in the 11th, and then allowed to slide into limbo.

Mommu (683–707). The 42nd ruler, reigned 697–707, a grandson of Tenchi and son of Empress **Gemmyō**. Mommu died at an early age, but during his reign the Taihō codes were issued and explainers dispatched to the provinces; the era name was changed to Taihō, Great Treasure, when gold was sent from Tsukushi; and the ambassador to T'ang China was singled out as a special position. A large mound in south Asuka is said to be Mommu's tomb.

Mononobe Early family of warriors, descended from the gods, arch opponents of the application of Buddhism in the 6th century. They appeared historically at the time of Emperor Yūryaku in the *muraji* rank. One of the three leading families when **Kimmei** was on the throne, the Mononobe objected to the acceptance of Buddhism and at the time of Mononobe-no-Moriya (?–587), then Ōmuraji (head of the rank), fought a pitched battle against the troops of the Soga. Moriya died, and the family went into bondage to the Soga and virtually disappeared from sight.

Munro, Neil Gordon (1863–1942). British physician who settled in Japan, excavated and wrote extensively on Japanese prehistory. Munro was born in Edinburgh, where he studied medicine. He traveled to India, then to Japan, arriving at the age of 30, and became head of the Yokohama Army Hospital. He also set up his own clinic. He became interested in Japanese culture and published a book on Japanese coins, did several excavations and produced the monumental *Prehistoric Japan* in 1908, reissued in 1911. In some respects he was years ahead of his time. By 1905 he believed there was an Old Stone Age and suggested excavating at Kō, but so much **Jōmon** material was found at Kō that the excavators forgot the original intention and the Old Stone Age had to wait for half a century to be discovered. Munro married a Japanese woman and worked among the Ainu in Hokkaido.

Murō-ji Major **Shingon** sect temple in Mt Murō, eastern Nara prefecture. The area was sacred to mountain worshipers at an early date and the Dragon Hole Shrine is the legacy of a rain-making spot. A temple may have been started here on a minor scale in the late 7th century, but as one of the three main Shingon centers, Murō-ji was commonly associated with **Kūkai** and today has the only two 9th-century buildings remaining in Japan, the pagoda and main hall.

Nakatomi Early family of professional priests, descended from the gods, arch opponents of the early application of Buddhism in the 6th century. Although they were in league with the Mononobe against Buddhism, their somewhat secondary position allowed them to survive despite the death of Nakatomi-no-Katsumi (?–587) in the Mt Shigi battle against the Soga. Katsumi's grandson, Nakatomi Kamatari (614–69), was in the conspiracy that led to the **Taika Reform** (646), following the avenging of his grandfather's death in the destruction of the Soga. Emperor Tenchi gave Kamatari the name of Fujiwara on his death-bed, his offspring forming the ancestors of the vast Fujiwara family and all its branches.

Names, Imperial and Personal Members of the imperial family were known by personal name, royal title or, as rulers, by the name of the palace where they lived. This last became too confusing when they all lived in the same place. For instance, Jimmu was Kamu-yamato-iharehiko, plus the title for deity, no-mikoto. The man in the Takamatsuzuka Tomb might be Prince Takechi. Emperor Kimmei was the emperor who lived in the Shiki-shima palace. Emperor Kammu assigned posthumous names to all the rulers, which gives us something understandable to use today. Hironuhime became Empress Jitō. Before the over-translated word *tennō* (emperor) was used, the leader of the Yamato tribe was *ōkimi* (great chieftain), designating him one notch above the others. There are many honorific terms and many implications. Family names were often occupation or place names, to which were added personal names with possessives. These possessives have been less commonly used with the passage of time. For instance, Soga-no-Umako, Fujiwara Michinaga. Today it is the custom when writing in English to use the family name last for recent personalities, such as Kōsaku Hamada.

Naniwa Old name for port, palace and capital, now Osaka. The "Naniwa dynasty" of 5th-century rulers lived in the area; Emperor Kōtoku announced the Taika Reform from Naniwa (646); and emperors Temmu and Shōmu both built palaces there in the 7th and 8th centuries. But after the capital was established at Heian and contacts with China slackened measurably, Naniwa lost much of its importance.

Nembutsu Contraction of *Namu Amida Butsu*, an incantation sometimes translated as Homage to Amida Buddha. It started as a magical expression and then became associated specifically with Amida Buddha worship. The *Kūya-nembutsu* was Kūya's advocacy of as much sincere recitation as possible, leading to greater happiness and therefore to a greater chance of rebirth in the Pure Land of Amida. The dancing *nembutsu* (*odori nembutsu*) added an even further dimension, progressively more distant from the Amidist philosophy.

Nihon Shoki, Kojiki, Fudoki Ancient histories and gazetteers, Chronicles of Japan, Records of Ancient Matters, and Records of Lands and Customs. A historical sense was acquired from the Chinese. The *Kojiki* was compiled from the memory of an elderly female chamberlain and consists primarily of brief mythology and genealogical lists. The *Nihon Shoki* or *Nihongi* is much fuller, and takes the account through the reign of Empress Jitō (696). Both were based on earlier written sources, the *Teiki* and *Kyūji*. They were followed by four more (to 888), making the Six Ancient Histories, which became the officially accepted chronicle for early Japan. The *Fudoki* started to appear after 713, but only parts are extant today. Fortunately one is the *Izumo Fudoki*, for Izumo was a contending area outside the Yamato cycle of myths in the official histories.

Nintoku The 16th emperor, fourth son of Ōjin, ruled from early to mid-5th century AD. His reign was long, studded with poetry on vegetable farming and unrequited love. Magnanimously, he waived his needs for a palace until agricultural levels could be raised. A great canal was dug and roads were built, while official granaries were established. The record has him starting to build his tomb in the 67th year of his reign and dying 20 years later. His is the largest mounded tomb, 486 m in length, at Sakai in south Osaka city.

Ōjin The 15th emperor, fourth son of Chūai and Jingū, from c.400 AD. The first of the "Naniwa dynasty" rulers, he was concerned with extending land for cultivation, improving communications and irrigation, and salt production. Seamstresses were to be brought over from China. Fishermen and mountain wardens were organized. He received two horses from the Korean king, cared for by Achiki who taught the Chinese classics. His wife was from Kibi in the Inland Sea, and he divided up Kibi for his successors. He is buried in the second largest tomb in Japan, 430 m in length, at Habikino city, Osaka prefecture.

Ōmiwa Shrine Mt Miwa is the actual object of worship, at the foot of which is Ōmiwa shrine. The mountain is said to be the oldest "shrine" in Japan. It is a perfect cone-shaped hill north of Sakurai and east of the Yamanobe-no-michi, the old road that led directly north to Heijō. There are special rocks on the mountain and the shrine is dedicated to Okuninushi, here called Ōmononushi. Two streams meet in front, forming a sacred triangle. All the families residing within the triangle were dedicated to the service of the shrine, which is today visited for many reasons, in particular by childless women.

Ōmori Place between Tokyo and Yokohama made famous by the presence of shell-mounds which were dug by Edward Morse in 1879. Now all continuous city, two sets of tracks run through Ōmori, passing a monument to Morse's work just north of Ōmori station. Morse recovered Late Jōmon material, now preserved by Tokyo University.

Ranks and titles There were many of these and they were often changed leaving unclear relationships. In pre-Buddhist times the ranking aristocrats at the court with blood connection to the imperial line were called *omi*; roughly equally ranked but without imperial kinship were the *muraji*. There were several locally ranked tribal heads, including the *kuni-no-miyatsuko*. Emperor Temmu abolished these ranks in 684 and introduced an eight-rank system, referred to as *kabane*, more or less hereditary titles, for which later modifications were made. Within these were grades, with costumes and colors set accordingly.

Richū The 17th emperor, son of **Nintoku**, ruled mid-5th century AD. Richū appointed four administrators of the country, a Heguri, Soga, Mononobe and Tsubura, apparently heads of the most powerful clans. He is the first emperor referred to as riding a horse. Richū is buried in a large tomb 360 m in length not far from Nintoku's mound.

Ritsu-ryō, Civil and Penal Codes Name given to several legal documents specifying the accepted social behavior and the punishments for infringements. The first was issued when Emperor Tenchi was living in the province of Ōmi, hence the Ōmi codes. These were superseded by the Taihō codes, dating to 701, and later the Yōrō codes (both era names), which were written by 718 but not applied until 757.

Ryōbu-Shinto Dual-aspect Shinto, the view that Buddhist and Shinto deities have common origins and can be identified with each other. Also called Honchi-suijaku (literally Original-place-passage), the Shinto *kami* were said to have had their beginnings in the homeland of Buddhism and lingered in Japan in the stage of passing through. This philosophy is usually attributed to priest **Gyōgi** (670–749), but its shape really took place under esoteric doctrines.

Ryōnin (1071–1132). Tendai priest,

posthumously named Shō-ō Daishi, founder of the Yūzū-nembutsu sect. He built a small temple on lower Mt Hiei, Raikō-in, and recited the Namu-Amida-Butsu (**nembutsu**) up to 60,000 times daily. The practice caught on and he built the Dai-nembutsu-ji in Sumiyoshi, Osaka, in 1124, a temple which became the headquarters of the sect.

Saga (785–842). The 52nd ruler, reigned 809–23, second son of **Kammu**. Saga followed his brother Heijō who had retired to Nara. Saga survived an attempt by Heijō to seize the throne and move back to Nara and came out stronger by forming a special council (*Kurōdo-dokoro*) for administrative business, and further improved his position by establishing the imperial police (*Kebiishi*) to combat lawlessness in the capital.

Saichō (767–822). Priest, posthumously known as Dengyō Daishi, founder of the esoteric **Tendai** sect in Japan. He studied in China from 802 to 805; on his return he transformed his earlier temple on Mt Hiei into the headquarters of the Tendai sect with support from Emperor Kammu. Later known as Enryaku-ji, it was the training ground for numerous priests, several of whom branched out to found their own sects.

Saimei (594–661). Empress and 37th ruler, reigned 655–61, resuming the throne after her brother **Kōtoku** died. She returned to Asuka to live, but was distracted from the reforms and resisted some. Word was received that China had attacked the Korean kingdoms. She went down to Kyushu to direct a Japanese expedition, but died there at the age of 68.

Samurai Originally guards, the professional soldiers. As pensioners, they formed a class of warriors of considerable importance in the feudal period, were noted for the strict training passed on from generation to generation and famed for their loyalty.

Sanage Low, hilly area between the old provinces of Mino and Owari, northeast of Nagoya, where pottery was made in great quantity. Starting in the 5th century AD, pottery was made in hundreds of kilns there, especially in the Nara and Heian periods when the courts and surrounding areas were supplied, and continuing until the 15th century. It was usually a light gray, in functional shapes, and, if glazed, had full coverage of monochromatic green or an ash glaze that appeared in the firing.

Seimu The 13th emperor, a son of Keikō, early to mid-4th century AD. His record is best known through the settlement of the province and district boundaries and the designation of the grades of their governors, according to the *Nihon Shoki*.

Shaka Gautama, Sakyamuni Buddha, the original Buddha who lived in the 6th century BC. Son of a leader of the Sakya tribe in northeast India, as Prince Siddartha he left the palace, practiced solitude and asceticism, and received enlightenment while meditating, hence the Buddha, the Enlightened One. He preached until his death or *Nirvana* (Japanese: *Nehan*), gaining many disciples, among whom the Ten Great Disciples are particularly well known. Shaka was an important Buddha in early Buddhism in Japan, but he lost importance in the Nara and Heian periods.

Shaku Foot unit introduced to Japan from Korea. It was used in laying out tombs, but when first applied precisely in the building of temples it was the north Korean *komajaku* which is slightly less than 1·2 of the English foot (36 cm). This became a little shorter, progressing through the *Karajaku* (T'ang *shaku*) and the *Narajaku*, to closer to 11 inches (28 cm) today. The chief multiples of this were 10 *shaku* = 1 *jo* (not the same *jo* as in *jōri* or *jōbō*), 6 *shaku* = 1 *ken* (used for area, equaling a *tsubo*), and 60 *ken* = 1 *chō*.

Shamanism Religious activity through a medium, practiced on behalf of the community in order to ensure its comfort and survival. An individual of supernatural powers was recognized by his or her group as being able to commune with and interpret the will of the *kami* through religious ecstasy. Early "abstainers" were shamans, and when shrines were first built, the *ichiko* were female shamans; but as shrines came to have priests (*kannushi*), shamanism yielded to a purely professional management of shrines. Many prominent women in early Japanese accounts were shamans.

Shingon Name of esoteric sect introduced by **Kūkai** (774–835) after his return from China in 806. Meaning True Word (Sanskrit: Mantra), it is a Tantric branch of Buddhism, using several sutras, one of which is the Mahāvairocana sutra, an exposition on the nature of **Dainichi**. Shingon stressed ritual, magical practices, verbal transmission of doctrines and the use of all the arts. Fierce deities from Indian sources abound. Kūkai set up a modest meditation retreat on remote Mt Kōya in 816 which expanded into the Kongōbu-ji, and built the Tō-ji in Kyoto into a large Shingon center after 823.

Shinto Kami-no-michi, the Way of the Gods, in Chinese style or Japanese pronunciation. The native animistic religion which sees higher spirits, **kami**, in all aspects of nature, and appeals to these spirits for beneficial rewards through purification, making offerings at shrines and participating in rituals and festivals. Its roots are very ancient, but its forms began to take their traditional shape after rice cultivation was introduced to Japan, and its

rituals were mixed with earlier shamanistic practices.

Shirakawa (1053–1129). The 72nd ruler, reigned 1072–86, succeeding his father Go-sanjō at the age of 10. Following the example of his father who died a year after Shirakawa took the throne, he pressed for greater imperial control of land and proof of legitimate ownership. He abdicated when 33 in favor of his son, then 9, and formed an administrative body that enabled him to rule another 43 years. This was the start of *insei*, the so-called "cloister rule" or "cloister government," though not all retired emperors actually entered the cloister. He supported his penchant for building temples by selling provincial governorships, at first for fixed periods, later for life. Once these became hereditary, the feudal system had its start.

Shōen Private manors or estates which developed in the Heian period and ultimately contributed to the feudal system. Loss of control over land allotments, permission for personal use if land was developed through private enterprise and rewards of land exempt from taxes all led to the *shōen* system. The government eventually recognized claims for land through officially issued deeds. *Shōen* are said to have constituted half the country in the 11th century.

Shōmu (699–756). The 45th ruler, reigned 724–49, son of Mommu, succeeding his aunt Genshō. Shōmu was the dominant imperial personality of the 8th century. His efforts to spread Buddhism culminated in an order for all the provinces to build temples in 741 and resulted in Buddhism becoming a state religion, as all the temple heads were court appointees. Internal conditions caused much local unrest, including a Dazaifu rebellion, but efforts toward improvement included examinations for public office. He built the **Tōdai-ji** with its large Buddha, acquired an unsurpassed personal collection and abdicated in favor of his daughter **Kōken**. His empress, Komyo, was the first to come from the Fujiwara family.

Shōsō-in Name originally used for storehouses, now referring to the wooden building in which the possessions of Emperor **Shōmu** have been kept since they were dedicated by his wife in 756. The Shōsō-in lies to the north of the main buildings in the Tōdai-ji compound. It is three joined, raised buildings, each with two floors and one entrance on the lower level, facing east.

Shōtoku (716–70). The 48th ruler, reigned 764–70, reascended the throne at the instigation of Priest **Dōkyō**. Shōtoku had been attended by Dōkyō when she was sick and her elevation of him antagonized Emi-no-Oshikatsu (ex-Fujiwara Nakamaro), who mustered troops but lost the battle and was killed. Junnin was forced off the throne and died shortly thereafter. Shōtoku took the throne and left the decision as to whether Dōkyō should be emperor to the *kami* at Usa Hachiman shrine, who failed to sanction the request. Crops were poor because of droughts and farmers were told to grow barley and wheat. Shōtoku died in office.

Shōtoku, Prince (572–622). Regent from 593 to 622 under Empress Suiko, 2nd son of Yōmei, and crown prince. Shōtoku was born and lived at Asuka, then moved to Ikaruga around 604 where he had built a palace earlier, A man of remarkable intellectual attainments and diplomatic skills, his energetic propagation of Buddhism through involvement with Korean priests, translations of the sutras and temple construction have ranked him foremost among religious personalities in Japan. He is regarded as the first Buddhist saint. A large cult grew up around him by the Kamakura period and the **Hōryū-ji** is now the headquarters of the Shōtoku sect, the prince's posthumous name. He and his wife died after an illness of one month and they, along with his mother, were buried at Shinaga in Taishi-chō, Osaka prefecture.

Six Sects of Nara Buddhism Term given by later writers to what were believed to be six Buddhist sects at Heijō in the 8th century. Jōjitsu and Sanron have disappeared, the former difficult to identify if even independent, the latter introduced by a Korean priest and taught at the Hōryū-ji, Gankō-ji and Daian-ji; Hossō (Fa-hsiang in China), introduced by Dōshō on his return in 654 and other priests later, a middle-path Buddhism, taught at the Gankō-ji, later at the Hōryū-ji and with its headquarters at the Kōfuku-ji; Kusha, introduced by Chitsū on his return from China in 658, since disappeared; Kegon (Hua-yen in China), brought by the Chinese priest Dōsen around 736, advocating discipline and unity of thought and substance, emphasizing sermons preached by Buddha, with headquarters at the Tōdai-ji; and Ritsu (Vayana Lii), brought by the Chinese priest Ganjin in 753, stressing rules, precepts and ethics, with headquarters at the Tōshōdai-ji.

Soga Family of long residence in Japan which supported Buddhism and acted as prime ministers to several rulers in the 6th and 7th centuries. Soga-no-Iname (?–570) accepted the Buddhist articles in 552; Soga-no-Umako (?–626) served as minister during the reigns of Bidatsu, Yōmei, Sushun and Suiko. The Mononobe were defeated in 587, ensuring the unimpeded development of Buddhism. Umako built the Asuka-dera. His Soga-no-Emishi served Jomei and Kōgyoku, but he and his son Iruka were killed in a conspiracy that brought on the **Taika Reform** (646). Soga

Stupa mound in cross-section

power lay in their control of Asuka and the country's tax system.

Stupa Mound that came to take on a sacred significance, indicating the presence of the Buddha. Japanese: *sotoba*, intended to be phonetically similar. Stupas are fundamentally reliquaries and take many forms, ranging from miniatures to large monuments, and have specialized names, one of which is the pagoda.

Sue Term used for the gray ceremonial pottery of the Tomb period and for the *be* which produced it. This high-fired, professionally made pottery was introduced from Korea and is quite similar to Silla ware. Made by the Suetsukuri-*be* in many places throughout the country, it was chiefly the ritual ware and was deposited in tombs, but in Buddhist times it was converted to domestic use.

Sugawara Michizane (845–903). Minister of the Right under Emperor Daigo, exiled to Kyushu by intrigues of the Fujiwara. Michizane was from a family of obscure origin that produced scholars, historians and readers of the Chinese classics. He moved up the political ladder, but was the object of a conspiracy by the Fujiwara who accused him of attempting to replace the emperor. He was exiled in 901. Twenty years later he was reinstated and the Kitano shrine built in his honor, where he is deified as the God of Calligraphy and referred to as Tenjin and Temmangū.

Suiko (554–628). Empress and 33rd ruler, reigned 592–628, the third daughter of Kimmei by a Soga mother, brother of Sushun. She married her half-brother Bidatsu in 576 to become the imperial consort. Described as comely and gracious, Japan's first empress set a precedent often invoked in the 8th century. The chief minister was Soga-no-Umako, but she appointed as regent her nephew, **Prince Shōtoku**, and supported his ardent propagation of Buddhism. She built palaces in Asuka and was buried in her son's tomb at Shinaga in Taishi-chō, Osaka prefecture.

Suinin The 11th emperor, third son of Sujin, late 3rd century A.D. He moved the shrine for the Sun Goddess to Ise, now the Inner Shrine,

and is best known for the story that rationalizes the existence of **haniwa**. He is buried in a large keyhole tomb at Amagatsuji, Nara prefecture, just south of Saidaiji.

Sujin The 10th emperor, with date of death perhaps 258 or 318 AD. He was probably the first Yamato ruler, at the start of the Tomb period, since the *Kojiki* calls him: "Mimaki, first ruler of the land." His tomb south of Tenri is the oldest keyhole-shaped tomb among the so-called imperial tombs. He entertained the first embassy from Mimana, constructed boats, took a census, fixed taxes, expanded canals and ponds for transportation and rice production, and built a shrine at Kasunui for the Sun Goddess.

Sumiyoshi Location and name of early shrine in south Osaka, dedicated to four *kami*, with four small buildings and closely fitting fences. It is the tutelary shrine of mariners because the *kami* of Suminoe, the old name of the area, were said to have aided Jingū on her Korean expedition. The early history is obscure, but Emperor Nintoku is credited with relocating the shrine where it is today. While the roof-top features of the buildings are now decorative and they have assumed Buddhist temple coloring, the form is the raised storehouse, prehistoric shrine type.

Sun Goddess Amaterasu-ō-mi-kami, the highest Japanese deity, the Heaven Great Shining Deity. She was spontaneously generated from the eye of her father **Izanagi** in one account, from a mirror he held in his left hand in another, and was sent up to rule

Empress Suiko

from Takamagahara, the High Plain of Heaven, and prepare earth for the coming of its mortal rulers. A series of events in the High Plain of Heaven include a power struggle with Susano-o, and until the narrative moves to earth, Takamimusubi, a supreme creator, determines the actions to be taken. An early symbol of the Sun Goddess is a spear, a later one a mirror.

Sushun (520–92). The 32nd emperor, reigned 587–92, twelfth son of Kimmei and brother of Yōmei. An old man, he was installed as a Soga pawn: during his reign the Soga destroyed Mononobe-no-Moriya and totally eliminated the Mononobe as contenders for power. Several qualified craftsmen from Korea started the Hōkō-ji (Asuka-dera) in 588. Supported at first by the Soga, Sushun was later assassinated by them when he showed signs of independence.

Sutra Buddhist scripture, *kyō* in Japanese. The Japanese normally read Chinese translations of the Indian sutras, which they constantly copied and distributed in Japan. Sutra-mounds are burials of sutras in containers with associated

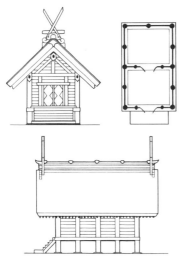

The shrine at Sumiyoshi

articles, intended to ensure the survival of the scriptures. The practice was known to 6th-century China and was in Japan by the 9th. It spread widely under Ryōbu-Shinto beliefs, particularly stimulated by the prospects of **Mappō** (1052).

Taika Reform Change in system of government carried out by a coup in 645 with the assassination of the Soga and the installation of Emperor Kōtoku in Naniwa, the Reform edicts promulgated in 646. Called Taika, Great Change, the first era name in use, it followed the abolition of old ranks and the taking of a census. The articles of the Reform dealt chiefly with the control of land, dissolution of the *be* system, and the prohibition of tomb construction except for

the highest ranks. The Reform was intended to establish a mode of government under the emperor similar to that of China.

Taira (also Heike or Heishi). Name of family of great prominence in the 11th and 12th centuries. The family can be traced to Prince Takamochi, a son of Emperor Kammu, who was given the name in 889. Under Taira Kiyomori (1118–81), who supported ex-Emperor Go-shirakawa and won the Heiji war (1159), the Taira reached their strongest point, but his subsequent extreme arrogance aroused such widespread hostility that several former allies turned against him. Following temporary victories, he died when the tide turned. Minamoto clansmen, summoned from all over the country, joined Yoritomo and the great naval battle of Dan-no-ura, spearheaded by Yoshitsune, climaxed a series of Taira defeats in southwest Japan in 1185.

Takamatsuzuka Tomb Small tomb with paintings on plastered walls and ceiling, located in south Asuka, Nara prefecture, dating to about 700. Designated as the tomb of Emperor Mommu on old maps, but redesignated at least a century ago, this tomb was excavated in 1972 when a nearby road was being improved, and was found to contain wall and ceiling paintings of groups of men and women, tutelary deities and constellations. It is the first and only tomb found in Japan with paintings in the current style.

Takuma Tamenari Relatively obscure artist working in the middle of the 11th century, sometimes regarded as the painter of the Phoenix Hall at Uji. Tamenari is associated with Yamato-e, or Japanese-style developments in painting, and the inclusion of landscape features in Buddhist subjects, a characteristic of his "school." Another tradition connects a painter by the name of Hirotaka with the Phoenix Hall's nine grades of Amida's paradise.

T'ang dynasty Expansive and prosperous period in Chinese history, from 618 to 906. There was much foreign trade, missionary and other activity which encouraged movement, spreading T'ang culture and arts to all surrounding areas. Buddhism reached its peak in the 7th and 8th centuries, but was suppressed in the 9th, partly because of the deep philosophical differences from Confucian thought. The Japanese welcomed many visitors and borrowed heavily from the art styles of T'ang China.

Temmu (622–86). The 40th emperor, reigned 673–86, third son of Jomei, brother of **Tenchi**. A short war, known as Jinshin-no-Ran, saw the defeat of Tenchi's son who had tried to seize the throne, despite Temmu having been designated heir apparent by his brother. In 680 the capital is said to have had 24 temples.

Temmu was deeply religious, he set the boundaries of the provinces and ordered the reading of sutras; people were forbidden to eat the meat of cattle, horses, dogs, monkeys and barnyard fowl. Among the decrees in his reign was a new system of eight ranks introduced in 684, clothing regulations and prescribing of the court ceremonies. He lived in the Kiyomigahara palace in Asuka.

Tenchi (626–71). The 38th emperor, ruled 662–71, ascending the throne in 668, the second son of Jomei and Empress Kōgyoku, succeeding his mother. As Prince Naka-no-Ōe, he was a key figure in the conspiracy that led to the downfall of the Soga and the **Taika Reform**. The Japanese were forced to evacuate completely from Korea, though they retained the hope of and made plans for returning, incessantly fortifying the south. Tenchi sent a mission to China to promote diplomatic relations in 666. Regarded as an able administrator, Tenchi issued the Ōmi-ryō codes, later superseded by the Taihō codes.

Tendai Name of sect introduced by **Saichō** (767–822) after his return from China in 805 which adopted esoteric practices in Japan. Tendai was founded in China by Chih-i in the 6th century, with temples adhering to his doctrines being built in the T'ien-t'ai mountains. The chief scripture was the *Lotus Sutra* (*Hokkekyō*), but value was seen in all, and each contributed to an ever-unfolding revelation, an eclectisicm that goes far in explaining why Tendai was the rich fount from which so many later sects sprang. The chief deity was **Dainichi**, but exoteric, non-mystical Buddhas, such as Yakushi and **Amida**, were equally worshiped. The headquarters were at the Enryaku-ji on Mt Hiei.

Three-color ware Pottery produced in the 7th and 8th centuries in Japan called *san-sai*, modeled after the Chinese Three-color ware. The materials for Three-color were probably under court control. Its occurrence in sites is limited to Heijō, imperial temples and a rare aristocratic temple. Lead glazes were used, with copper oxide employed for the green and iron oxide for the yellow. White was called the third color. Three-color ware is not very common, but a monochromatic green was used widely as late as the 12th century.

Tiles Meaning roof tiles, as used here, high-fired gray ceramic in two shapes: sharply curved tiles, rows of which give the ribbed effect to a roof, and long arc tiles, called pantiles, laid between. The pantiles take the runoff and guide the water to the edge of the roof. A specially decorated circular tile is attached to the row at the edge of the roof, and frequently its corresponding pantile is decorated. These are valuable for dating the buildings. The tiles are laid on boards. If the roof slope is not too great the tiles hold by sheer weight, otherwise by holes and wires. Well-laid tiles under normal conditions may give up to 200 years of service, although less than 100 is considered average. Temples were tiled when first built, but palaces not for another century, until the capital was at Fujiwara.

Tiles from the Hōryū-ji

Tōdai-ji Immense temple built by Emperor **Shōmu** on the eastern edge of Heijō city begun in 745 and dedicated in 752. The headquarters of the Kegon sect, the Tōdai-ji was to be Japanese handiwork *par excellence*. A large bronze Roshana Buddha was installed in the Daibutsu-den, the Great Buddha Hall. Twin pagodas and a huge gate gave access to the precinct. In the pilgrimage period it was the chief of the Seven Great Temples of Nara. The Tōdai-ji was burned in the civil war in 1180, rebuilt by priest Chōgen, burned again in 1567 and again rebuilt, each time on a more modest scale.

Tōhoku Northeast, the northern part of the island of Honshu, comprising the prefectures of Aomori, Akita, Iwate and usually including Miyagi and Yamagata.

Tokugawa Name of family which controlled the government under 15 *shōguns* after 1603 until the Meiji Restoration in 1868. The family was traceable to a son of Emperor Seiwa of the 9th century. Under Tokugawa Ieyasu (1542–1616) at the battle of Sekigahara in 1600 the Tokugawa defeated the troops of Toyotomi Hideyori (1593–1615). The first and third *shōguns* were buried at Nikko, the others in Tokyo. A local governor, Tokugawa Mitsukuni (1628–1700), lord of Mito (Ibaragi prefecture), grandson of Tokugawa Ieyasu, achieved much local popularity through his disobedience to the central government. He expended one third of his domain's income in having a 240-volume history of Japan compiled by distinguished scholars, the *Dai-nihon-shi*. He excavated tombs, the first to do so out of curiosity and not for loot. Tokugawa: period name, from 1603 to 1868.

Tori Member of the saddlers' *be*, active as a bronze sculptor between 605 and 623. Tori's grandfather was an immigrant from China who brought Buddhist relics with him; his father took the priestly vows at the time of Yōmei; and his aunt was the first nun in Japan. Tori was commissioned by Empress **Suiko** to cast a *jōroku* statue, that is a 16-foot (meaning large) Buddha for the Asuka-dera in 605. For this he was rewarded with a title and land. He was called upon to cast an image when **Prince Shōtoku** was sick in 622. This is the Shaka triad in the Hōryū-ji, completed after the prince's death in a span of 13 months. At the end of the long inscription he gives his name as "Shiba no Kuratsukuri no obito Tori Busshi." Shiba was the family name, Kuratsukuri the saddlers' *be*, Tori his personal name, and Busshi a title of master, given him for his contributions to the Buddhist church.

Tōshōdai-ji Head temple of the Ritsu sect, built by priest **Ganjin** and his followers on the west side of Heijō from 759. After Ganjin's arrival from China, following the ordination ceremony, he was given land on the west side of the city, due north of the Yakushi-ji—which apparently tried to resist the threatened encroachment of its domain—and the Chinese monks set about building a temple. The Tōshōdai-ji preserves the original main hall and lecture hall and many 8th- and 9th-century images.

Uji Clan, the broadest kinship group, such as Soga, Fujiwara, Tokugawa. The head of the clan was for long referred to as *uji-no-kami*, while the tutelary deity is the *uji-gami*. *gami*.

Yakushi Bhaishajyaguru, the Buddha of healing. Of obscure origin, there developed increasing regard for this Buddha in east Asia as a healer, to whom temples were built and named. A major deity in Hosso and Tendai, he came to be viewed as the eastern counterpart of Amida, offering relief in this world as Amida offered salvation for the next. After the 13th century he is virtually unknown. A medicine jar or bowl held in the left hand is a main attribute. He became associated with the number 7 by the 8th century, and also with the number 12, after his 12 vows to aid mankind which were identified with the times of day and months and were personified as the 12 Divine Generals (Jūnishin-shō).

Yamabushi Ascetics involved with the spirits of mountains through religious exercises. Traditional mountain worship was stimulated by esoteric Buddhism in the 9th century and eventually came to be known as Shūgen-dō. White-clothed ascetics climb holy mountains, perform rituals and exorcise evil spirits by means of supernatural powers. Many mountains with the names of Kinbusen, Kinposan, Kimbusan and Mitake are sacred to Shūgen-dō. The main ones today are Mts

Three-color ware from the Shōsō-in

Kinbu, Kumano, Haku and Haguro in Nara, Wakayama, Ishikawa and Yamagata prefectures respectively.

Yamanouchi, Sugao (1902–70). Lecturer in archaeology at Tokyo University, Jōmon pottery specialist. Yamanouchi was a student at Tokyo Imperial University, an assistant in the Faculty of Medicine of Tōhoku Imperial University, and then organized a Society of Prehistoric Studies in Tokyo in 1933. As editor of the short-lived *Sanshi Kōkogaku* (Prehistoric Archaeology) he published in 1937 the five divisions of the **Jōmon** period on the basis of pottery types, still in standard use today: Sō-ki, Zen-ki, Chū-ki, Kō-ki and Ban-ki. After World War II he was lecturer at Tokyo University until his retirement at the age of 59, when he became a professor at Seijō University.

Yamato Name of the dominant tribe and source of the imperial line; the plain from the Kizu river extending south to the Yoshino mountains, bordered on either side by mountains, often called the Nara Basin; and the name of the province, now Nara prefecture. Yamato is a word synonymous with Japan, evoking a strong nationalistic, traditional spirit. It was the nucleus of the Go-Kinai, the Five Home Provinces, where Japan came into being as a state.

Yayoi Place name in Tokyo, now applied to a cultural period in which rice and metals were introduced to Japan, dating from about the 3rd century BC to the 3rd century AD. The agricultural practices and accompanying crafts and ceremonies set fundamental patterns for later social life in Japan. The Mukōhara shell-mound was in the area that is now Yayoi-chō; it was the first site to yield recognizable Yayoi material.

Index